Inheriting Wisdom

Inheriting Wisdom

Readings for Today from Ancient Christian Writers

EVERETT FERGUSON

HENDRICKSON PUBLISHERS

© 2004 by Everett Ferguson

Hendrickson Publishers, LLC
P.O. Box 3473
Peabody, Massachusetts 01961-3473

1-56563-354-7

Printed in the United States of America

First Printing — September 2004

Cover Art: The cover photo is of an oil painting by Leonid Malishov, titled *Pechory*, that is a depiction of a scene from the grounds of the ancient Pskovo-Pechersky Monastery of the Caves located on historically Russian land west of the city of Pskov, near the border of Estonia. Used by permission of the Rev. Viacheslav Kharinov, St. Petersburg, Russia.

Library of Congress Cataloging-in-Publication Data

Inheriting wisdom : readings for today from ancient Christian writers / [compiled by] Everett Ferguson.
    p. cm.
  ISBN 1-56563-354-7 (alk. paper)
  1. Christian literature, Early. I. Ferguson, Everett, 1933–
BR60.I54 2004
230—dc22

                                        2004013738

To the memory of
LeMoine Gaunce Lewis and George Huntston Williams,
my mentors in the study of church history,
who taught and lived by the wisdom of the past
and its relevance for the present.

TABLE OF CONTENTS

INTRODUCTION

We examine nothing except what is fitting and virtuous, and we do so according to the standard of the future more than of the present. We declare nothing to be useful except what is of use for the grace of eternal life, not what is of use for the enjoyment of the present life. . . . Our literary work is not superfluous, because we judge duty according to a different rule from what others do. They include the advantages of this world among the good things, but we consider them to be harmful. . . . Those who do not read other writings may wish to read ours, as long as they do not require literary quality of words or a skillful manner of speaking but only the simple grace of the subject itself.
— Ambrose, *Duties* 1.9.28–29

A BOOK SUCH AS THIS ONE has a long literary tradition. Collections of wisdom sayings and writings were made in ancient and medieval times. Among the ancient Christian works from which we draw our selections were John Cassian's *Conferences*;[1] the *Apophthegmata Patrum*, Alphabetical Collection[2] and Anonymous Collection[3] (collected wisdom of the "Desert Fathers" of early Egyptian monasticism), and Defensor of Ligugé's *Book of Sparkling Sayings*.[4] The popularity of such collections stems from the fact that so many issues of contemporary life—practical, moral, and spiritual—are not peculiar to modern times. Political, economic, social, and technological circumstances may differ and vary across time and place; but human nature, personal relations, and spiritual needs remain remarkably constant across the centuries. It is our hope that our collection may serve to introduce modern readers to the literature produced during the early centuries of

Christianity and increase awareness of the rich resources of the past that may provide direction and guidance for life in the twenty-first century. More importantly, modern readers may glean universal truths from these ancient masters of religious life.

Christianity grew and developed in a pluralistic world and was itself highly diverse. Thus of necessity, our selections often refer to competing systems of thought both within Christianity and within the broader context of the Greco-Roman world. Within Christianity there was a broad consensus of thought on some topics but wide variation on others. Any viewpoint, therefore, must be considered only *a* perspective among many, and not necessarily *the* Christian perspective. As Christianity competed with various pagan philosophies and religions, as well as with Judaism, Christian writers offered insight and different perspectives both on matters that are of universal concern and on those that are distinctly Christian. It is our hope that awareness of the alternative beliefs and lifestyles that were at work in the ancient world may deepen and sharpen our awareness of what it means to choose the Christian life. The selections we present here are also intended to provide food for thought, broaden the readers' perspective, and provide devotional reading and a starting point for deeper exploration of the spiritual life.

For the most part, we have sought to let the early Christian writers speak for themselves. Our work provides an appropriate structure and arrangement so that the writings are more accessible. Introductory comments are kept to a minimum so that the emphasis remains on the ancient words rather than on modern comment. An alphabetical list of Sources Cited at the end of the book identifies the authors as well as the time and place of original documents.

Our collection begins with writings that concern common circumstances of life and formal social institutions. Thus Chapter I (Social Existence) includes sayings and writings related to vocation, marriage, family, friendship, education, the human relationship with the natural world, the human body and its care, the use of money and time, and a Christian's relationship with civil government. Chapter II (Good and Bad; Right and Wrong) considers psychological and moral categories: the inner person (the heart, motives, thoughts, conscience, attitudes) as well as individual expressions of positive and negative attitudes and behavior. In Chapter III (Conversion and Salvation) we take up ethics and faith. For the Christian, the power to live an ethical life is rooted in God and his saving work in Christ, applied through the Holy Spirit. Hence this chapter introduces early Christian thought on the means of grace whereby a change in life is effected. For Christians, belief and behavior are closely related. Thus Chapter IV (Life-

Nourishing Doctrines) focuses on beliefs that direct and empower a converted life. The topics include God, Christ, the Holy Spirit, angels, human nature, church, revelation, and the last things. Finally, Chapter V (Christian Living) forms a kind of inclusio with the first, since both concern the way a Christian's activity and behavior in life, both individually and socially, is oriented toward God. Here we include a broad range of topics and principles that relate to Christian living—the spiritual disciplines, worship, prayer, challenges to Christian living, and specific Christian qualities.

Although our original intention was to begin with matters of more general human interest and proceed through conversion to a God-centered existence and its more specifically Christian topics, in practice this proved to be impossible. Early Christians looked at all things, including those that today we would consider to be secular in nature, from a doctrinal perspective. That is, the Christian worldview saw everything through the lens of God and Christ, so that we could not separate out writings of more general secular interest from those that are more distinctly Christian. Perhaps the reader will find this way of viewing the world, where there is little separation between the sacred and the profane, sufficiently attractive to enter deeper into Christian existence.

The translations are my own, except in the few instances where another source is acknowledged. I am grateful for and indebted to previous translators for their role in helping me understand the ancient writers and for often supplying appropriate words and phrases to express the thought. In addition to earlier translators, special thanks are due to those who helped make original texts accessible to me for translation. The libraries of Abilene Christian University and Dallas Theological Seminary have been most cooperative. Professor D. Jeffrey Bingham and John Brown at Dallas Theological Seminary provided special assistance.

CHAPTER I

Social Existence

> Neither is any religion to be adopted that lacks wisdom, nor any wisdom to
> be approved that lacks religion.
> —Lactantius, *Divine Institutes* I.I.25

WHEN WE SPEAK OF A PERSON'S social existence, we are referring to the way he or she experiences the institutions, concerns, and relationships that are shared by all human beings. These include vocation, marriage, family, friendship, the care of the body, the use of time and money, and government. While the writings of ancient Christian preachers and moralists placed a priority on spiritual concerns and one's service to God, they did not neglect these other aspects of life. Rather, they viewed all of their activities, relationships, and responsibilities from a Christian perspective. A person's occupation, for instance, was viewed as work done both for the Lord and in the sight of the Lord.

The influence of Christian thought is especially pronounced in those writings that discuss family relationships and responsibilities. Hence John Chrysostom's striking reference to the home as a little church. Parents were admonished to view child rearing as fashioning wonderful images for God, much in the same way that a painter or sculptor daily shapes his work by adding paint or removing stone. The model that parents were to follow in rearing their children was God's treatment of human beings; by the same token, the foundation of a child's character—the foundation for the development of a virtuous life—was honor and reverence for parents. Children were to be taught the Scriptures from earliest childhood, for these would provide them with examples for living. Early Christian texts strongly affirmed the innocence of small children.

Friendship was a favorite theme of both secular writers and Christian authors. A notable example that our selections draw on is the friendship between Basil of Caesarea and Gregory Nazianzus, two Christians who enjoyed the best that pagan education and culture had to offer. While friends are needed for advice and guidance, the preservation of a friendship was never to be placed above doing right. Christian writers discussed different kinds of friendship and companionship, as well as different reasons for entering into friendship, in order to teach that true friendship be based on virtue and foster the development of virtue in both participants.

In general, early Christian writers expressed a negative view of "profane," or secular, education, cautioning against its dangers even when their tone took a more positive turn. Still, Clement of Alexandria noted the contributions to human development made by music, arithmetic, geometry, astronomy, dialectics, and philosophy. Origen refuted forcefully the charge brought by the pagan critic Celsus that only uneducated persons became Christians. Gregory the Wonderworker, one of Origen's students, praised his teacher for both his educational program and his teaching skills (Origen was a one-man university). And Jerome included elementary education among those things that are necessary for the proper upbringing of a daughter (see his letter to Laeta regarding the proper upbringing of her daughter Paula).

Most Christian authors viewed the design of the natural world as proof of God's existence and evidence of God's goodness. Hence the natural world is good. The tree of knowledge in the garden of Eden, for instance, was not evil in and of itself; rather, the point of the story was that knowledge could be used toward either good or bad ends. Even opposites in the world, because they exist in harmony with one another, point to God. God was affirmed as the source of the natural world, including all arts, skills, and sciences. Still, the natural world was never to be deified, and this was especially true with regard to skills—a warning necessitated by the use of the arts in the service of idolatry. The apologists in particular reasoned from the natural world to the Creator but, again, warned that human beings must worship the Creator alone and not the works of creation.

Like the rest of creation, the early Fathers affirmed that the human body was good, and they viewed the design of the body as pointing to the Creator. Although the body can be used for sinful purposes, the body is not the cause of sin. Concern over the body and its care stimulated thought and writing about practical matters such as food and drink, clothing, and entertainment, as well as more ethical concerns such as the relationship between medicine and prayer, materialism, and the use of time and money. Although the body is good, it is still subject to illness; medical science does not make prayer unnecessary nor does prayer make medical science dispensable. While much of what these ancient authors propose along these lines is unacceptable today, some of their admonitions are still worth consideration and heeding.

With respect to government, Christians were admonished to pay taxes and to honor their rulers but not to worship them. Personal and civil oaths that were part of the legal foundation of society were to be taken seriously. Where the law of the state and the law of God conflicted, however, Christians were clearly to choose the law of God since it is far superior. Christians considered their true citizenship to be in heaven, and this sometimes caused problems. Celsus—the famous critic mentioned above—strongly objected to Christians' refusal to participate in the government and defense of the empire. He called on Christians to aid the emperor on the grounds that if the world fell into the hands of barbarians, it would no longer be possible for them to practice the Christian religion. In his reply, Origen upheld the pacifism advocated by many early church leaders.

Discussing rule according to God's law, the *Discourse* attributed to Melito speaks in the political context of its time about the "king," but the words are applicable to government leaders in other political systems. The author, however, expresses too much confidence in the power of a ruler to influence people toward godliness. Throughout the course of history, the efforts of religious people to use government power to advance the cause of righteousness has led to abuses equal in severity to those inflicted by unrighteous rulers. In this respect Melito represents many who tried to impose their beliefs on others. Christian apologists in the early church advocated religious liberty with arguments that continue to be relevant. They made their pleas within the context of an empire that required religious expressions of loyalty, both to the emperor and to the Roman gods; they spoke out eloquently against religious persecution. Unfortunately, when Christianity became the favored religion of the Empire, Christians often forgot the fundamental premise of these arguments for religious liberty, that is, that religion is a voluntary response to deity.

Work

I do not forget that many artisans are standing around us. They barely earn a living from their daily labor, and so they make me shorten my discourse lest they be kept too long from their labor. What shall I say to them? The time that you lend to God is not lost, but he returns it to you with large interest. The Lord will dismiss any circumstances that create difficulties for you. For those who make spiritual affairs a priority, he gives strength to the body, eagerness to the soul, opportunity in business, and success in all affairs of life. And, even if the things that we work hard on do not turn out as we hope in this life, the Spirit's teaching is a good treasure for the age to come. Remove from your heart, then, every care of life and join yourself wholly together here with me. What good is it for you to be here physically if your heart is distressed about your earthly treasure?

—Basil of Caesarea, *Hexaemeron* 3.1

⌒he young people of the church should be eager to serve as needed; devote yourselves to your work with all seriousness so that you may always have enough to support yourselves and the needy and not be a burden to the church of God. For we ourselves [the apostles], although devoted to the word of the gospel, nevertheless do not neglect our temporal jobs. For some of us are fishermen, some tentmakers, some farmers, so that we may never be idle. . . . For the Lord our God hates those who are idle. None of those who are dedicated to God ought to be idle.

—*Apostolic Constitutions* 2.63

Everyone should know that for the faithful, trades are their lesser jobs but their true work is service to God. Pursue therefore your trade as secondary work for sustenance and practice your service to God as your main work.

—*Apostolic Constitutions* 2.61

If anyone is unwilling to work, let him not eat" [2 Thess 3:10]. Paul was not required to work but had a right to be idle, since he had been entrusted with such a great task. Nevertheless he not only worked but did so night and day, so as to be able to help others. How much more necessary it is for others to do the same! . . . To have leisure for the sake of prayer and fasting does not mean that one is not to do the manual work Paul speaks about [1 Cor 4:12; 2 Thess 3:6–13]. . . . That is why he did not say, "If they are disorderly, let them be sustained by you." Instead, he requires two things: "to be quiet and to work" [2 Thess 3:12].

—John Chrysostom, *Homilies on
2 Thessalonians* 5.2, on 2 Thess 3

There was in the Cells [of Scetis] an old man named Apollo. If someone asked him to do a particular job, he would set out joyfully, saying, "I have to work with Christ today on behalf of my soul, for this is the soul's reward."

— *Apophthegmata Patrum*, Alphabetical
Collection, Apollo # 1

Marriage

So MUCH has been written about an early Christian emphasis on virginity that the many positive statements about marriage are often neglected. Likewise, the attention paid to the patriarchal nature of ancient society often leads one to overlook what was said about mutuality between men and women. Yet in comments on 1 Corinthians 7, for instance, one finds explicit advice on sexual relations in marriage. And ancient wedding ceremonies sometimes include sentiments to the effect that "When sorrows are shared, they are halved; when joys are shared, they are doubled." A similar thought is expressed by Gregory Nazianzus, a fourth-century bishop, whose writings introduce our selections on the topic of marriage.

Through marriage we become one another's hands, ears, and feet. Marriage doubles what had been weak. It is a great joy to our friends, a distress to our enemies. Sorrows shared hurt less; joys shared are sweeter for both; wealth brings greater joy to those who are like-minded. To those who are in need, being like-minded brings greater joy than wealth. Marriage supplies a lock of self-control over desires and sets a seal on our natural need for friendship. . . . It is a drink from the household spring from which strangers cannot taste; it does not flow forth outside nor can another collect it from outside. The mutual love of those who are united in the flesh and are of one soul sharpens their piety to a fine point.

— Gregory of Nazianzus, *Carmina*
1.2.1.262–275

GREGORY described the marriage of his parents in ecstatic terms.

For I think that if anyone sought out the best marriage from the ends of the earth and among every human race, it would not have been possible to find one that is better or more harmonious than this. For the most excellent of men and women were so united into one that their marriage was as much a union of virtue as of bodies. While they excelled all others, they could not excel each other since they were quite equally matched with regard to virtue. . . . She who was given by God to my father became not only his coworker—which is less wonderful—but even his leader, drawing him forward to the highest excellence by her influence in word and deed. She thought it best in all other respects to be excelled by her husband according to the law of marriage, but was not ashamed to present herself as his teacher with regard to piety.

—Gregory of Nazianzus, *Oration* 18.7–8

It is good for a wife to reverence Christ through her husband, and it is good for a husband not to dishonor the church through his wife. Let the wife, [as the Apostle Paul says in Eph 5:22–33], reverence her husband just as she does Christ; but also let the husband treat his wife well, just as Christ does the church.

—Gregory of Nazianzus, *Oration* 37.7

How great is the marriage between two believers! They have one hope, one desire, one way of life, the same religion. They are brother and sister, fellow servants, divided neither in flesh nor in spirit—truly "two in one flesh," for where there is one flesh there is also one spirit. They pray together; they prostrate themselves together; they carry out fasts together. They instruct one another, and exhort one another. They are present in the church of God and at the banquet of God side by side; side by side they stand in difficulties and in consolations. Neither one hides anything from the other; neither one avoids the other; nor is either one a grief to the other. Freely the sick are visited and the poor are sustained. Without anxiety, misgivings, or hindrance to one another, they give alms, attend the sacrifices [of the church], and carry out their daily duties [of piety]. They are not secretive about making the sign of the cross; they are not fearful about greetings, nor silent in offering benedictions. They sing psalms and hymns to one another, challenging one another as to who sings better to God. When Christ sees and hears such things, he rejoices.

—Tertullian, *To His Wife* 2.8

We [Christians] avoid unrestricted intercourse to such an extent that for us it is unlawful even to look upon another with lust [Matt 5:28]. . . . How could anyone doubt that we, for whom a look with pleasure is adultery, practice self-control? . . . We exercise the greatest care that the bodies of those we regard as brothers and sisters, and those we call by other names of kinship, remain undefiled and uncorrupted. . . . Each of us who has married a woman according to the laws laid down by us considers her to be his wife only for the purpose of bearing children. . . . One should remain either as he was when he was born or in one marriage, for a second marriage is only a socially acceptable form of adultery.

—Athenagoras, *Plea for the Christians* 32–33

CLEMENT of Alexandria marked out a middle ground between those who insisted upon celibacy and those who advocated sexual libertinism.

A wise woman then should first try to persuade her husband to become a partner with her in the things that lead to true happiness. If that should be impossible, then alone she should be diligent about virtue, being obedient to her husband and doing nothing against his will except with regard to those things that affect virtue and salvation.

So a marriage that is fulfilled according to reason is sanctified if the union is subject to God. . . . A truly happy marriage must be judged according to neither wealth nor beauty but according to virtue.

—Clement of Alexandria, *Miscellanies* 4.19, 20

We [Christians] consider that abstention from sexual intercourse is blessed when undertaken by those to whom God has given this state. We honor monogamy and the dignity of one marriage, saying that we ought to suffer together and "bear one another's burdens" [Gal 6:2] lest one "who seems to stand firmly should fall" [1 Cor 10:12]. Concerning a second marriage, the apostle says, "If one burns, he should marry" [1 Cor 7:9].

—Clement of Alexandria, *Miscellanies* 3.1.4.3

Both states—singleness and marriage—have their own distinctive ministries and services to the Lord. With regard to the care of a wife and children, for instance, marriage provides the occasion for the perfect man to make provision for all the things pertaining to the household that are shared in common. For example, Scripture says that those are to be appointed bishops who have learned from their own household the care of the whole church. Let each one therefore fulfill his ministry through the work in which he was called, in order that he might be free in Christ and receive the fitting reward for his ministry.

—Clement of Alexandria, *Miscellanies*
3.12.79.5–7

Let us learn to be reasonable and gentle toward all, especially our wives, and to be very diligent so that if they rebuke us—whether rightly or wrongly—we may not be too exacting but may make our sole concern the removal of the cause of sadness and establish deep peace in the home. Then the wife may turn her attention toward her husband, and the husband may take refuge in his wife and find consolation at home, as in a harbor sheltered from external difficulties and troubles. The wife was given as a helper in order that the husband, strengthened by her encouragement, might be able to withstand whatever comes his way. . . . Those who are thus bound together will have no grief in this life nor will their pleasure suffer any harm. Wherever harmony, peace, and the bond of love exist between a wife and husband, all good things will flow together, and they will become impregnable to every assault, being fortified by the great and unassailable wall of divine harmony. This will make them stronger than steel, harder than iron, and supply them with more benefits than all wealth and possessions; this will lead them to the highest distinction and recommend them to God's abundant favor.

I urge therefore that we not prize anything more than this, but that we labor and do everything we can to bring about calm and peace in marriage. Then the children who are born will follow the virtue of their parents, the servants will imitate them, and in every respect the affairs of the household will contribute toward virtue, and there will be much happiness in our affairs. When we honor first the things of God, then all other things will come to us smoothly and we will experience no distress, for the goodness of God supplies us with all things in abundance. In order then that we may pass our present lives without distress and—above all else—win the favor of the Lord and hold fast to virtue, let us be diligent in bringing about harmony and peace in our households, in being attentive to the orderly behavior of our children and the conduct of our servants. Thus, in addition to being rewarded beyond all other favors, we may be found worthy of the good things promised by the grace and loving-kindness of our Lord Jesus Christ.

—John Chrysostom, *Homilies on Genesis* 38.7 [22], on Gen 16:1ff.

Is marriage a theater? It is a mystery and a type of something great [Christ and the church, Eph 5:32]. Even if you do not hold marriage in awe, hold in awe that of which it is a type. . . . How is marriage a mystery? Two come together and make one. . . . When they come together, they make neither a lifeless nor an earthly image but an image of God himself. They come [to the wedding] in order that they might become one body. Behold again the mystery of love! If the two do not become one but remain as two, they do not make many. But when they come together in unity, then they make [another]. What do we learn from this? The great strength of unity. The ingenuity of God divided one person into two at the beginning and, desiring to show that after the division they remained one, he did not leave one person sufficient for generating a child. . . . Do you see therefore the mystery of marriage? God made one out of one, and again, having made these two into one, he also makes one so that even now one person is born of one. For wife and husband are not two human beings but one. . . .

The child is a sort of bridge that connects each one to the other, so that the three become one flesh. . . . What happens then when there is no child? Does this mean they remain two? The answer is quite clear: conjugal intercourse itself accomplishes this [unity] through the pouring forth and commingling of both bodies.

—John Chrysostom, *Homilies on Colossians* 12.5–6

IN THE selection below, John Chrysostom comments on 1 Cor 7:3.

And what is "the debt of honor" ["obligation" or "conjugal rights" in NRSV]? A wife does not have authority over her own body but is her husband's slave and mistress. If you avoid proper service, you offend God. If you wish to abstain, even if for a short time, [do so] with the consent of your husband. [The apostle] called conjugal relations a "debt" in order to convey that husband and wife are not their own lord, but they are both slaves of one another. Husband, when you see a prostitute tempting you, respond, "My body is not mine but my wife's," and likewise let the wife respond the same to those who desire to undermine her self-control: "My body is not mine but my husband's." If husband and wife do not have authority over their own bodies, they have even less over their possessions. Hear, you married women and married men, if you do not have control over your body as your own, how much less do you have control over your possessions as your own. . . .

Suppose a wife abstains from marital relations without her husband's consent. What then? He might commit fornication or—if he does not—he is pained, raises a disturbance, becomes inflamed, fights, and makes many demands on his wife. What is the gain of fasting and continence if love is broken into pieces? Nothing at all. . . .

[In 1 Cor 7:5] Paul speaks about periods of intense prayer. . . . It is certainly possible to have intercourse with one's wife and be attentive to prayer. But prayer is made more disciplined by abstinence. For Paul did not say, "in order that you may pray," but he said, "in order to devote yourself to prayer." His point is not that sexual relations make prayer impure but that they occupy one's attention.

—John Chrysostom, *Homilies on*
1 Corinthians 19, on 1 Cor 7

Husbands

Because of wisdom, those who have run to the Father become good fathers to their children; those who have known the Son become good sons to their parents; those who remember the Bridegroom become good husbands to their wives; and those who have been ransomed from the ultimate slavery become good masters to their slaves.

—Clement of Alexandria, *Exhortation* 10

Let the husband be neither arrogant nor boastful toward his wife; but be compassionate, generous, desiring to please only his own wife, flattering her with honor and endeavoring to be pleasing to her; not adorning himself in a way that would entice another woman to him.

—*Apostolic Constitutions* 1.3.2

You have seen the measure of obedience [Eph 5:22–24]; hear the measure of love [Eph 5:25–30]. Do you [husband] want your wife to obey you as the church obeys Christ? Then exercise providential care for her as Christ does for the church. Even if it is necessary to give up your life for her, to be cut into thousands of pieces, to endure and suffer anything whatever, do not refuse to do it. Even if you suffer these things, you have not done what Christ did. . . . Even if you see her despising you, putting on airs, and being disdainful, you will win her submission through much care for her, through love and kindness. No bonds are stronger than these, especially between husband and wife. One can control a slave through fear, but only for a while, and then he quickly seeks to escape. But one's companion for life, the mother of one's children and the basis of all one's joy, must never be bound through fear and threats but through love and a good attitude. If the wife is afraid of her husband, what kind of a marriage can they have? What kind of pleasure can a husband enjoy if he lives with his wife as though she were a slave instead of a free woman? Even if you suffer for her sake, do not reproach her. For Christ never did this. . . .

The wife is a second authority, endowed with much authority and equal dignity, but the husband has more. This is beneficial to the household. . . . Seek the things of God, and human things will follow easily. Train your wife, and thus your household will be well disciplined. . . . If we administer our households in this way, then we will be fit for leadership of the church, for the household is a little church.

—John Chrysostom, *Homilies on Ephesians* 20.1, 6, on Eph 5:22ff.

Wives

You instructed the women to perform everything with a blameless and pure conscience and to be properly affectionate toward their own husbands. You taught them to fulfill their household duties honorably and to live according to the rule of submission, being altogether prudent.

—*1 Clement* 1.3

Let us direct our wives toward what is good. Let them manifest the habit of purity, which is most worthy of love; let them demonstrate the innocence of their will through meekness; let them make the gentleness of their tongue evident through their silence; let them show their love in a holy manner, not with partiality but equally toward all those who reverence God.

—*1 Clement* 21.6–7

Therefore, an unmarried woman devotes her time to God alone, and her attention is not divided. A chaste woman who marries divides her life between God and her husband. Another kind of woman devotes herself wholly to marriage (that is, to passion). Thus it seems to me that a chaste wife who devotes her time to her husband sincerely serves God, but if she loves adornment, she falls away from both God and a chaste marriage by exchanging the things of her husband for adornment.

—Clement of Alexandria, *Instructor* 2.10.109

Family Roles and Relationships

Fathers

And let the husband repeat [at home] the words said here in church. Let the wife hear; let the children learn; let the servants be taught; and let your household become a church. Do this in order that the devil may be banished and that evil demon—the enemy of our salvation—may run away. The grace of the Holy Spirit will rest there at once, and all peace and harmony will surround the residents.

—John Chrysostom, *Homilies on Genesis*
2.4 [13], on Gen 1:2

Mothers

A mother experiences more than one death, even though she herself will die only once. She fears for her husband; she fears for her children; again, she fears for the women and children who belong to her children; her cares multiply according to the number of leaves put forth by the root of the family tree. For each of these—whether for loss of possessions, bodily illness, or undesired misfortune—she mourns and grieves no less than those who suffer. If all depart from this life before she does, her grief is unbearable; even if some remain while others are carried away by untimely deaths, this circumstance brings her no real consolation. For fear on behalf of the living disturbs the soul as much as grief over those who have died; indeed—what is even more surprising—fear for those who are living is more difficult. For time eases our sorrow over those who have died, but anxiety over the living remains always and ceases only with death.

—John Chrysostom, *On Virginity* 56.1–2

Parents

Just as an artist who paints pictures and portraits exercises great care in his work, so each of you, mothers and fathers, must be attentive to these wonderful images [children]. Each day, a painter adds what is necessary to the picture. Sculptors do the same, removing excess stone and adding what is lacking. You should do the same: as makers of images, devote all your time to the task of fashioning wonderful images for God. Remove the excess; add what is lacking. Each day, examine the images closely. Cultivate the natural excellence that each one has, removing what is by nature inferior. Take care to root out first the thought of licentiousness, for sex is especially troublesome to young souls. Instead, before they encounter this temptation, teach them to be sober, vigilant, watchful in prayer, and to place everything that is said and done under the sign of the cross.

—John Chrysostom, *On Vainglory and the*
Education of Children 22

Let us persuade them with this blessed exhortation: "Bring them up in the discipline and admonition of the Lord" [Eph 6:4]. Let us give them examples by having them spend time reading the Scriptures from earliest childhood.

—John Chrysostom, *Homilies on Ephesians*
21.2, on Eph 6:4

Let our children receive the instruction that is in Christ. Let them learn why humility prevails before God, why pure love is strong before God, how reverence for God is beautiful and great and saves all those who conduct themselves in a holy manner and with a pure mind.

—*1 Clement* 21.8

IN THE following passage a heavenly messenger, who appears in the form of a woman, reproves Hermas:

God is not angry with you because of this, but he desires the conversion of your family, who sinned against the Lord and against you, their parents. Out of affection for your children, you did not correct your family, and it became corrupt. The Lord is angry with you on account of this, but he will heal all the past evils in your family. Because of their sins and transgressions your daily affairs were brought to a sorry plight. However, the Lord's great mercy on your family will make you strong and establish you in his glory. Do not be negligent, but be of good courage and strengthen your family. For as a smith shapes the object he desires by striking it with a hammer, so also a righteous word spoken daily overcomes all wickedness. Do not cease then to admonish your children, for I know that if they repent with their whole hearts, their names will be inscribed with those of the saints in the book of life.

—Hermas, *Visions* 1.3.1–2 [3.1–2]

Even we human beings, when we teach slaves or children, we restrain them with threats and fear as long as they are incapable of listening to reason because of their age; but when they begin to understand what is truly good, useful, and honorable, then the fear of punishment may cease, and they can be persuaded by word and reason to obey willingly everything that is good.

—Origen, *First Principles* 3.5.8

And teach your children trades that are useful and appropriate according to the word in order that they may not through leisure become unruly and rebel against the good, going uncorrected by parents who indulge them for a time. Do not be cautious about chastising them and instructing them with severity, for you will not kill them by disciplining them but will save them. . . . Whoever is reluctant to exhort and punish his son hates his own child. Therefore, teach your children the word of the Lord, punish them with beatings, and bring them into subjection, teaching "the sacred Scriptures from childhood" [2 Tim 3:15]. . . . If, through the negligence of their parents, they do this [commit fornication], their parents will be held accountable for their souls; for if the children are undisciplined because of their parents' indifference, then the children who sin will not be the only ones punished, but the parents also will be punished on account of them. Therefore when the time for marriage comes, be diligent about drawing up a marital contract and joining them in marriage lest in the prime of youthful ardor they follow common practices and become fornicators.

— *Apostolic Constitutions* 4.11

Children

GREGORY of Nazianzus, in a funeral oration for his friend Basil, paid tribute to Basil's parents for the children they raised.

There were many other characteristics of the union of [Basil's] parents, a union that was as much a union of equally honorable virtue as of bodies. . . . It seems to me that the greatest and most notable characteristic is the excellence of their children. . . . Even if parents themselves were not so eminent in virtue, they who have produced such children would surpass all others through the excellence of the children. If one or two children become praiseworthy, then this might be ascribed to the nature of the children themselves, but when all are eminent, then this is a clear tribute to those who have brought them up.

— Gregory of Nazianzus, *Oration* 43.9

Paul lays a marvelous foundation for a virtuous life: honor and reverence for parents. Leading away from evil practices and entering into good ones, he commanded (I say) that we honor first of all our parents, since— after God—they before all others are the authors of our being. So it is fitting that the enjoyment of our good deeds should first be theirs, and after them all other people. If one does not honor parents, one will never be fair to those outside the family.

— John Chrysostom, *Homilies on Ephesians* 21.1, on Eph 6:1–3

Those who believe are like innocent infants, in whose heart no wickedness enters and who do not know what evil is but remain always in innocence. Those who are like this will undoubtedly live in the kingdom of God because they do not in any way defile the commandments of God but remain in the same childlike frame of mind throughout their lives. All of you then who continue on and remain as infants, with no wickedness, will be more honored than all others; for all infants are honored before God, occupying the first place before him.

— Hermas, *Similitudes* 9.29.1–3 [106.1–3]

I have heard that the death of your child greatly afflicted you. For a grandfather, such a loss is naturally grievous. But for a man who has attained such a degree of virtue, who knows human nature from long experience and from spiritual teaching, separation from those nearest to us is not altogether unbearable. The Lord does not require the same things from us as he does from ordinary people. They live according to custom, but for our rule of life we rely on the commandment of the Lord and the examples of blessed men from earlier times, whose nobility of mind was demonstrated in severe circumstances. Toward the end, then, that you may bequeath an example of fortitude and a true disposition toward the things hoped for, show that you are not overwhelmed by your grief and rise above your sorrows, patiently endure affliction, and rejoice in hope. . . . Indeed children are held blameless on account of their tender age; but you and I bear the responsibility of serving the Lord as he commands us, and in all things we must be ready to administer the affairs of the churches.

— Basil of Caesarea, *Letters* 206

Youth

Let us speak of the duties that must be observed from our youth, so that they may grow along with our age. It is the nature of good youths to fear God, to be subject to parents, to honor older persons, to preserve chastity, not to despise humility, and to love clemency and modesty. All of these are ornaments of our younger years. For as older persons are characterized by seriousness and young people by enthusiasm, so also nature entrusts the gift of modesty to youths.

—Ambrose, *Duties* 1.17.65

Old Age

Nearly everything that is excellent about the body changes with age, and while wisdom alone increases, other things decline. . . . Young people endure many struggles with their bodies; just as fire is stifled by green fuel, so also when youth is stifled by the enticements of vice and the titillations of the flesh, it cannot display its own brilliance. But certainly—I remind you again—those who were taught about honorable pursuits during their youth and who meditate on the law of the Lord day and night become more learned with age, more experienced with practice, wiser with the passage of time, and in old age reap the sweetest fruits from past pursuits.

—Jerome, *Letters* 52.3

When those who are covetous reach old age and intemperance no longer brings enjoyment, and the fear of death comes upon them, consider the fears they suffer! It is not so for those who live according to virtue: they rejoice and feel glad when they reach old age, for their enjoyment does not wither away but blossoms. Old age brings the decay of enjoyment to those who are adulterers, licentious, covetous, and gluttonous; but for those who live virtuous lives it brings the height of enjoyment.

—John Chrysostom, *Commentary on the Psalms* 7.16

Friends

IN THE following selection we find a modern-sounding thought that relates loving others to one's self-esteem.

How can someone love another person if he does not love himself? And if a person cannot be a friend to himself, will he not be an enemy to everyone else?

—Pseudo-Clement, *Recognitions* 3.53

How much wiser it is to spend money on human beings than on gems and gold! How much more profitable to acquire suitable friends than lifeless ornaments! Who has benefited as much from lands as from the granting of favors?

—Clement of Alexandria, *Instructor*
2.13 [2.12.120]

GREGORY of Nazianzus speaks of his friendship with Basil of Caesarea:

Envy was far from us, and sincere imitation made us more earnest. We competed against each other not to gain precedence but in order to confer precedence on the other; for we made each other's reputation our own. In both of us there seemed to be one soul that extended through two bodies. . . . In both there was one work: to practice virtue and to live for the hope to come, removing ourselves from this world before departing from it. We devoted all our attention and activity toward this goal and, being guided by the commandment, we sharpened virtue in each other. And—if it is not too great a thing for me to say—we became each other's rule and standard for discerning what is right and what is not. Our associates were not the most dissolute but the most sober, not the most rowdy but the most peaceable, whose companionship was most profitable; we knew that it is easier to become a participant in evil than to impart virtue.

—Gregory of Nazianzus, *Oration* 43.20

There is one kind of love between persons that is indissoluble, because the unity is based neither on esteem nor the greatness of one's position or favors, nor on a business obligation, nor on natural need, but only on likeness with respect to virtue. This love, I say, is never broken off for any reason. Not only are distance and time unable to separate and destroy it, but even death itself cannot disrupt it. This is the true and unbroken love that grows by means of the twofold perfection and virtue of the friends. Once this relationship has begun, neither different desires nor contentious disagreement caused by personal inclinations can disrupt it. . . .

True friendships, then, have as their first foundation contempt for worldly wealth and a disdain for all the material goods that we possess. . . . The second foundation is each person's curtailment of his own inclinations, so as not to consider himself wise and skilled. Neither one insists on having his own way but both prefer to do what his neighbor wishes. The third is that each person knows that all things—even those he values as useful and necessary—are to be treated as secondary to the value of love and peace. The fourth is that each person believes from the bottom of his heart that he must never become angry for any cause, whether just or unjust. The fifth is that each one desires to assuage the anger that the other may have toward him—even if for no reason—in the same way as he would his own anger. . . . The last is something not to be doubted with regard to vice in general—namely, a person must believe each day that he is going to depart from this world.

—John Cassian, *Conferences* 16.3.1–2; 16.6.1–2

The greatest freedom, and the greatest reputation one can have, is freedom from self-concern. We are weak and easily overcome by both people and the devil because we promote our own interests and do not protect one another. We are not fortified by God's love, but seek comrades and friends out of other motives—some because of family, some out of habit, some for the sake of partnership, some because they are neighbors. Instead—above all—we should be friends on account of piety. Friends ought to be bound together by this alone.

—John Chrysostom, *Homilies on Matthew* 59.5, on Matt 18:7ff.

Anthony the Great] said, "Life and death depend on our neighbor. If we gain our brother or sister we gain God, but if we cause our brother or sister to fall we sin against Christ."

—*Apophthegmata Patrum*, Alphabetical Collection, Anthony # 9

Abba Agathon said, "If someone were very specially dear to me, but I realized that he was leading me to do something less good, I should put him from me."[1]

—*Apophthegmata Patrum*, Alphabetical Collection, Agathon # 23

Concerning Prov 11:14] You see the force of this saying, brothers and sisters. You see what holy Scripture teaches us. It fortifies us lest we become satisfied with ourselves, lest we consider ourselves experts, lest we trust that we are able to manage our own affairs. We need help; in addition to God, we need others to guide us. There are none more miserable, none more vulnerable, than those who have no one to guide them on the road that leads to

God. . . . Scripture says, "In an abundance of counselors there is safety." It does not mean by "an abundance of counselors" that one should seek counsel from everyone, but it is evident that in all things one should seek advice from those in whom one has confidence and not remain silent about some things while speaking of other things.

—Dorotheus of Gaza, *Teachings* 5.61

Nothing then should be preferred over integrity, which is not to be neglected out of devotion to friendship.

A friend is never obliged to gratify someone by doing wrong, nor to plot against the innocent. . . .

Certainly, if it is necessary to give testimony, if one is aware of any fault in a friend, one ought to rebuke the friend secretly; if he does not listen, one must rebuke him openly. For rebukes are good, and much better than a silent friendship. . . . Rebuke then your erring friend; do not desert one who is innocent. For friendship ought to be constant and to persevere in affection. We ought not to change our friends childishly, on a whim.

—Ambrose, *Duties* 3.22.125–127

Education and Areas of Knowledge

Secular and Religious Education

For profane education is truly barren; it is always in labor but never gives birth. What fruit does philosophy bring forth that is worthy of such birth pangs, being so long in labor? Do not all of those who are full of wind and never come to term miscarry before they come to the light of the knowledge of God . . . ? Now Moses, after living with the Egyptian princess for so long a time that he seemed to share in their honors, had to return to his natural mother. Indeed—as history states [Exod 2:6–10]—he was not separated from her while he was being brought up by the princess but was nursed on his mother's milk. This teaches us, it seems to me, that if we become involved with profane teachings during our education, we should not separate ourselves from the nourishment of the church's milk, that is, from her laws and customs. On these the soul is nourished and matured.

—Gregory of Nyssa, *Life of Moses* 2.11–12

I think that all reasonable people will acknowledge that education is our foremost advantage. [This is true] with respect not only to our more noble Christian education, which disdains all rhetorical subtlety and ambition and clings to salvation and beautiful thoughts alone, but also with respect to non-Christian culture, which many Christians ill-advisedly despise as treacherous, dangerous, and likely to drive us away from God. It is the same with regard to heaven, earth, air, and everything that pertains to these: these things are not to be despised simply because some have wrongly understood them and worship the things of God rather than God himself. Rather, we enjoy whatever they provide that is useful for life and refreshment and avoid whatever is dangerous. We do not—as those who are foolish do—raise creation to the place of the Creator, but we apprehend the Creator from the works of creation and, as the divine apostle says, we "bring every thought into captivity to Christ" [2 Cor 10:5]. Likewise, we know that fire, food, iron, and other things are neither most useful nor most harmful in and of themselves, but they seem useful or harmful to the one who uses them. Indeed, just as we have compounded healing medicines from certain reptiles, even so we have received from secular education those things that pertain to inquiry and speculation, but we have despised whatever involves demons, error, and the depth of destruction. We profit with respect to godliness even from these things, since we learn what is better from what is worse and strengthen our doctrine according to the weakness of theirs. Therefore, education is not to be dishonored simply because some consider it dishonorable. One must suppose that those who hold such views are stupid and uneducated. They wish that everyone were like themselves so that their nature might be hidden among the general mass and their lack of culture might escape criticism.

—Gregory of Nazianzus, *Oration* 43.11

Avoid the thorns; pick the rose.

—Gregory of Nazianzus, *Poems* 2.2.8

Most people are as frightened of Hellenic philosophy as children are of masks, being afraid that it will lead them astray. If their faith—I would not call it knowledge—is such that it can be dissolved by plausible speech, then let it be dissolved, since by this they acknowledge that they do not possess the truth. For the truth is immovable, but false opinion is dissolvable. . . . Dialectics is like a bulwark that prevents the truth from being trampled upon by Sophists.

—Clement of Alexandria, *Miscellanies* 6.10

IN THE following selection, Origen responds to the criticism of Christians by the pagan philosopher Celsus.

It is also untrue that the teachers of the divine word "wish to persuade only the foolish, low born, stupid, slaves, women, and children." Indeed the Word calls such as these in order to make them better. But it also calls those who are very different from these, since Christ is "the Savior of all people, especially of those who believe" [1 Tim 4:10], whether intelligent or simple. . . . Truly "it is no evil to have been educated," for education is the way to virtue. But to count among the educated those who hold erroneous opinions is something even the wise among the Greeks will not do. Again, who would not acknowledge that it is good to have studied the best teachings? But what shall we say are the best teachings if not those that are true and foster virtue?

— Origen, *Against Celsus* 3.49

A STUDENT paid this tribute to Origen, his teacher:

Origen was the first who urged me with words to study philosophy, but his deeds anticipated his verbal exhortation. . . . He endeavored to portray himself as being like the one who lives well, whom he describes in his discourses, using himself—I would say—as an example of the wise man. . . . I am not saying that he was a perfect example but that, as one who wanted to be like the perfect example and lead others to it, he diligently and earnestly made every effort, even—if I may say so—going beyond human capacity out of his desire to shape us who are so different from him. His concern was not that we become masters of words, persons who have understanding about our impulses, but that we might master and understand the impulses themselves. . . .

How can I enter into the very disposition of this man and thereby in my discourse describe his diligent, laborious practice of piety and teaching about God? How shall I describe the degree of intelligence and preparation he brought to his desire for us to learn all the doctrines concerning the divine, guarding us against being in any danger concerning what is most necessary of all, namely knowledge of the Cause of all things? He considered it good for us to study philosophy, and he diligently collected all the writings of the ancient philosophers and poets, eliminating and rejecting nothing—for we ourselves did not yet have the power of judgment—except what belongs to the atheists, those who turn aside from the common opinion of humanity and say that there is no God or Providence. . . . He counted it worthwhile to encounter and be conversant with all others, neither preferring nor rejecting any one kind—whether philosophical discourse or not, whether Greek or barbarian—but listening to all. He did this wisely and with great skill lest any one of these teachings when it alone is heard and valued—even if it should happen not to be true—be considered by us to be true and, being considered in isolation, deceive us and make us its own. . . . The human mind is easily deceived by speech and often assents before it examines carefully and exercises judgment. The mind is often taken in by false words and doctrines, either because of its own dullness and weakness or because of the subtlety of the discourse, being weary of going to the trouble of making precise inquiry.

—Gregory Thaumaturgus, *Panegyric
to Origen* 11, 13

Jerome offered this advice on the education of a friend's daughter:

Thus a soul that is to become a temple of God must be educated. It must learn to hear nothing and to say nothing except what pertains to the fear of God. It must have no understanding of indecent words, and no knowledge of the world's songs. While still at a tender age its tongue must be introduced to the sweetness of the Psalms. . . . And let her have companions in her lessons, with whom she may compete and be stimulated when they are praised. She must not be punished if she is slow to learn; rather, natural ability must be aroused by praises, so that she may be glad when she surpasses others and sorry when she is surpassed by them. Above all, care must be taken that she not dislike her lessons lest bitterness acquired in early childhood continue into the future. . . . What young souls imbibe is hard to eradicate. . . . There is an inclination toward imitating bad things, and where you may be unable to attain virtue, you are able quickly to imitate faults. . . .

Let her have you for a teacher; let her naiveté hold you in admiration. Let her see neither you nor her father do anything that would be a sin if she did it too. . . . You can teach her more through example than through words.

—Jerome, *Letters* 107.4.1, 3–4, 6, 7; 107.9.1

The naive and simple-minded brother who knows nothing must not for that reason consider himself a saint; and he who is learned and eloquent must not count that as sanctity. Of these two imperfect things, it is much better to be unsophisticated and holy than to have sinful eloquence.

— Jerome, *Letters* 52.9.3

Arts and Crafts

THE GREEK word *technē* ("art") also means "skill," so it includes more than our modern notions of "art."

God gave to human beings the power of discovery, sowing it in their nature, together with wisdom and the faculty of art. . . . Contemplative wisdom is a gift from God. By it we are impelled toward the arts and other pursuits. And we all—just and unjust alike—have it [wisdom] in common; if we are rational creatures, we have this capacity.

— Methodius, quoted by Nicetae,
Catena on Job 19

The good things in the arts have their source in God. For, even as to do something artistically is included in theories of art, so also to act prudently is included in prudence.

— Clement of Alexandria, *Miscellanies* 6.17

What handicraft or work made by builders and stonecutters can be holy? . . . Works of art are neither sacred nor divine.

— Clement of Alexandria, *Miscellanies* 7.5

Scripture calls by the same name of wisdom every secular knowledge and art, for many additional things are invented by human reason, and artistic and wise inventiveness is from God [adducing Exod 31:2–6]. . . . Those who pursue the common arts have exceptional sensory enjoyment: a musician enjoys the sense of hearing; the sculptor, of touch; the singer, of the voice; the perfumer, of smell; the engraver of designs on seals, of sight. Instructors teach the perception of poetic meters; the sophists teach perceptiveness regarding words; dialecticians, syllogisms; and philosophers, their theories. Perceptiveness persuades one to apply what one discovers and invents. Through application, training grows into knowledge. Appropriately, the apostle has said that the wisdom of God is "manifold" [Eph 3:10].

— Clement of Alexandria, *Miscellanies*
1.4.25.4–27.1

The Word] allows a signet ring only for the purpose of sealing things for safety. . . . Our seals should be a dove, a fish, a ship sailing with a fair wind, a harmonious lyre (which Polycrates used), or a ship's anchor (which Seleucus had engraved as an emblem). And a seal of someone fishing should remind us of the apostle [Peter] and the children [baptizands] drawn out of the water. We are not permitted to make any impression of an idol's face, since at no time are we even to pay attention to them. Nor may we impress a sword or bow since we pursue peace, nor drinking cups since we practice temperance. Many licentious people have had engravings made of their male lovers or their courtesans, as if they wanted to make it impossible to forget their erotic passions by means of these continual reminders of their licentiousness.

—Clement of Alexandria, *Instructor*
3.11.58–60

Science and the Natural World

NOVATIAN was opposed to Christians attending gladiator contests, offering them "nobler exhibitions" instead.

A Christian has the beauty of the world to look upon and admire. He may observe the rising of the sun and again its setting, as it causes day and night in their turn; the sphere of the moon, signifying by its waxing and waning the course of time; the chorus of stars, glittering and gleaming from on high with their regular movement; the division of the entire year through its changing seasons; the days and nights themselves arranged and ordered into hourly periods; the earth like a millstone balanced by the mountains; the flowing rivers with their sources; the expanse of seas with their waves and shores. At the same time, he may observe the air, existing equally everywhere in perfect harmony . . . , now pouring forth showers from dense clouds, now calling back the refreshed serenity of the sky by thinning and disbursing the clouds; and in all these elements appropriate inhabitants dwell—birds in the air, fish in the water, human beings on the earth. I say, let the spectacles for faithful Christians be these and other divine works. . . . No one who is recognized as a child of God will ever be amazed at the works of human beings. Anyone who is more amazed by these things than by the works of God causes himself to fall away from God's noble eminence.

—Novatian, *On the Shows* 9

If the rationale of these sciences is accessible to you and you are knowledgeable about these things, examine the different kinds of plants also, even the ingenuity of the leaves; they are exceedingly pleasing to look at and are extremely useful to the fruit. Examine also the variety and abundance of fruits, and especially the great beauty possessed by those that are most necessary. And also examine the roots, juices, flowers, and fragrances, which are not only so very sweet but also useful as medicine; the grace and quality of color; and again the value and brilliance of precious stones. Nature has set all things before you—both the necessities and luxuries of life—as a full public banquet so that, if nothing else, you might know God from his benefits and by reason of your sense of need might become wiser than you were.

Next, walk with me the length and breadth of the earth, the mother of all things: the gulfs of the seas bound both to one another and to the land; the beauty of the forests; the plentiful and ever flowing rivers and springs that flow not only on the surface of the earth, with waters that are cold and fit for drinking, but also run in caverns beneath the earth, which are either thrust out by a violent blast and repelled or, when heated by the violence of agitation and resistance, burst out little by little wherever possible, supplying our need for hot baths in many parts of the earth and—in conjunction with the cold—provide healing that is spontaneous and free. Tell me how and whence are these things? . . . How does the earth stand firm and unswerving? On what is it carried? What supports that, and on what does that rest? For reason has nothing upon which it rests, except the will of God. . . . Is this not the clearest sign of the magnificent working of God?

— Gregory of Nazianzus, *Oration* 28.26

The world is beautiful, . . . but its Maker—not the world—is to be worshiped. When your subjects approach you [emperors], they do not neglect to pay homage to you, their rulers and masters, from whom they would obtain what they need and have recourse to the majesty of your residence. And if they come upon the royal house, they admire its beautiful adornments, but they bring glory to you as one who is "all in all." You emperors adorn royal residences for yourselves, but the world was not created as if God needed anything. For God is everything in himself—light unapproachable, a perfect world, spirit, power, reason. If then the world is a melodious instrument that moves rhythmically, I do not worship the instrument but the One who gives it harmony, strikes its notes, and sings the unison melody line. For the judges at contests do not pass over the kithara players and crown the kitharas. As Plato says, "Admiring the beauty of God's art, I come before the Artist." . . . If then, although I admire the heavens and its elements for their art, I do not worship them as gods, knowing that the law of dissolution applies to them, how much less shall I call "gods" the things I know human beings have made.

—Athenagoras, *Plea for the Christians* 16

Like beauty, so also a flower when looked at brings delight; it is necessary to glorify the Creator through enjoying the sight of beautiful things.

—Clement of Alexandria, *Instructor* 2.8.70

Upon seeing things that are opposite in nature combine and exist in harmonious concord—as for example, fire mixed with cold and dry with wet—and these not in conflict with one another but one thing performing as one body, who would not think that there exists outside of these things One that united them? Upon observing that winter gives way to spring, spring to summer, and summer to autumn, and that these things are contrary by nature—for one chills and the other burns, one nourishes and the other causes decay—yet all are equally and harmlessly useful to humanity, who would not think that there exists One who is superior to these things, who apportions and guides all things, even if he cannot see this One? . . .

Therefore, things that are of conflicting and opposite natures would not have reconciled themselves if there were not One superior and Lord over them, who unites them and to whom the elements themselves yield obedience as slaves to a master. . . . If these things occurred [one part of nature striving against another], we would no longer see an ordered universe but disorder, not arrangement but confusion, not a system but a chaos of the whole, not proportion but disproportion. For in the general discord and conflict either all things would be destroyed or the stronger alone would appear. . . .

Since then there is everywhere not confusion but arrangement, not disproportion but proportion, not disorder but order, and a completely harmonious arrangement of the cosmos, one must necessarily be led to comprehend and perceive the Master who reconciled and bound together all things and produced harmony in them. For even if he is not seen with the eyes, yet from the arrangement and harmony of contrary things it is possible to perceive their Ruler, Arranger, and King. [Athanasius proceeds with two illustrations: observing a city of many diverse peoples living in concord and concluding from this the presence of a wise ruler, and the harmony of the members of a human body.] So in the arrangement and harmony of the universe it is necessary to perceive God the Governor of it all, and to see that he is one and not many.

—Athanasius, *Against the Pagans* 36, 37, 38

Scripture says that the heavens and its order are a guide to faith, for through it we see the Artist himself. Again, beholding the beauty of the earth will cause faith in God to grow within you. We believe in God; we cannot see him with human eyes, but through the power of the mind we can perceive the Invisible One through those things that are visible. All his works then are occasions for faith. Even a stone bears some mark of the power of its Creator. The same goes for an ant, a mosquito, or a bee; the wisdom of the Creator is often manifest in the smallest creatures. He spread out the heavens. He poured out the vast expanse of the seas. He also hollowed out like a pipe the tiny stinger of a bee so that it might sting. God's works therefore are all occasions for faith. Let nothing be an occasion for unbelief in you.

—Basil of Caesarea, *Homilies on the Psalms*
32.3, on Ps 33:6

Reflect with me, beloved, how all the plants on the earth came into existence by the word of the Lord. There was no human being to act as the laborer, no plough, no assistance from oxen, no other diligence provided; but only upon hearing the command, immediately the earth brought forth crops from itself. From this we learn that even now it is not the diligence of those who till the ground, not the labor and toil put forth by the farmer, that provides us with a fruitful harvest; but before all these efforts, the word of God was spoken to the earth at the beginning. . . . For even if human beings work the earth, even if they have the assistance of animals and diligently care for the earth, even if the weather is favorable and everything else is cooperative, without the will of the Lord everything is fruitless and in vain. Unless the hand from above participates and brings to fruition the things undertaken, we have only toils and troubles.

—John Chrysostom, *Homilies on Genesis* 5.4
[12–13], on Gen 1:11–12

The Tree of the Knowledge of Good and Evil

God gave human beings a law so that they might exercise free will. This law took the form of a commandment as to which plants could be eaten and one which could not be touched. This latter was the tree of knowledge. This Tree was not created evil from the beginning nor was it forbidden out of jealousy—let not the enemies of God send their tongues in that direction, nor imitate the serpent. [Gregory then offers his own speculation.] The Tree would have been good if partaken of at the proper time, for in my view the

Tree was contemplation, which is safe only for those more mature in habit but not good for those who are still somewhat simple and desirously curious.
— Gregory of Nazianzus, *Oration* 45.8

SEE CHAPTER IV, under The Knowledge of God, for the relationship between faith and knowledge.

The Human Body and Its Care

OUR SELECTIONS on the human body reflect two different viewpoints. In his terminology of flesh and spirit and in his view of the unity of a human person, Hermas's view is more Semitic in character. For Hermas, human beings are a combination of flesh and spirit, and both must be kept pure, for what affects one also affects the other. Gregory of Nyssa's viewpoint, however, was more influenced by Greek philosophy, which drew a contrast between body and soul. A comparison of the body to a musical instrument was common in Gregory's day; he used this in his argument that the principle that governs the human body is not located in only one part but instead permeates every part.

With regard to the human body and entertainment, a passage from Tertullian refers to the places of public entertainment that were most popular among the Romans: the circus (not the modern circus but the place for chariot races), the theater (plays and mimes), the arena (or amphitheater, where gladiator and wild beast contests were held), and the exercise grounds (athletic events). Christian moralists protested against the sexual immorality and violence that were associated with the entertainments of their time, especially in the theaters and gladiatorial contests. Today our forms of entertainment may be different, but sex and violence are still present, so the warnings issued by these ancient writers remain pertinent. The reader may also wish to consult Chapter V (Christian Living) for other relevant passages.

Flesh and Spirit

INSTRUCTIONS of the heavenly Shepherd to Hermas:

Keep your flesh pure and undefiled so that the spirit that lives within it may bear witness on its behalf, and your flesh may be justified. Take care lest the idea enter your heart that the flesh is mortal and you misuse it in some defilement. If you defile your flesh, you also defile the Holy Spirit; and if you defile your flesh, you will not live. . . . Keep the present things, and the Lord, who is assuredly full of mercy, will heal the former sins of ignorance, if you, for the rest, defile neither your flesh nor your spirit. For both are in communion, and it is impossible for one to be defiled without the other. Keep both pure, and you will live unto God."

—Hermas, *Similitudes* 5.7.1–4 [60.1–4]

The whole body has been made like a musical instrument, yet as often happens to those who know how to make melody but are unable to show their skill because the instrument is unfit to receive their art, . . . so it is with the mind, which passes over the whole instrument of the body and, touching each of the parts according to their nature and in a manner corresponding to its intellectual activities, produces the proper effect on those parts that are prepared according to their natural condition, but remains inactive and ineffective upon those parts that are too weak to receive its artistic movement.

—Gregory of Nyssa, *On the Making of Man* 12.8

The Goodness of the Body

What is blameworthy about the way your body was created? Control yourself and nothing evil will come from any of your members. At the beginning, Adam was naked in paradise with Eve, but he was not cast out because of the members of his body. The members, therefore, are not the cause of sin, but those who use their members wrongly. The Maker of the members is wise. Who prepared the womb for child bearing? Who gave life where there was no life within it? . . . As soon as the baby was born, who brought streams of milk out of the breasts? How does a baby grow into a child, and a child into a youth and then into a man, and the same again passes into an old man, while no one notices the exact change from day to day? . . . See, O human, the Maker! See the wise Creator!

—Cyril of Jerusalem, *Catechetical Lectures* 9.15

There is nothing polluted in the way a human being is created unless one defiles the body through adultery and licentiousness. The One who formed Adam also formed Eve; the male and the female were formed by divine hands. From the beginning, none of the bodily members was polluted.

Let all the heretics who slander their bodies, or rather him who formed them, be silenced.

—Cyril of Jerusalem, *Catechetical Lectures* 12.26

Do not tell me that the body causes sin. For if the body causes sin, then why is it that a dead body does not sin? . . . The body does not sin by itself, but the soul causes sin through the body. The body is an instrument, like the soul's garment or robe. If because of the soul the body is given over to fornication, then it becomes impure; but if it lives together with a holy soul, it becomes a temple of the Holy Spirit.

—Cyril of Jerusalem, *Catechetical Lectures* 4.23

When we consider everything that we have taught and continue to teach about human nature, we are led to see the wisdom of the Creator manifested in us. Observe the different activities of the senses—sight, hearing, smell, taste, touch—which all function from one brain but contribute different perceptions. Observe also all the members of the body, both internal and external. Observe the memory, which recalls numerous disparate elements from the past and keeps them unaltered, producing whatever was received at different times without confusing them. The many thoughts do not cancel one another, but the memory exhibits each one at the proper time. We cannot refrain from exclaiming with the psalmist, "Such knowledge is too wonderful for me, O Lord; it is so high, I cannot attain it" [Ps 139:6]. What teaching is sufficient for tracing out either the harmony that is displayed in our bodies or the wisdom that is perceived in our souls? Many have written on these things. . . . Many more things remain to be said, for human reason cannot fathom the works of divine wisdom. On account of this, the prophet [psalmist] praises God. Unable to apprehend all the things perceived in human beings, he confesses that he is clearly inferior and thinks such a confession [of inability] is a worthy hymnody.

—Theodoret, *Cure of Pagan Diseases* 5.81–82

It is profitable for us to avoid the harmful aspects of medical practice, to take advantage of those things it offers that are useful, and to keep its prescriptions. Let the recovery of the flesh from illness to health encourage us not to despair of the soul, as if it were not able to return to its customary wholeness through repentance from sins. Therefore, let us neither simply avoid the medical arts nor place all our hopes in them. But just as we practice agriculture and ask God for the harvest, or as we entrust the helm to the ship's pilot and pray to God to be delivered from the sea, so also let us go to the doctor for assistance but not abandon hope in God.

—Basil of Caesarea, *Greater Rule* 55.5

Food and Drink

Some persons live in order to eat, as if they were indeed irrational animals for whom life consists in nothing but the stomach. Our Instructor, however, commands us to eat in order to live. For food is not our work nor pleasure our goal, but these things are the result of our existence here. The word instructs us toward incorruptibility, and we select our food accordingly. It is to be simple and plain, corresponding to truth, suitable for simple and plain children, useful for living and not for luxury. Living consists of two things, health and strength, to which corresponds an amount of food that is sufficient for digestion and lightness of the body and from which growth, health, and proper strength—not the improper, dangerous, and wretched strength of athletes that comes from a compulsory diet—result. . . . For they have not learned that God furnished food and drink not for pleasure but as sustenance for his creatures—I mean human beings. Bodies by nature do not benefit from an extravagance of foods. On the contrary, those who eat the most frugal fare are stronger, healthier, and more energetic. . . .

We were brought into being not in order to eat and drink but in order to come to the full knowledge of God.

—Clement of Alexandria, *Instructor*
2.1.1–2, 5, 14

Clothing

Wear plain clothing—not for ornamentation but for necessary covering, not for vanity but for warmth in the winter and to hide the unseemliness of the body, lest under the pretense of hiding unseemliness you fall into the unseemliness of extravagant dress.

—Cyril of Jerusalem, *Catechetical
Lectures* 4.29

Let the adornment of the body not be artificial but natural and plain, unstudied rather than sought after, not enhanced by costly and bright clothing but by what is ordinary.

—Ambrose, *Duties* 1.19.83

ALTHOUGH Clement of Alexandria often addressed women and their clothing and cosmetics, he also spoke to men.

In no way is it permitted for women to expose and reveal any part of the body lest both should fall—the men by being aroused to gaze and the women by enticing the eyes of men to themselves.
— Clement of Alexandria, *Instructor* 2.2.33

For I am truly ashamed when I see how much wealth is expended for the covering of nakedness.
— Clement of Alexandria, *Instructor* 2.11 [10.111]

Just as smoke signifies the presence of fire, and as good color and a steady pulse are signs of health, so also proper clothing indicates the condition of our character.
— Clement of Alexandria, *Instructor* 3.11.55

Entertainment

The Instructor will not lead us to the spectacles. One might appropriately call the stadiums and theaters a "seat of plagues" [Ps 1:1]. . . . Therefore, we should renounce the spectacles and performances that are full of ribaldry and gossip. For what shameful deed is not exhibited in the theaters? What shameless word is not uttered by the comedians? Families that enjoy the evil in these activities imitate their clear images. . . . For even if people say that they attend the spectacles as a kind of amusement for recreation, I say that cities in which amusement is diligently pursued are not wise. For merciless contests that are staged for the love of fame and that even end in death are not amusements. The zealous pursuit of frivolity, the irrational love of honor, what is more the useless expense, and indeed the riots at these events are not amusements. Relaxation is not to be bought with the pursuit of frivolity. No sensible person would choose pleasure over what is more excellent.
— Clement of Alexandria, *Instructor* 3.11.76–78

We renounce all your [pagan] spectacles. . . . Among us [Christians] nothing is said, seen, or heard with regard to the madness of the circus, the immodesty of the theater, the violence of the arena, or the futility of the exercise grounds. Why are you offended if we anticipate other pleasures?
— Tertullian, *Apology* 38.4–5

Since all frenzied behavior is forbidden to us, we avoid all public spectacles, including the circus, where wild behavior is particularly at home. . . . [The spectators there are characterized by] fury, anger, discord, and everything forbidden to those who are priests of peace. There one hears curses and abusive words with no cause for hatred; also cries of applause with no basis in affection.

—Tertullian, *On Shows* 16

In like manner, we are instructed to rid ourselves of all immodesty. Because of this we are excluded from the theater, which is the special home of immodesty, where nothing is approved except what has no approval elsewhere. . . . If we are to abhor all unchastity, why would it be lawful for us to hear what is unlawful for us to speak, since we know that all offensive humor and every idle word is judged by God? Why, in the same way, would it be lawful for us to see what is scandalous for us to do? Why would those things that are considered to defile a person when they come out of the mouth [Mark 7:20] not defile a person when they are admitted through the ears and eyes?

—Tertullian, *On Shows* 17

Money and Time

Wealth and Poverty

CLEMENT of Alexandria represented the well-to-do class, but he voiced a Christian attitude toward possessions.

One must partake of wealth in a reasonable manner, sharing it out of love for humanity, not unworthily nor boastfully, and not changing the love of honor into self-love and vulgarity lest anyone should say of us something like, "His horse, his field, his slave, or his gold is worth fifteen talents, but he himself is overpriced at three bronze coins." . . .

It is necessary, therefore, constantly to celebrate this excellent teaching: "The good man who is wise and just lays up treasures in heaven" [cf. Matt 6:19–21]. The one who sells his earthly possessions and gives to the poor discovers an indestructible treasure, for here is "neither moth nor robber." This one is truly blessed, even if he is unimportant, weak, and obscure, for he is truly rich and possesses the greatest riches. . . .

A precious stone, silver, clothing, a beautiful body—these things are not of great value; but virtue, which is the word the Instructor delivers for our training, is. This word renounces luxury, encourages working with one's hands as a servant, and praises thrift as the offspring of prudence. . . .

Hence, it is not the one who has and keeps but the one who shares who is rich; and the sharing, not the possessing, exhibits happiness. Generosity is the fruit of the soul; in the soul, therefore, is wealth. . . . Christians alone are rich. Righteousness is true wealth, and reason (which is not a product of animals or fields but is given by God) is more valuable than all treasure, for it is wealth that cannot be taken away (the soul alone is its treasure).

—Clement of Alexandria, *Instructor* 3.6.34, 35, 36

CLEMENT interpreted Jesus' command to the rich young ruler, "Sell your possessions" (Mark 10:21), as meaning that he must rid himself of the love of money.

It is not what some hastily assume, that Jesus commands him to throw away everything he owned and to abandon his property; rather, Jesus commanded him to banish from his soul his attitudes about property, his affinity for these things, his excessive desire, his terror and distress over these things, his anxieties (the thorns of life) that choke the seed of life. For it is neither great nor desirable to be generally without property, except for the sake of the word of life. . . .

For what sharing among people would there be if no one had anything? . . .

Property that is beneficial to our neighbors is not to be thrown away, for possessions (being a possession) and property (being property) are supplied by God for people to use. They have been made available to us and placed under our control as means and instruments to be used well by those who understand. . . . Money is to be used righteously; it is to serve righteousness. If someone uses it unrighteously, then it becomes a servant of unrighteousness. Its nature is to serve, not to rule. One must not, then, accuse what does not in and of itself have the ability to be good or bad—and so is guiltless—but accuse the one who is able to use these things either well or badly by reason of free choice. . . .

It is no great gain for one to be poor in property who is rich in passions. . . .

A person who is truly and nobly rich is one who is rich in virtues and able to use every good fortune in a holy and faithful manner. The person who is falsely rich is one who is rich according to the flesh and has altered life into what is perishing and belongs to one person, then to another, and in the end to no one at all. Or—to put it another way—there are genuinely poor persons and there are persons who are falsely and improperly called poor. The former are poor in spirit and thus are properly called poor; the latter are poor according to the world's standard and thus their poverty is alien.

> —Clement of Alexandria, *Who Is the Rich Man Who Is Saved?* 11; 13; 14; 15; 19

POVERTY is defined by the extent of a person's wants.

That many of us are called poor is not our disgrace but our glory, for even as the mind is relaxed by luxury so it is strengthened by frugality. Who can be poor who has no wants, does not covet what belongs to another, and is rich toward God? But the poor person is he who, although he has much, desires more.

> —Minucius Felix, *Octavius* 36

The person is rich enough who is poor—with Christ.

> —Jerome, *Letters* 14.1.3

What shall I say about Paula's distinguished, noble, and one-time very wealthy house, practically all the riches of which she spent on the poor? What shall I say about her very compassionate attention and widespread kindness toward all, which was extended even to those whom she had never seen? What poor person, while dying, was not wrapped in clothing provided by her? What bedridden person was not supported by her resources? She diligently searched throughout the city for such people and counted it a loss if any hungry or sick person was supported by another's food. The result was that she despoiled her children and when they rebuked her, she told her relatives that she was leaving them a better inheritance—the mercy of Christ.

> —Jerome, *Letters* 108.5

How much better it is to have health without wealth than wealth without health! . . .

Moreover, humans are so accustomed to admiring riches that no one is thought worthy of honor unless he is rich. . . .

Avarice, then, is fatal. Money is seductive. It contaminates those who have it and is of no help to those who do not have it. . . . We possess what we use; whatever is beyond our use brings us no fruit of possession but only the danger of keeping it safe.

—Ambrose, *Duties* 2.25.128; 2.26.129, 132

To many people poverty seems evil, but it is not. If someone is self-controlled and practices philosophy, poverty can destroy evils. On the other hand, to many people wealth seems good. But it is not altogether good unless one uses it as it should be used. If wealth were a good thing in and of itself, then everyone who possesses it ought to be good. If not all rich people are virtuous, but only those who use their wealth in a good way, then it is evident that wealth in and of itself is not good but is only an instrument of virtue.

—John Chrysostom, *Commentary on Isaiah* 45.7.3

IN CONTRASTING material and spiritual wealth, Gregory reflects a theory of economics that was popular in his time, namely, that there is only a fixed amount of wealth in the world.

The distribution of virtue is such that it is shared by all who seek after it, and all of it is present in each one; it is not diminished in those who partake of it. In the distribution of earthly wealth, however, the one who hoards more for himself wrongs those who must share the same goods. For the one who increases his own portion of this world's goods surely diminishes the portion of the one who shares with him.

—Gregory of Nyssa, *On the Beatitudes* 1

Gold is sought after by people not primarily because of its usefulness but to serve their pleasures through it.

A love of possessions is caused by three things: a love of pleasure, vanity, and a lack of faith. Lack of faith is harder to deal with than the other two.

A lover of pleasure loves silver in order to live luxuriously by means of it; a vain person, in order to be glorified through it; a person who lacks faith, in order to hide and guard it, fearing hunger, old age, sickness, or exile. The latter person places more hope in himself than in God, the Maker of all creation, whose providence extends to the smallest and most remote of living things.

There are four kinds of people who acquire money. I have mentioned three. The fourth kind is the frugal steward. Only this last clearly acquires money correctly, in order that there might always be enough to help those in need.

—Maximus the Confessor, *Charity* 3.16–19

SEE ALSO Chapter II, under Mercy, for further selections on the proper use of money.

Materialism

The best kind of wealth is poverty of desire, and true magnanimity consists not in being boastful about wealth but in despising it. To boast about one's material goods is altogether shameful. For it is not at all proper to be diligently attentive to those things that anyone can purchase in the marketplace. Wisdom is not purchased with earthly money nor is it sold in the marketplace but in heaven, where it is sold with genuine money—the incorruptible word, the royal gold.

—Clement of Alexandria, *Instructor* 2.3.39

HERMAS was especially conscious the way entanglements in business affairs and worldly concerns could sap a Christian's spiritual energy. The heavenly Shepherd instructs him:

Listen," he said, "some people have never inquired about truth or searched out the Godhead; they have never progressed beyond merely believing, being entangled in business affairs, riches, pagan friendships, and many other worldly pursuits. Those involved in these things do not understand the parables about the Godhead. They are darkened and corrupted by these affairs, and become barren. Just as a good vineyard becomes barren from thorns and various weeds when neglected, so also believers who fall into the aforementioned practices become deceived in their understanding and comprehend nothing at all about righteousness. Even when they hear about the Godhead and truth, their minds remain fixed on their business affairs and they understand nothing. But those who reverence God, inquire about the Godhead and truth, and have their hearts set on the Lord, understand and quickly perceive the things said to them, because reverence for the Lord exists within them."

—Hermas, *Mandates* 10.1.4–6 [40.4–6]

Evil desire consumes those who are not clothed with the garment of good desire but are entangled in this world; it delivers them to death." I said, "Lord, what are the deeds of evil desire that deliver people to death? Tell me so that I may avoid them." "Hear," he said, "the sort of activity evil desire uses to put the servants of God to death.

"Foremost of all, desire for another person's wife or husband, for extravagant riches, for gourmet foods and intoxicating drinks, and for many other foolish luxuries. For all luxury is foolish and empty for the servants of God. These, then, are the evil desires that put the servants of God to death. Evil desire is the daughter of the devil. One must avoid evil desires in order to live for God. Those who do not resist them and become ruled by them will die in the end, for these desires are fatal. But put on the desire for righteousness and resist them, arming yourself with the fear of the Lord. For the fear of God thrives on good desire."

—Hermas, *Mandates* 12.1–2 [44.2–45.4]

It ought not to surprise anyone that a kingdom [Rome], although founded through great effort and long increased by many men of great stature—in sum, well established with great resources—would nevertheless collapse at some time or other. There is nothing that human strength has labored to produce that human strength cannot also destroy. The works of mortals are mortal.

—Lactantius, *Divine Institutes* 7.15.12

THE FALL of Rome that was contemplated by Lactantius in the preceding selection came to pass during Augustine's time, when the Goths sacked Rome in 410. This event sparked Augustine's great work on philosophy and history. Much of his work sounds very contemporary, for the attitudes are similar. In the passage below, Augustine expresses what he perceives to be the prevailing attitude among the people—materialism.

Let the Republic stand, they say, let it flourish with abundant resources, be glorious in victories, or—even better—be secure in peace. What is that to us human beings? Are we not more concerned that everyone increases in wealth, wealth that lavishly supports the ongoing expenses by which the powerful subjugate the weak? Let the poor submit to the rich for the sake of their surplus, so that under their patronage they may be peacefully idle. Let the rich in their arrogance abuse the poor who are their clients and ministers. Let the people applaud not those who advise them for their welfare but those who liberally provide for their pleasure. Let no strenuous work be required nor any impurity forbidden. . . . [He then discusses the desire that prostitutes, banquets, dancers, theatrical entertainments, and other pleasures be available.] Let the one who speaks out against these pleasures be a public enemy. Let the one who attempts to change or take away these things be silenced, banished, or killed.

—Augustine, *City of God* 2.20

The Use of Time

An old man said, "If one loses gold or silver, more can be found to replace it, but the one who loses time cannot find more."

—*Apophthegmata Patrum,* Anonymous
Collection, # 265 Nau

Government and Authority

Paying Taxes

JUSTIN Martyr, an apologist for Christianity, addressed the Roman emperor Antoninus Pius and his associates.

Everywhere and beyond all other people we are careful to pay both regular tribute and special taxes, as Jesus taught [referring to Matt 22:15–21]. . . . Hence we worship God alone but in other matters we gladly serve you, acknowledging you as emperors and rulers of human beings and praying that along with your imperial power you may possess sound reasoning.

—Justin Martyr, *1 Apology* 17

Praying for Those Who Hold Civil Authority

I will honor the emperor not by worshiping him but by praying for him. I worship God, the only one who is really and truly God, since I know that the emperor was made by him. If you ask me, "Why do you not worship the emperor?" I will respond that he was not made to be worshiped but to be honored with lawful honor. For the emperor is not God but a human being appointed by God, not to be worshiped but to judge justly. . . . "Honor the emperor" [1 Pet 2:17] by thinking well of him, by being submissive to him, and by praying for him, for in doing these things you do the will of God [1 Pet 2:15].

—Theophilus, *To Autolycus* 1.11

We are always praying on behalf of all the emperors: that they may have long life, a secure empire, a safe home, brave armies, a faithful senate, an honest people, a quiet world, whatever anyone and a Caesar would wish. . . .

I have good reason for saying that Caesar is more ours than yours, since he was appointed by our God. . . . Because he is more mine, I do more for his welfare not only because I ask it from God who is able to give it, or because I am such a person as deserves to receive what I ask for, but also because in taking a moderate position with regard to Caesar's majesty—I place him below God alone—I commend him to God all the more. I place him under One who truly surpasses him. For I will not call the emperor God.

—Tertullian, *Apology* 30; 33

Oaths

A person whose godliness has been proven must be very transparent with respect to lying and swearing an oath. For an oath is a definitive profession with the addition of divine invocation. How could one who has been proven once for all to be trustworthy offer himself as untrustworthy, as if he needed an oath or as though his life itself were not a firm and definitive oath? He lives, conducts himself, and demonstrates the trustworthiness of his profession by his unwavering and steadfast life and word. . . . He will neither lie nor commit perjury for his own benefit, since he will never willingly wrong himself. He will not swear an oath but will choose instead to respond in the affirmative with a simple "Yes" and in the negative with a simple "No" [Matt 5:37]. For to swear is to make an oath openly, or something intended to be like an oath. For the benefit of those who do not perceive the certainty of his answer, it is enough for this person simply to add "I speak truthfully" to his assent or his denial. . . . To swear truly then consists in properly fulfilling one's duties. For the person who lives the truth to the utmost, what need is there for an oath?

—Clement of Alexandria, *Miscellanies* 7.8

Divine Law and Human Rulers

Now in general when two laws—one a law of nature legislated by God and the other a civil law—are presented to us, if the civil law is not opposed to the law of God, then it is good not to distress the citizens by our observing customs that seem strange to them. But if the law of nature, that is, God's law, commands something that is contrary to civil law, is it not reasonable to bid farewell to the civil law and to the will of its legislators and to commit oneself to the God who is *the* Lawgiver, and to choose to live according to his word, even if this brings the possibility of danger, suffering, death, and dishonor?

—Origen, Against Celsus 5.37

The law itself has been delivered to us by God, the one Master and Emperor of all. . . .

The first requirement of this law is to know God himself, to obey and to worship him alone. For it is impossible for someone who is ignorant of God, the parent of his soul, to hold onto the qualities of a human being; such ignorance is the greatest impiety. . . . If someone wishes to follow justice but is ignorant of divine law, he gladly accepts as true justice the laws of his own nation, laws that surely were devised for the sake of utility rather than justice. For why are different laws instituted among various peoples if not because each nation enacts for its own benefit what it considers useful?

—Lactantius, Divine Institutes 6.8.12–6.9.3

THE FOURTH century was a time of conflict in the church over the divinity of Christ. Basil, the bishop of Caesarea in Cappadocia, maintained the full deity of Christ. Because he defended this viewpoint, Basil was called before the prefect of the emperor, who took a "lower" view of Christ, and he was accused of resisting the will of the emperor.

Why do you not follow the religious observances of your emperor, when all others are in subjection and have yielded?" [Basil] replied, "Because these things are not the will of my Emperor. Nor do I dare to worship any creature, since I am a creature of God and have received orders to be a god." "And what do we," asked the prefect, "seem to you to be? Or, are we who give you these commands nothing?" . . . "You may be a prefect and a person of distinction," Basil replied, "I will not deny this, but you are not more honorable than God. . . . For Christianity is characterized by faith and not by outward appearances."

—Gregory of Nazianzus, Oration 43.48
[Panegyric on Basil]

Ruling According to God's Law

Perhaps one who is a king may say: I cannot behave myself aright, because I am a king; it becomes me to do the will of the many. He who speaks thus really deserves to be laughed at: for why should not the king himself lead the way to all good things, and persuade the people under his rule to behave with purity, and to know God in truth, and in his own person set before them the patterns of all things excellent—since thus it becomes him to do? For it is a shameful thing that a king, however badly he may conduct himself, should *yet* judge and condemn those who do amiss.

My opinion is this: that in 'this' way a kingdom may be governed in peace—when the sovereign is acquainted with the God of truth, and is withheld by fear of Him from doing wrong to those who are his subjects, and judges everything with equity, as one who knows that he himself also will be judged before God; while, at the same time, those who under his rule are withheld by the fear of God from doing wrong to their sovereign, and are restrained by *the same* fear from doing wrong to one another. By this knowledge of God and fear of Him all evil may be removed from the realm. For, if the sovereign abstain from doing wrong to those who are under his rule, and they abstain from doing wrong to him and to each other, it is evident that the whole country will dwell in peace. Many blessings, too, will be *enjoyed* there, because amongst them all the name of God will be glorified. For what blessing is greater than this, that a sovereign should deliver the people that are under his rule from error, and by this good deed render himself pleasing to God? For from error arise all those evils *from which kingdoms suffer;* but the greatest of all errors is this: when a person is ignorant of God, and in God's stead worships that which is not God.[2]

—Pseudo-Melito, *Discourse*

Freedom of Religion

PSEUDO-MELITO (above) stated the view advocating that rulers have responsibility for the religious life of their subjects. Other Christian thinkers held the view that religion was a matter of the individual conscience and not to be imposed by political authorities.

Consider whether or not the charge of irreligion may also consist in this—to take away freedom of religion, to forbid the right to choose a divinity, so that I am forbidden to worship whom I want but am forced to worship whom I do not want. No one, not even a human being, desires to be worshiped unwillingly. . . . In fact, we [Christians] alone are forbidden to have a religion of our own. We offend the Romans and are excluded from the rights and privileges that belong to Romans because we do not worship the Roman gods. It is good that there is a God of all, to whom we all belong whether we desire this or not. But among you it is lawful to worship anything except the true God—as if he were not the God of all, to whom we all belong. . . .

It might seem an injustice that free people are compelled to sacrifice against their will when the performance of other divine services requires a willing mind. Certainly it should be considered foolish for someone to force another to honor the gods whom he ought to please for his own sake.

—Tertullian, *Apology* 24.6–10; 28.1

It is not the nature of religion to compel religion. Religion ought to be adopted voluntarily and not by force, since even sacrificial animals are required to be offered from a willing mind. Thus when you require sacrifices from us, your gods are presented with nothing. For unless they are of a contentious nature, they do not desire sacrifices from the unwilling; but God is not contentious.

—Tertullian, *To Scapula* 2.2

Why do you direct your efforts against the body's frailty? Why do you contend with the earthly weakness of the flesh? Fight against us with strength of soul, win us over through the power of the mind, demolish our faith and conquer us—if you are able—through debate, through reason. Or, if your gods possess anything awesome or powerful, then let them arise to their own defense, let them defend themselves by their own majesty. What can they offer their worshipers if they cannot avenge themselves on those who do not worship them? For if the one who avenges is greater than the one who is avenged, then you are greater than your gods. And if you are greater than those whom you worship, then you ought not to worship them, but instead be worshiped by them. Your vengeance defends them when they are harmed, just as your custody protects those who are shut up lest they perish. You should be ashamed to worship those whom you yourself defend, to hope for protection from those whom you yourself protect.

—Cyprian, *To Demetrianus* 13–14

It is not necessary to use force and injury because religion cannot be compelled; it can be accomplished only by words and not by blows, so that it may be voluntary. Let them [the pagans] draw the weapon of their mental powers. If their system is true, let it be affirmed. We [Christians] are ready to listen if they will teach. Certainly we remain unconvinced by their silence, since we do not yield to their violence. Let them imitate us by setting forth their whole system. For we do not entice them to obedience; but we teach, we prove, we demonstrate. No one is retained by us against his will, for those who lack devotion and faith cannot be used by God; yet no one departs from us, being retained by the truth itself. . . .

Religion is to be defended not by killing but by dying, not by violence but by patient endurance, not by wicked acts but by faithfulness. . . . For if you try to defend religion with bloodshed, tortures, and evil, it is not defended but becomes polluted and defiled. For nothing is so much a matter of free will as religion; if the mind of the one who sacrifices is estranged, then religion is eliminated and amounts to nothing.

—Lactantius, *Divine Institutes* 5.19 [20]

I want to question [the pagans] who in particular they think benefits by compelling those who are unwilling to sacrifice to do so. Is it those whom they compel? But it is not a kindness if it is done to one who refuses it. . . . Or do they truly benefit the gods? A real sacrifice is not extracted by force, unwillingly. For unless it is done voluntarily and intentionally, it is a curse. . . . But we, on the contrary, do not desire that anyone unwillingly worship our God, who is the God of all whether they are willing or not; nor are we angry when someone does not worship him. For we trust in the majesty of him who is able to avenge both the contempt that is shown him and the sufferings and injuries of his servants.

—Lactantius, *Divine Institutes* 5.20 [21]

Christian Pacifism

The more pious a person is, the more effectively he or she assists those who rule, even more than soldiers who go forth in the line of battle and kill the enemy. . . . We fight for the emperor more than others. Indeed we do not join his army even if he requires it, but we do serve in the army on his behalf by enlisting a special legion of piety through our petitions made to the divine. . . .

Christians are benefactors of their country more than other people since they educate the citizens and teach them piety toward the real guardian deity, restoring those who live well in the least cities to a divine and heavenly city. . . .

If those who are called rulers, or "those who exercise control," in the church rule well over the divine nation (that is, the church), they rule according to the commands issued by God and do not stain their office by adopting secular laws. Christians avoid common public duties, not to escape from these but to keep themselves for the more divine and necessary ministry of the church of God, which is human salvation.

—Origen, *Against Celsus* 8.73, 74, 75

Heavenly Citizenship

As for this mortal life, which passes in a few days and comes to an end, what difference does it make to a person who is going to die what empire he lives under as long as those who rule do not force him to commit unholy and unjust deeds? . . . With regard to safety and virtues, which are true human values, I cannot see what difference it makes—except for that completely empty esteem that some have for human glory—that some conquer and others are conquered. . . . Let us consider that the city where it is promised that we Christians will reign is as far removed from Rome as heaven is from earth, as eternal life is from temporal joys, as true glory is from empty praise, as the society of angels is from mortal society, as the light of him who made the sun and moon is from the light of the sun and moon themselves. We who are citizens of such a homeland ought not to view ourselves as having done something great, as if we accomplished good works or endured evils in order to attain that homeland, for the Romans accomplished similar deeds and experienced similar sufferings in order to possess this earthly homeland.

—Augustine, *City of God* 5.1

CHAPTER II

Good and Bad; Right and Wrong

Abba Isidore said, "The insight of the saints is this: to recognize the will of God. For in obedience to the truth a human being is superior to all, because this is the image and likeness of God. But to follow one's own heart—that is, one's own reasoning and not the law of God—is the most dangerous of all spirits."
— *Apophthegmata Patrum,* Alphabetical Collection, Isidore of Pelusium # 9

MORAL DECISION MAKING is a recurrent feature of human life. In the following sampling of moral teaching by Christians in the early centuries of our era we begin with descriptions of the inner self. It is the inner person who is the source of moral choices, who makes decisions concerning right and wrong. This inner self is variously referred to as the heart, the seat of motives, thought, conscience, or the source of attitudes. These motives, thoughts, and attitudes may in turn be either positive or negative, and they give rise to positive or negative decisions and actions.

The selections on positive and negative qualities offered here have been organized alphabetically to help the reader locate passages, but there is an interconnectedness with regard to the virtues such that one topic often leads to another. The number of selections included under each quality should not be interpreted as an indication of the relative importance attached to it by early Christian moralists, although humility and love certainly occupied a central place in their understanding of proper attitudes. Christian writers took pains to distinguish both qualities from pagan ideas. For "humility" commonly meant "humiliation," and, although "active good will" was not a foreign idea, "love" was not a common word.

The writings of early Christian authors help us distinguish the ancient meaning of the virtues from our more modern notions and word usage. They point out, for instance, that the basis for practicing love is God's love for humanity, as expressed in the example of Christ. The Golden Rule (Matt 7:12) was closely related to Jesus' teachings on love, so we have included comments on it in our selections on love. One practical expression of love in the early church was the common meal by which charity was shown to the poor. The active doing of good was so closely associated with love that the Greek word for love *(agapē)* was given to the meal itself; thus today we often refer to this meal as the "love feast." The quality of mercy, especially as it was extended to the poor, was closely related both to love and kindness.

The section entitled "Saying and Doing" includes several aphorisms from the ancient church that juxtapose speech with thought and deed. Discussions about sexual morality included discussion of lascivious thoughts and speech; sexual morality called for much comment, as it has in other periods of history. But unlike the approach often taken for these matters, early Christians appealed to theological reasons in determining proper sexual conduct. Finally, comments on wisdom distinguished spiritual wisdom from worldly wisdom.

In general—though not completely—the negative attitudes and actions that early Christian moralists condemned were the antitheses of the positive attitudes that they commended. Similarly, Christ is the prototype for positive attitudes and actions, while the devil is the prototype for those that are negative.

Divisiveness, idolatry, and passion were negative qualities that deserve special mention. Division among believers is not just a modern phenomenon; ancient authors spoke to this problem in a way that sounds remarkably relevant to the church today. Envy was named as one cause of divisions, as well as many other problems. All Christian authors were concerned about idolatry, which was a major problem then and remains a problem in many parts of the world today. Some authors, such as Tertullian, associated many aspects of negative conduct with the pervasive presence of idolatry in Roman society. The word "passion" tends to be used today to refer to sexual passion, but ancient authors included all of the drives and desires that characterize human nature under this term. Those authors who wrote about sexual immorality sound quite modern in their comments on fornication, adultery, and homosexuality. Warnings were issued against pride and the pursuit of honor and fame. Sins of the tongue—lying, perjury, slander, and licentious talk—were frequently condemned.

Sins, it was believed, were like diseases: they were contagious and must be treated accordingly. And like fame, sins were transitory. Sin often found its own punishment within the person who committed it. Some authors made the important distinction between the sin committed and the sinner. Early Christian moralists also stressed that the very existence of sin and evil testifies to the existence of the good. They repeatedly affirmed the power of the good and the strength of the virtues. Unlike transitory sins, the virtues are lasting. Christian virtue is based on one's relationship with God. Unlike material possessions, virtue was something one could "take with you" into the afterlife.

The Inner Self

THE HEART, in the sense of motives, must be pure; in the sense of one's own inclinations, the human heart can deceive. Different persons engage in good conduct out of different motives; motives, in turn, determine the moral worth of behavior. Discussion of different motives—fear of punishment, the hope of reward, doing the right thing for its own sake or out of love—for doing right and serving God was common among early Christian thinkers.

The Heart

THE FOLLOWING passage is addressed to persons receiving instruction in preparation for baptism.

Sincerity of purpose makes you one of those whom God has called; for if your body is here but your mind is not it profits you nothing. . . . May none of you enter saying, "Come, let us see what the faithful are doing. . . ." Do you think you can see and not be seen? Do you think that while you are examining what is going on, God is not examining your heart?
— Cyril of Jerusalem, *Procatechesis* 1; 2

Abba Poemen said, "Do not give your heart's attention to whatever does not fully satisfy your heart."
— *Apophthegmata Patrum,* Alphabetical Collection, Poemen # 80

A brother asked Abba Tithoes, "How can I guard my heart?" The old man replied, "How can we guard our heart when our mouth and our stomach are open?"
— *Apophthegmata Patrum,* Alphabetical Collection, Tithoes # 3

Motives

WITH respect to different reasons for abstaining from wrong conduct, in this example on adultery, Origen writes:

You see then that what is considered the same conduct—that is, the avoidance of adultery—is not the same for everyone but differs according to the principles held by the one who avoids it, whether from sound opinions or from bad and impious ones.

—Origen, *Against Celsus* 7.63

By THE third century the church had grown so much that sometimes suspicions arose over whether or not those who held positions of leadership in the church did so out of ambition and a desire for earthly gain.

No one can say that Christians undertook to spread the word throughout the world for the sake of financial gain, when sometimes they refused to accept even basic provisions. . . . In the present day, perhaps on account of the multitude of those who come to the word—indeed persons who are rich or hold rank, as well as women who are wellborn and well-off, welcome teachers of the word—some dare to say that there are those who become leaders in teaching the Christian faith for the sake of a little glory. But how could one reasonably think that this was the case at the beginning, when the danger was especially great for teachers?

—Origen, *Against Celsus* 3.9

Let us fear the coming wrath of God or love the present grace—one of the two—only to be found in Christ Jesus for the true life.

—Ignatius, *Ephesians* 11.1

WHILE Ignatius spoke of two motives for doing good, others more frequently analyzed motives in three categories.

We must, in my view, approach the saving word neither out of the fear of punishment nor the promise of a gift, but because of the good itself. . . .

The work of a [true] gnostic [Clement uses the word in an orthodox rather than a heretical sense] is not to abstain from evil deeds (which is a stepping stone to the highest perfection) nor to do something good out of fear. . . . Nor should one act out of hope for a promised reward. . . . For a gnostic, the doing of good is chosen only for the sake of love, and he chooses it because of its intrinsic excellence.

— Clement of Alexandria, *Miscellanies* 4.6, 22

Those who are steadfast in the confession of their calling are like this not because they choose to endure lesser dangers for fear of even greater ones—as other people do—nor because they fear censure from their equals and those who are like-minded, but because of their love for God. They willingly trust in their calling and set as their goal not the reward for their labor but only to be well pleasing to God. For some endure suffering because they love glory, some because they fear a more severe punishment, and others remain as children in the faith because their goal is the pleasure and joy that are promised after death (they are indeed blessed but they are not yet men and women who are mature in love like the gnostic). . . . Love is not to be chosen for any reason other than itself.

— Clement of Alexandria, *Miscellanies* 7.11

This is true perfection: not to avoid a wicked life out of servile fear of punishment—like slaves—nor to do good because we hope for rewards, as if cashing in on the virtuous life in some business-like or contractual arrangement. Instead, disregarding all those things for which we hope and have been promised, the only thing we dread is to fall from God's friendship, and the only thing we consider worthy of honor and desire is to become God's friend. This, as I have said, is the perfection of life.

— Gregory of Nyssa, *Life of Moses* 2.320

For some, salvation comes about through fear, when contemplation on the threats of punishment in hell causes them to depart from evil. Others become good examples of virtue because they hope to receive the recompense reserved for those who have lived well, not because they love the good but because they expect a reward. The one who pursues the goal of perfection with his soul rejects fear, for servile persons do not choose to remain with the master through love but are afraid to run away for fear of punishment, and disdains rewards, as though the reward seemed more valuable than the Giver. Rather, this one loves from the whole heart, soul, and strength none of the things created by God but only God himself, the One who is the fountain of good things.

—Gregory of Nyssa, *Commentary on Canticles* 1

1 know of three classes of people among those who are being saved: slaves, employees, and sons. If you are a slave, fear punishment; if you are an employee, look only for wages; if you are more than these—if you are a son—then revere God as Father. Do what is good because it is good to obey a Father. And even if there will be no reward for you, it is reward enough to have pleased your Father.

—Gregory of Nazianzus, *Oration* 40.13

COMPARE the above to Maximus the Confessor, *Mystagogy* 24.

Thoughts

Above all we should know that our thoughts arise from three sources: God, the devil, and ourselves. Thoughts come from God when he sees fit to visit us with an illumination of the Holy Spirit and raises us up to a higher level of progress; in those things where we have made little gain or acted slothfully and been overcome, he corrects us with healthy compunction. Or, God may display the heavenly mysteries for us and change our way of life for the better, in act and will. . . . A whole series of thoughts is born of the devil, when he attempts to overthrow us through delight in wickedness or hidden snares. With the most subtle cunning he fraudulently presents evil things as good and transforms himself for us into an angel of light. . . . Thoughts also originate with us, when we naturally recollect those things that we are engaged in, have been engaged in, or have heard. . . .

We must be continually aware of this three-fold classification and wisely discern all of the thoughts that emerge within our hearts, first ascertaining their origin, cause, and author, so that we may consider according to their merit what quality we ought to assign those things they suggest to us. . . . First, we should diligently scrutinize whatever enters our hearts. For instance, if some doctrine is introduced to us, we ought to ascertain whether it has been purified by the Holy Spirit's divine and heavenly fire, or pertains to Jewish superstition, or comes from the pride of worldly philosophy and thus has only the superficial appearance of piety. . . . Secondly, it is fitting that we carefully explore, lest a wicked interpretation that is covered over with the pure gold of Scripture deceive us by the precious appearance of the metal.

[The author then proceeds with examples of things that appear good but are used by the devil to lead us away from what is best.] . . .

Therefore all of the secret places of our heart must be constantly scrutinized, and the tracks of whatever enters them must be carefully reconsidered and investigated. . . . At every single hour and moment we should make a furrow in the earth of our heart with the gospel plow—that is, by the continual remembrance of the Lord's cross.

—John Cassian, *Conferences* 1.19–20, 22

My sons, before you act, think; and when you have thought for a long time, then do what you regard as right.

—Ambrose, *Duties* 2.30.153

An old man said, "We are not condemned because of the thoughts that enter us but because we use our thoughts badly; our thoughts can cause us either to suffer shipwreck or to be crowned."

—*Apophthegmata Patrum*, Anonymous Collection, # 218 Nau

Abba Anoub asked Abba Poemen about vain desires and the impure thoughts that the heart of a person brings forth. Abba Poemen said to him, "Is an axe honored unless someone cuts with it [Isa 10:15]? If you do not make use of such thoughts, they too will do nothing."

—*Apophthegmata Patrum*, Alphabetical Collection, Poemen # 15

Abba Theodore of Scetis said, "A thought comes to me that troubles me and gives me no rest. It is not strong enough to make me act; it only hinders my progress toward virtue. A vigilant man would shake if off and arise for prayer."

—*Apophthegmata Patrum*, Alphabetical Collection, Theodore of Scetis # 1

Amma Syncleitica [one of the Desert Mothers] said, "There are many people living on the mountain who act as if they were in town and are perishing. One can be among many people and live as a solitary in one's mind, and one who is alone can live life with many things on his mind."

—*Apophthegmata Patrum*, Alphabetical Collection, Syncleitica # 19 (Guy, supp. 1)

Thoughts can be simple or composite. Simple thoughts are those that have no passion. Composite thoughts have passion, since they are compounded out of thought and passion. It is possible for many simple thoughts to accompany composite thoughts, when the latter begin to be moved to sin in the mind. An example is money. The thought of someone's money arises in the memory with passion. In the mind, this sets in motion an urge to steal, and in one's mind the sin is committed. Accompanying the memory of the money there is also the memory of the pouch, the vessel, the living quarters, and so forth. The memory of the money was composite, for it came with passion; but the memory of the pouch, the vessel, and so forth was simple because the mind had no passion for these things. Every thought is similar, whether it be of vainglory, the opposite sex, or other things. . . .

There are three principal moral conditions. The first condition is to abstain from sinful acts. The second is to abstain from spending time on passionate thoughts in the soul. The third is to consider in your mind without passion the form of a woman or past offenses that others have committed against you.

—Maximus the Confessor, *Charity* 2.84, 87

Conscience

The conscience is best for accurately discerning what to choose and what to avoid. A correct life and appropriate instruction provide a firm foundation for conscience. To follow others who have already been approved and serve as the best examples is an excellent way of understanding the truth and the practice of the commandments.

—Clement of Alexandria, *Miscellanies* 1.1.5.2

IN THE following selection Origen comments on Rom 2:15: "They show that what the law requires is written on their hearts to which their own conscience also bears witness" (NRSV).

Since the conscience possesses such freedom, which always rejoices and glories in good deeds and in bad deeds is not convicted but rebukes and convicts the soul with which it is connected, I think conscience may be the spirit, which the apostle says is with the soul [1 Thess 5:23]. . . . Conscience is like a pedagogue and guide that is associated with the soul, advising it with regard to better things and chastising and convicting it with regard to sin.

Concerning conscience, the apostle also said that "no one knows a human being—the things that are in a person—except the human spirit within that person" [1 Cor 2:11]; and he may have been speaking about the spirit of conscience when he said, "That very Spirit bears witness with our spirit" [Rom 8:16].

—Origen, *Commentary on Romans* 2.10

We infer that if a person's life is formed according to the direction of nature, so as to be obedient to her, then that person can never injure another. One who injures another violates nature. And whatever is acquired through injury to another is not an advantage but a disadvantage because it came about through that means. For what punishment is harder to bear than the interior wound of conscience? What judgment could be more severe than the internal one in which each person accuses and convicts himself of wrongfully harming a brother?

—Ambrose, *Duties* 3.4.24

We are to seek nothing except what is virtuous. A wise person does nothing except what can be done with straightforwardness and without deception. Nor does this person do anything that may involve any misdeed, even if it is possible to remain unobserved. For one is accused by one's own self before being judged by others, and the publicity of the crime is no more shameful than one's own consciousness of it.

—Ambrose, *Duties* 3.5.29

Attitudes

The fear of God is the purpose to be sought in everything we do or experience. If one first plants this root deeply, then not only relaxation, honors, glory, and services but also insults, oppression, insolence, dishonor, tortures, and, in a word, everything, will produce the fruits of pleasure in you. Even if the root of a tree is bitter, it bears for us the sweetest fruits. In the same way, great sorrow that is godly bears pleasure within us. Those who have prayed in pain and poured forth tears know how much good cheer they enjoyed, how their conscience was purified, how they were lifted up in good hope. What I always say is that it is not the nature of things but our own attitude that causes us to be either sorrowful or cheerful. . . . External things involve the necessities of nature but within the soul everything is done according to free will. . . .

If you desire contentment, then do not pursue possessions, bodily health, glory, power, luxury, costly tables, silk clothing, expensive fields, magnificent and conspicuous houses, or anything such as these. But seek divine philosophy and virtue, and nothing—neither things present nor things expected—will make you sad. What do I mean by "make you sad"? The things that make others sad will increase your pleasure. . . . For no one can make us unhappy if we do not make ourselves unhappy, nor happy if we do not make ourselves so, that is after the grace of God.

—John Chrysostom, *On the Statues* 18.3–4

Positive Attitudes and Actions

Confidence Against Despondency

Careful thought is a good thing but despondency, despair, and loss of hope for our salvation are harmful to the soul. Trust therefore in the goodness of God and look for his support, knowing that if we turn to him rightly and sincerely, not only will he not throw us away completely but even as we utter the very words of prayer he says to us, "Behold, I am with you."

—Basil of Caesarea, *Letters* 174

Discernment

THE FOLLOWING selection speaks about the futility of the external disciplines of renunciation and devotion without spiritual insight and commitment. The second selection offers a definition and explanation of spiritual discernment.

An old man was asked, "How can I find God?" He replied, "Through fasting, vigils, labor, mercy, and—above all—through discernment. I tell you, many have afflicted their flesh when they lacked discernment and have gone away from us fruitless, having achieved nothing. We have bad breath from fasting, we recite the Scriptures by heart, we perform the Psalms of David, but we do not have what God seeks—love and humility."

—*Apophthegmata Patrum*, Anonymous
Collection, # 222 Nau

In beginners, discernment takes the form of true self-knowledge. In those who are on the way, it is spiritual perception that unfailingly discerns what is truly good by nature and what is its opposite. In those who are perfect, discernment is knowledge that stems from divine illumination, which enlightens by its own lamp the dark things in others. Or, to speak briefly and in general, discernment is—and is recognized to be—the sure understanding of the divine will in every time, in every place, and in every matter. It is present only in those who are pure in heart, body, and speech. . . .

Discernment is an uncorrupted conscience and pure perception.

— John Climacus, *Ladder of Paradise* 26

Forgiveness

THE NEXT selection, which is addressed to those who were coming to be baptized and to receive forgiveness of sins, reflects a double truth: the foundation of forgiving others is our reception of God's forgiveness; forgiving others then thus becomes the condition for receiving further forgiveness from God.

If you hold anything against anyone, forgive it. You come here to receive forgiveness of sins; you must also grant forgiveness to anyone who has sinned against you. How can you say to the Lord, "Forgive me of my many sins," if you yourself have not forgiven your fellow servant for a few sins.

— Cyril of Jerusalem, *Catechetical Lectures* 1.6

Gregory of Nazianzus describes his father:] Indeed, many of those who caused him pain encountered neither payment in kind nor, as the poet [Pindar] says, "attendant vengeance." At the very moment they did these things, they were struck with remorse, were changed, came forward, knelt before him, and obtained pardon. They went away having been clearly shown that they were inferior, and they were made better through the correction and forgiveness they received. Indeed, a forgiving spirit often has great saving power, bringing a sense of shame on the wrongdoer and transforming his fear into love, which is a far more secure state of mind.

— Gregory of Nazianzus, *Oration* 18.26

We consider it important to obtain justice from those who have wronged us, important—I say—because this is also useful in correcting others; but it is far greater and more godlike to bear suffering patiently. For the former course curbs wickedness but the latter persuades one to be good, which is much better and more perfect than merely not being wicked. Let us pursue the great mercifulness that is set before us. Let us forgive the wrongs that have been done to us so that we also may obtain forgiveness, and let us promote kindness through kindness.

— Gregory of Nazianzus, *Letters* 77

Humility

THE HUMILITY of Christ provided the pattern and standard for Christian humility. After quoting Phil 2:5–7, Gregory of Nyssa proceeds with these rhetorical paradoxes:

What greater poverty could come to God than the form of a slave? What greater humility to the King of the universe than willingly to enter into fellowship with our poor nature? The King of kings and Lord of lords [1 Tim 6:15] willingly submitted to servitude. The Judge of all became subject to rulers. The Lord of all creation was brought down into a cave. The one who holds the universe in his hand found no place in the inn but was cast aside into a manger with the irrational animals [Luke 2:7]. The pure and undefiled one accepted the filth of our human nature, and having passed through all of our poverty, he proceeded even to experience death. Behold the extent of his voluntary poverty! Life tasted death! The Judge was brought to judgment. The Lord of all creation was sentenced by a judge. The King of all cosmic powers did not free himself from the hands of executioners. He said, let this example of humility be the standard for your humility.

— Gregory of Nyssa, *On the Beatitudes* 1.4

Having condescended to become a man, Christ went through every demeaning experience: his mother was not registered as a queen; when wrapped in swaddling clothes, he was not placed in a bed of gold but in a manger; he was not raised in a luxurious house but in the humble dwelling of a workman. Again, when he chose his disciples, he did not choose orators, philosophers, and kings but fishermen and tax collectors. He shared this frugal life, not owning a house, nor wearing expensive clothing, nor similarly enjoying expensive food, but was nourished by others, insulted, despised, driven out, and pursued. He did these things out of his great superiority in order to trample human vanity underfoot.

— John Chrysostom, *Commentary on the Psalms* 45.2

Ambrose invokes Christ's example in a different way to encourage humility.

> Let no one strive to outshine others; let no one be conceited; let no one boast. Christ did not desire to be known here. He did not want his name preached in the gospel while he lived on earth. He came so that he might be hidden from this world. Let us therefore in the same way hide our life after the example of Christ; let us avoid boastfulness; let us not desire praise. It is better to live here in humility and there in glory.
>
> —Ambrose, *Duties* 3.5.36

Celsus, the pagan critic of Christianity, took exception to the penitential practices of Christians. Origen responded by contrasting the outward show of humility with true, inner humility.

> One who is truly humble does not humble himself shamefully and unworthily, groveling on his knees, throwing himself prone on the ground, wearing the clothing of those who are destitute, and covering himself with dust. According to the prophet [Ps 131:1–2], the one who is humble, "although walking in great and marvelous things" that are above him—that is, great doctrines and marvelous thoughts—"humbles himself under the mighty hand of God" [1 Pet 5:6]. [Origen then proceeds to discuss the teaching and example of Jesus.]
>
> —Origen, *Against Celsus* 6.15

> Pursue humility and patience with a pure heart, not pretending, as some do, with false humility, which consists of words and an affected and superfluous inclination to engage in certain bodily activities. . . .
>
> Preserve true humility of heart, which is brought about not through affected humility of the body and words but through a deep abasement of the mind. Its patience shines forth when one does not brag to others about one's crimes—which are not to be believed—but disregards what another insolently says against him and endures insults inflicted upon him, all with a gentle equanimity of spirit.
>
> —John Cassian, *Conferences* 18.11.1, 5

Theodora, one of the few Desert Mothers, also spoke about humility.

> Theodora again said, "Neither asceticism, nor vigils, nor any kind of suffering saves without true humility. There was a certain anchorite who drove away demons. He asked them, 'What makes you go away? Is it fasting?'

They replied, 'We neither eat nor drink.' 'Is it vigils?' They replied, 'We do not sleep.' 'Is it withdrawal from the world?' 'We live in the deserts.' 'Then what makes you go away?' They replied, 'nothing overcomes us, except humility.' Do you see how humility is victorious over the demons?"

— *Apophthegmata Patrum,* Alphabetical
Collection, Theodora # 6

⟨The devil, transformed into an angel of light, appeared to one of the brothers and said to him, "I am Gabriel and I was sent to you." The brother said to him, "See if you were not sent to someone else, for I am not worthy." And immediately the devil disappeared.

— *Apophthegmata Patrum,* Anonymous
Collection, # 310 Nau

GREGORY of Nazianzus speaks of his father as an example of true humility, which he contrasts to humility that is feigned by external appearances.

Who more than he held vanity in check and loved humility? And he did this in a way that was neither feigned nor superficial, as is the case with many who pretend to live a philosophical life: they are refined in appearance like the most foolish of women, who being deprived of their own beauty have recourse to makeup and are—if I may say so—made up like an actress, ugly in their outward show of beauty and more shameful in their shame. For his humility was not in his clothing but in the condition of his soul. He did not make a show of humility by bending his neck or lowering his voice, by having a downcast appearance, by length of beard or a closely shaved head, or by his manner of walking—things that can be assumed for a time but are very quickly exposed, for nothing that is pretended is lasting. He was most exalted in his manner of life but most humble in mind; unapproachable in virtue but exceedingly approachable in conversation. His custom in manner of dress was to avoid equally both the stately and the lowly. His inner splendor exceeded all others.

— Gregory of Nazianzus, *Oration* 18.23

TRUE moral, spiritual authority is demonstrated in humility that has great power to elicit a response in others.

An old man said, "If someone humbly and in the fear of God orders a brother to do something, then the word that goes forth for the sake of God causes the brother to submit and do what was ordered. But if someone desires to command a brother not according to the fear of God but out of a desire to have authority and exercise control over him, then God, who sees the secrets of the heart, does not give the brother confidence to hear and do it. Work that is done for the sake of God is evident; what is done out of authoritarianism is also evident. The work of God is humble and done with encouragement; work done out of authoritarianism is full of anger and trouble, for it proceeds from evil.

—*Apophthegmata Patrum,* Anonymous
Collection, # 315 Nau

An old man said, "I prefer a defeat with humility over a victory with pride."

—*Apophthegmata Patrum,* Anonymous
Collection, # 316 Nau

One person said, "Humility is constant forgetfulness of one's accomplishments." Another said, "It is reckoning oneself less than others and a greater sinner." Another said, "It is the mind's knowledge of its own weakness and helplessness." Yet another said, "It is preventing your neighbor from becoming provoked and first to put an end to wrath." Again another said, "It is knowledge of the grace and sympathy of God." Another said, "It is the feeling of a broken heart and the denial of one's own will." . . .

I gave my definition: "Humility is a grace of the soul that is difficult to describe and is honored only by those who have received the experience of it—an indescribable wealth, a name, and a gift of God." . . .

A citron tree that has no fruit naturally lifts its branches high. When the branches bend low, they will soon bear fruit. The one who has gained spiritual insight knows what this means. . . .

The fathers we hold in everlasting remembrance defined physical labor as the foundation and way of humility. I am speaking of obedience and righteousness of the heart, qualities that are naturally opposed to pride. If pride made demons out of angels, then surely humility can make angels out of demons. So, let those who have fallen take courage.

—John Climacus, *Ladder of Paradise* 25

No one can learn humility in a high position unless he ceases to be proud when in a lowly position. No one who learned to long for praise when it was missing knows how to flee from praise when it abounds.

—Gregory the Great, *Pastoral Rule* 1.9

Joy

THE HEAVENLY Shepherd commands Hermas:

Remove sorrow from yourself. . . . Sorrow is more evil than all the spirits; it is most terrible to the servants of God, ruins a person beyond all other spirits, wears out the Holy Spirit—and again it saves. . . . Hear now, foolish man, how sorrow wears out the Holy Spirit and again saves. When a double-minded person engages in any work and fails because of his double-mindedness, sorrow enters into the person and grieves and wears out the Holy Spirit. Again, when for any reason hot temper cleaves to a person and he becomes exceedingly bitter, sorrow again enters into the heart of the hot tempered person and he is sorry for what he has done and repents because he did wrong. Therefore, this sorrow appears to contain salvation, because one who did wrong repented. . . .

"Therefore, put on joyfulness, which always has favor with God and is acceptable to him, and he delights in it. For every joyful man does good deeds, thinks good thoughts, and despises sorrow. But a sorrowful person always does wrong things. He does wrong first because he grieves the Holy Spirit who was given to us for joy; second, he grieves the Holy Spirit by working wrong, by not interceding and confessing to the Lord. For the intercession of a sorrowful man is never powerful enough to ascend to the altar of God. . . . Therefore, purify yourself from evil sorrow and you shall live in God. And all who cast sorrow away and put on all joyfulness shall live in God."

—Hermas, *Mandates* 10.1–3 [40.1–2;
41.1–3; 42.1–2, 4]

Let us mourn, then, while the pagans rejoice, so that when they begin to mourn we may rejoice; lest sharing now in their rejoicing, we then also share in their mourning. You are given too much to comfort, oh Christian, if you also desire pleasure in this life; more correctly, you are exceedingly foolish if you think that what pagans do is pleasure. . . . Your joy is where your hope is.

—Tertullian, *On Shows* 28

As he was dying, Abba Benjamin said to his sons, "If you practice the following you can be saved, 'Rejoice always, pray without ceasing, and in everything give thanks' [1 Thess 5:16–18]."

—*Apophthegmata Patrum*, Alphabetical
Collection, Benjamin # 4

Justice

THE FOLLOWING selections are extracted from an extended discussion of justice written by Ambrose of Milan.

Justice has to do with the society of the human race and the community at large. What holds society together is divided into two parts—justice and philanthropy (also called liberality and kindness). . . .

Nature has produced a common right for all, but avarice has made it a right for only a few. . . .

The glory of justice is great, for justice exists for the good of others rather than the good of self, and in this way it fosters the bond of union and community among people. . . .

How can someone who tries to take from another what he wants for himself be just? . . .

Justice must be preserved even when dealing with enemies. . . .

It is the facts of the case, and not personal feelings, that we must consider. . . .

Nothing is so harmonious as justice and impartiality.[1]

—Ambrose, *Duties* 1.28.130, 132, 136, 137;
1.29.139; 1.30.150; 1.33.172

THE GREEK word for justice was the same word that was used for righteousness (see selections quoted below), thus Gregory of Nyssa's discussion of Matt 5:6 speaks first about the philosophical virtue of justice and then calls attention to the higher righteousness of the gospel.

Those who have investigated these matters say that justice [righteousness] is the practice of apportioning equally to each one what is deserved. For example, if someone were in charge of distributing money, then he would be called just if he were mindful of equality and apportioned the contribution according to the needs of each recipient. And if anyone who has the authority to judge renders a judgment that is not according to favor or enmity but according to the facts of the case, and if he punishes those who deserve punishment and renders a judgment of deliverance to the innocent, and judges other disputed matters truthfully, then this person is called just. . . .

But when I reflect on the sublimity of divine laws, something more than the things we have said with regard to this justice forces itself into my consideration. For if the saving word is common to every human being but the things said do not apply to everyone—for few rule, hold office, judge, or have authority over money or some other stewardship, because the majority are in subjection and are objects of regulation—how can one attain true justice if it is not equally applicable to all human beings? If, according to the teachings of non-Christians, the goal of the just person is equality, but authority presupposes inequality, then this definition of justice cannot be true since it is immediately refuted by the inequality that is a characteristic of life.

What then is the justice that anyone attains—the common desire that is held by everyone who looks to the spiritual food of the gospel, whether rich, poor, slave, master, nobly born, or bought with money—since there is no circumstance that enlarges or restricts the quality of a just person? . . . If to be just involves ruling, distributing, or administering something, then the person who is not involved in those things is excluded from being just. . . . Therefore, we must inquire about the kind of justice that, when it is desired, brings the promise of refreshment. . . .

If we know what the Lord hungered for, we will surely learn the meaning of the beatitude we are considering . . . [John 4:34; 1 Tim 2:4]. If God desires our salvation and Christ's food is our life, then we learn what the hungry soul needs. What is it? Let us hunger for our salvation; let us thirst for the divine will, which for us is to be saved. The beatitude teaches us how this hunger is to be directed in us, for the person who desires the justice of God has found the true object of desire. . . . We have already learned that when the divinely inspired word speaks of one thing, it includes many things. Therefore, when the word speaks about the blessedness that is set before those who hunger for justice, it signifies by justice every kind of virtue. There is an equal blessedness for prudence, courage, self-control, and anything else that is understood by the word "virtue." . . . If the concept of justice is not mixed with anything bad, then it assuredly includes in itself everything that is good, and every good is what is contemplated by virtue. Therefore, the word justice here signifies every virtue.

—Gregory of Nyssa, *On the Beatitudes* 4

Love

UNLIKE our modern ideas of love, in early Christian literature love is not primarily an emotion; it is "active good will." The first selection is inspired by Paul's words about love in 1 Cor 13.

Let the one who loves in Christ do the commandments of Christ. Who can explain the bonding power of God's love? Who is capable of expressing the greatness of its beauty? The height to which love leads us is inexpressible. Love binds us to God; "love hides a multitude of sins"; love bears all things, "endures all things." There is nothing arrogant in love, nothing haughty. Love does not cause division; love does not form factions; love does everything in harmony. In love, all of those who are chosen by God are brought to perfection. Without love, nothing is pleasing to God. In love, the Master received us. Because of the love he had for us, Jesus Christ our Lord, by the will of God, gave his blood for us, his flesh for our flesh, his soul for our souls. See, beloved, how great and marvelous love is, and its perfection is beyond description! . . . Blessed are we, beloved, if we do the commandments of God in the harmony of love, so that through love our sins may be forgiven.

— *I Clement* 49–50

EARLY Christian writers recognized that there is a distinction between loving and liking.

It is possible to show the love that is called *agapē* to all . . . [Gal 6:10]. This love must be shown to all in general to such an extent that our Lord commands that we grant it even to our enemies . . . [Matt 5:44]. But *diathesis* (affection) [propensity, disposition] is shown to very few, to those who are united to us by a similarity of disposition or by the bond of virtue. And *diathesis* itself seems to have many different degrees. For we love our parents in one way, our spouses in another way, our brothers in another, and our children in still another.

— John Cassian, *Conferences* 16.14.1–2

THE TRIAD of "faith, hope, and love" (1 Cor 13:13) continued to be basic to Christian thought and conduct.

To have knowledge of one's own ignorance is the first lesson learned by those who walk according to the Word. A person who was ignorant seeks; and when he seeks, he finds the Teacher; and when he finds, he believes; and when he believes, he hopes; and when he loves, he is made like the Beloved, endeavoring to be the object that has been loved.

— Clement of Alexandria, *Miscellanies* 5.3

WITH reference to 1 Cor 13:13, it was observed that love is greater than faith and hope because it endures even in eternity.

For faith departs when we see God and are persuaded by the vision. And hope vanishes when the things hoped for are received. But love becomes complete and even increases when the perfect things are given to it.
— Clement of Alexandria, *Who Is the Rich Man Who Is Saved?* 38

A perfect person does not encounter anything that causes fear, since he considers none of the things of this life to be fearful, nor can anything remove him from his love for God . . . [1 John 4:18]. He has no need of anything to cheer him up because he does not fall into sorrow, being persuaded that all things turn out well. Nothing provokes anger, for there is nothing that moves him to anger since he always loves God and turns to him alone; because of this he hates none of God's creatures. He does not envy, since he lacks nothing that would make him become truly excellent. Therefore he is fond of nothing, in the usual sense of this word. Rather, he loves the Creator through the creatures. . . .
— Clement of Alexandria, *Miscellanies* 6.9

CLEMENT of Alexandria further explained that one does not desire what one already possesses, and the true gnostic already possesses what is desired.

Love is not desire on the part of the one who loves but an affectionate kinship that restores the gnostic to "the unity of the faith" that is independent of time and place. Through love he is already coming into those things in which he will be, and he anticipates hope through knowledge. He desires nothing since he already has—in a sense—the object he desires. It is appropriate then that by loving in the gnostic manner he remains in one unchangeable habit. He will not seek to be like the beautiful since he possesses beauty through love. What further need is there of courage and desire in one who, because of love, has been given a likeness to the good God, one who through love has enrolled himself among the friends of God?
— Clement of Alexandria, *Miscellanies* 6.9

EARLY Christian writers recognized the principle of a balance between loving the sinner and hating the sin, though this balance was difficult to maintain.

It is therefore necessary for a perfect person to practice love, to hasten from there to divine friendship, fulfilling the commandments because of love. To love one's enemies does not mean to love evil—neither impiety, adultery, nor robbery—but to love the robber, the impious, and the adulterer; and this not as one who sins and defiles the identity of a human being through such activity, but as a human being who is the work of God. Without doubt, sin pertains to the actions of a person, not to one's essence.

— Clement of Alexandria, *Miscellanies* 4.13

THE PAGAN world marveled at Christian love.

To your regret, our love for one another is mutual because we do not know how to hate. Thus—to your envy—we call one another brothers and sisters, those who share a common Parent, who is God, as companions in faith and fellow heirs in hope.

— Minucius Felix, *Octavius* 31.8

TERTULLIAN was given to exaggeration and sharp contrasts, thus he often overstated his case, but he believed that there was something distinctive about Christian love and that Christians could claim greater consistency than others in their practice of love.

For our [Christian] teaching commands us to love even our enemies and to pray for those who persecute us, so that our teaching may be perfect and our goodness be distinctive rather than such as is common. For everyone loves his friends, but only Christians love their enemies.

— Tertullian, *To Scapula* 1

ORIGEN commented on the different words used for love; he especially sought to distinguish passionate love from the Christian meaning of love as active good will.

It must therefore be understood that in whomever this love—which is God [1 John 4:8]—exists, nothing earthly, nothing material, nothing corruptible is loved; for it is contrary to its nature for this love to love anything corruptible, since it is itself the source of incorruption. . . .

This love considers all persons as neighbors. . . . [Luke 10:29–37 is referred to]. For by nature we are all one another's neighbors, but a person truly becomes a neighbor when, through works of love, he is able to benefit another who is in need. . . .

The name of love belongs first to God—the One, that is, from whom we have the very ability to love—and for this reason we are commanded to love God with all our heart and with all our soul and with all our strength [Matt 22:37]. And this command undoubtedly implies that we should equally love wisdom, justice, piety, truth, and all the other virtues; for to love God and to love good things is one and the same. In the second place, by an adapted and derived use of the word, we are also commanded to love our neighbor as ourselves. A third use of the word "love," which is a false use of the word, is to love money, pleasure, or anything that pertains to corruption and error. . . . It must be understood that everyone who loves money—or anything in the world that is corruptible and draws the power of love, which is of God, down to earthly and perishable objects—misuses the things of God for purposes contrary to God's will; for God gives things to human beings to be used, not to be loved. . . .

It is impossible for human beings not to feel the passion of love for something. Everyone who reaches the age of puberty loves something—either incorrectly when one loves what should not be loved, or rightly and beneficially when one loves what should be loved. But some people misuse passionate love, which is implanted in the rational soul through the kindness of the Creator. Either they dissipate it in passion for money and the pursuit of avarice; or they strive for glorious deeds and desire glory; or they chase after prostitutes and become prisoners of impurity; or they squander the strength of this great good on other things like these. And when love's passion is channeled into artistic works, whether manual crafts or endeavors that are useful for this present life—for example, the art of wrestling or running track—or even when it is devoted to the study of geometry, music, arithmetic, and disciplines similar to these, it does not seem to me to be wholly commendable. . . . Consequently, love is commendable only when it is applied to God and the powers of the soul. . . .

Suppose, for example, that a woman with ardent, passionate love for a certain man wants to marry him. Does she not act in all respects and manage her every movement in a way that will please the man she loves, lest any act contrary to his will cause that excellent man to refuse or scorn marriage to her? Will this woman, whose whole heart and soul and strength are on fire with passionate love for that particular man, be able to commit adultery when she knows that he loves purity? Or murder when she knows that he is peaceful, or theft when she knows that he is pleased with liberality? Or will she desire the goods of others when all of her own desire is absorbed in passionate love for that man? It is in this sense that every commandment is said to be summed up in the perfection of love, and the power of the law and the prophets to depend on it [Matt 22:40].

—Origen, *Homilies on the Song of Songs*, prologue

After love for God we are commanded first to love our parents, second our children, and third our servants . . . [Matt 22:37–39]. He does not say, "Love God as yourself, and your neighbor with all your heart, soul, strength, and mind." Again he said, "Love your enemies" [Matt 5:44], and he does not add "with your whole heart." The divine Word is not disordered, nor does he command what is impossible. He does not say, "Love your enemies as yourself."

—Origen, *Homilies on the Song of Songs* 2.8, on Song 2:4

The Lord, wishing to awaken our souls to this command [John 13:34], required that the proof of discipleship not be signs and marvelous powers (although he granted the working of these by the Holy Spirit), but what one says [in John 13:35]: "By this everyone will know that you are my disciples, if you have love for one another." And so he everywhere joins these commandments so that he takes the good done to a neighbor as though it were done to himself [Matt 25:25, 40]. To observe the first commandment [to love God, Matt 22:37–38] is to observe the second [to love one's neighbor, Matt 22:39]. The fulfillment of the second is also the fulfillment of the first. Accordingly, to love the Lord is also to love one's neighbor. . . . Again, to love one's neighbor is to fulfill the love of God.

—Basil of Caesarea, *Greater Rule* 3

JOHN Chrysostom did not consider the "Golden Rule" to be something new but only a sharper formulation of what is known by nature within us. After quoting Matt 7:12, he writes:

Do you see how he introduced nothing strange, but only what nature had anticipated him in prescribing? He says, "However you wish your neighbors would treat you, put into practice yourself." Do you desire to be praised? Give praise. Do you desire not to be robbed? Do not rob. Do you desire to be honored? Give honor. Do you desire mercy? Show mercy. Do you desire to be loved? Love. Do you desire to hear nothing bad? Say nothing bad. Note the precision. He did not say, "Whatever you do not desire that people do, do not do yourselves" but "Whatever you desire." In other words, since there are two paths leading to virtue, one the avoidance of evil and the other the practice of the virtues, he proposes the latter, while making evident the former by means of the latter.

—John Chrysostom, *Commentary on the Psalms* 5.1

THAT love involves activity is well demonstrated by the use of this word as the name for the church's meal of fellowship and charity.

The *agapē* [love feast] is truly heavenly food, a rational banquet. . . . The meal takes place because of love, not love because of the meal, which is proof that a generous good will is shared by all. . . . He who eats of this meal shall obtain the best things that pertain to reality, the kingdom of God, since he has cared about the holy assembly of love, the heavenly church. Thus love is a pure thing and worthy of God, and its work is generosity. . . . Love is not the meal itself, but the banquet is held because of love.

—Clement of Alexandria, *Instructor*
2.1.5.3; 2.1.6.1–2.1.7.1

The motive for our feast is evident in its name, which is the Greek word for love. Whatever the cost, money spent in the name of piety is gain, since with that refreshment we benefit the needy. . . . Here we show greater consideration for the lowly, just as God does. Our common meal is held for honorable reasons, and you may discern that the way it is carried out is consistent with its purpose. Since it is a religious duty, nothing vile or immodest is permitted. We recline at the table only after first tasting prayer to God. We eat the amount that satisfies our hunger; we drink as much as is beneficial to the modest. We satisfy ourselves as people who remember that even during the night we must worship God; we converse as people who know that the Lord is listening. After we wash our hands and light the lamps, each one who is able is called into the center to chant praise to God, either from the holy Scriptures or from his own talent. This is proof of how much is drunk. In like manner, prayer concludes the meal.

—Tertullian, *Apology* 39.16–18

Mercy

Since we have so many examples, let us imitate the kindness of God rather than learning from ourselves the great evil of making retribution for sin. Observe the sequence of God's goodness. First he makes laws. Then he commands, makes promises, threatens, reproaches, holds out warnings, restrains, threatens again, and—when forced to do so—strikes the blow, but this little by little, leaving room for correction. Therefore let us not strike at once (for this is not safe) but, being self-controlled in our fear, let us conquer through kindness and make others indebted to us because of piety, tormenting them more through their conscience than through wrath. . . . Let us desire to demonstrate that we are kind rather than unblemished, lovers of the poor rather than of justice.

— Gregory of Nazianzus, *Letters* 77

Some of the fathers related that there was a great old man and if someone asked him for a word, he would skillfully say, "Look, I take the place of God and I sit on the throne of judgment. What then do you want me to do for you? If you say, 'Have mercy on me,' God will say to you, 'If you want me to have mercy on you, then you yourself have mercy on your brother; if you want me to forgive you, then you forgive your neighbor.' Can there be injustice in God? Certainly not. But our salvation depends on whether we want to be saved."

— *Apophthegmata Patrum*, Anonymous
Collection, # 226 Nau

THE FOLLOWING selection comments on Matt 5:7. The concluding part of the selection supposes that those who have benefited from the merciful acts of others will commend their benefactors to the Judge at the final judgment.

Mercy is voluntary sorrow that involves itself in the suffering of others. . . .

Mercy is a loving disposition toward those who are distressed over anything painful. For just as cruelty and brutality arise from hatred, so mercy grows out of love and cannot exist without it. If anyone carefully inquires into the distinctive character of mercy, he will find an intensely loving disposition commingled with a feeling of sorrow. For all—enemies and friends alike—seek to share in the good things of others, but a desire to share in the suffering of others is characteristic only of those who are ruled by love. Love is acknowledged as the best thing that can be pursued in this life, and mercy is the intensifying of love. Therefore, a person who has this disposition of soul is properly and truly most blessed, having attained the height of virtue. . . .

Just as a cruel and brutal person makes enemies out of those who experience his fierceness, so also those of us who experience the opposite behavior are kindly disposed to the one who shows mercy on us, because mercy naturally causes love in those who share in it. Therefore, as the teaching shows, mercy is the parent of kindness, the pledge of love, and the common bond in every friendly disposition. What greater strength for life can be imagined than the security provided by mercy? . . .

For those who have been participants in grace, the good will that springs up in souls toward those who have shown them mercy surely endures beyond this life and into eternal life. If at the time of judgment benefactors are recognized by those who have experienced their goodness, then what is their soul likely to feel when they are acclaimed by grateful voices before the Judge of all creation? . . . When they see others dragged down by an evil conscience—as by an executioner—into that gloomy darkness, while they, shining with confidence, are led to the Judge by their works and the praise and thanks of those who have experienced their good deeds, will they consider material wealth equal to this good fortune?

—Gregory of Nyssa, *On the Beatitudes* 5

ᗰercy is also a good thing because it makes people perfect, in that it imitates the perfect Father. Nothing commends the Christian soul so much as mercy: first of all toward the poor, as sharers with you in the produce of nature, which generates the fruits of the earth for use by all. Thus freely give what you have to the poor, and help your partner and companion. Freely give a coin; the one you help receives life. Give money, as it is everything to the recipient. For that person, your denarius constitutes his property.

In this regard, the person you help bestows more on you, since your salvation may depend on him. When you clothe the naked, you clothe yourself with righteousness. When you bring a stranger under your roof, when you support the needy, that person acquires the friendship of the holy ones and eternal dwelling places for you [Luke 16:9]. That is no small favor. You sow material things and reap spiritual things. . . . You are clearly blessed if no poor person ever goes away from your house with empty pockets. And no one is more blessed than the one who understands the needs of the poor and the distress of the weak and indigent. On the day of judgment such a person will have salvation from the Lord, who will owe him a debt of mercy.

—Ambrose, *Duties* 1.11.38–1.12.39

Patient Endurance

THE GREEK and Latin words for "patience" primarily emphasize endurance. The following quotations from Latin authors include this element of long-suffering but also approximate the English usage for the calm attitude with which one exercises forbearance toward others. For other quotations related to endurance, see Perseverance below.

Patience protects faith, governs peace, aids love, instructs humility, waits for repentance, assigns confession, rules the flesh, watches over the spirit, controls the tongue, restrains the hand, suppresses temptations, repels scandals, brings martyrdoms to completion, and consoles the poor; it moderates the rich, does not devour the weak, does not increase the strong, pleases the believer, attracts the pagan, commends the servant to the master and the master to God, adorns a woman, makes a man agreeable, is loved in childhood, is praised in youth, is admired in old age, and is beautiful in both sexes at every age in life. Come now; let us apprehend the appearance and manner of patience. Her features are tranquil and peaceful: her forehead is pure, not contracted by wrinkles of sorrow or anger; her eyebrows are evenly relaxed in a glad manner; her eyes are downcast in humility, not in unhappiness; her mouth is sealed in the dignity of silence; her color is that of one who is without worry and guilt. . . . Where God is, there also is his child—I mean, of course, patience. Thus whenever God's Spirit descends, patience inseparably accompanies him.

—Tertullian, *On Patience* 15

IN DEVELOPING his own thoughts and comments on patience, Cyprian depended heavily on Tertullian.

We have this virtue [patience] in common with God. Patience originates in him; its renown and dignity have their source in him. The origin and greatness of patience proceed from God as its author. . . .

Although God is provoked by numerous—indeed continual—offenses, he moderates his indignation and patiently awaits the day of retribution, which has been fixed once for all. And although revenge is within his power, he prefers to keep patience for a long while, mercifully—I might say—enduring and delaying so that if it be possible, the much-prolonged wickedness might be at some time changed and human beings who are immersed in the contagion of errors and crimes might be converted to God, even if only tardily. . . .

Patience commends us to God and preserves us in him. It is patience that moderates anger, controls the tongue, governs the mind, maintains peace, rules discipline, breaks the impulse of lust, restrains the violence of arrogance, extinguishes the fire of animosity, limits the power of the rich, relieves the needs of the poor, and preserves blessed integrity in virgins, diligent modesty in widows, and inseparable love in those who are united in marriage. It makes persons humble in prosperity, strong in adversity, mild in the face of injuries and insults. It teaches us to forgive quickly those who do wrong; and if you yourself do wrong, it teaches you to make long and frequent entreaties. It overcomes temptations, submits to persecutions, and brings sufferings and martyrdoms to completion. It is patience that guards firmly the foundations of our faith. It is this that carries our hope ever higher. It is this that directs our actions so that, walking by his patient fortitude, we are able to hold fast to the way of Christ. When we imitate our Father's patience, this causes us to persevere as children of God.

—Cyprian, *On Patience* 3; 4; 20

Righteous persons have always possessed patient fortitude. The apostles took this discipline from the law of the Lord: not to murmur in adversity but to accept bravely and patiently whatever happens in this world. . . . Beloved, we must not murmur in adversity but endure patiently and bravely whatever happens.

—Cyprian, *On Mortality* 11

True patience and tranquility are not acquired or kept without deep humility of heart. . . . For patience that has never been attacked by enemy spears does not deserve praise or admiration, but it is splendid and glorious when it remains unmoved while violent disturbances and trials rush in upon it. Just when patience seems to be distressed and broken by adversities, it grows stronger; and at the very moment that it seems to be battered, it is sharpened even more. For everyone knows that patience is so named from suffering and endurance, and therefore it is clear that no one can be called patient except the person who endures without indignation everything that is inflicted upon him.

—John Cassian, *Conferences* 18.13.1–2

Peace—External and Inner

IN THE following selection Gregory of Nyssa comments on Matt 5:9.

Of those things that we pursue for enjoyment in life, what is sweeter to human beings than peace? Every pleasure in life that can be named requires peace in order to be pleasurable. For if those things that are valued in life—whether wealth, good health, marriage, children, house, parents, servants, friends, land and sea each producing its own wealth, gardens, animals, baths, exercise grounds, gymnasiums, or places of luxury and pleasure; and let us add to these the theatrical shows, musical recitals, and anything else by which life is made pleasurable for those who live in luxury—if all of these things are present but the blessing of peace is absent, if war cuts off the enjoyment of these good things, then what is their benefit? Peace itself then is sweet to those who share in it, and it sweetens all the things that we value in life. Even if we suffer human misfortune, when there is peace those who are affected bear it more easily, since it is mixed with some good. When life is accompanied by war, we become somewhat insensitive to those things that cause grief, for common misfortune surpasses each individual's pains. . . .

A peacemaker is one who gives peace to another, but one cannot provide another with what he himself does not have. Hence, the Lord desires that you first become full of the good things peace provides and then extend what you possess to those who need it. . . . Is peace anything other than a loving disposition toward one's neighbor? What is the opposite of love? Hatred, wrath, anger, envy, malice, hypocrisy, and the misfortunes of war. Do you see how many different kinds of illness peace can cure? For peace opposes equally each of the things mentioned, and its presence makes their evil disappear. . . .

Peacemakers imitate the divine love for humanity. They demonstrate in their own lives the activity characteristic of God. The Lord and Worker of all good things completely removes everything that is strange and foreign to the good, causing it to exist no longer. He commands that you also do this work: cast out hatred, abolish war, destroy envy, root out conflict, remove hypocrisy, extinguish malice that smolders within the heart. . . . Should not the one who dispenses divine gifts, who imitates the gifts of God and patterns his own good deeds after God's generosity, be called "Blessed"? . . . I think a person is properly called a peacemaker when he brings the discord of flesh and spirit within himself into peaceful harmony.

—Gregory of Nyssa, *On the Beatitudes* 7

THE NEXT passage comments on Isa 2:3 and its fulfillment in Christianity.

We who formerly killed one another not only refuse to make war against our enemies but also readily confess Christ and die so as not to lie or deceive our examiners. . . . Those who take an oath and are enrolled as your [Roman emperors'] soldiers place adherence to that oath above their own life, parents, homeland, and all their kindred, even though you can offer them nothing that is incorruptible; it would be ridiculous for those of us who desire incorruption not to endure all things in order to receive our desire from the One who is able to grant it.

—Justin Martyr, *1 Apology* 39

THE FOLLOWING words were written about monks, but they are applicable to others.

A brother asked Abba Rufus, "What is inner peace, and what is its benefit?" The old man replied, "Inner peace is sitting in one's cell with the fear and knowledge of God, avoiding haughtiness and the remembrance of wrongs. Inner peace is the mother of all the virtues, and it protects the monk from the fiery darts of the enemy [Eph 6:16], not allowing him to be injured by them. Yes, brother, obtain this. Remember your departure in death because you do not know at what hour the thief will come [Luke 12:39]. Finally, then, exercise self-control over your soul."

—*Apophthegmata Patrum*, Alphabetical
Collection, Rufus # 1

Abba Poemen said, "If you think little about yourself, you will have rest wherever you reside."

—*Apophthegmata Patrum*, Alphabetical
Collection, Poemen # 81

When Abba Romanos was dying, his disciples gathered around him and asked, "How should we conduct ourselves?" The old man replied, "I do not think I have ever told one of you to do something without first deciding that I would not become angry if what I asked were not done; and so we have lived all our days in peace."

—*Apophthegmata Patrum*, Alphabetical
Collection, Romanos # 1

Perseverance

PERSEVERANCE is closely related to Patient Endurance (above), but here we stress the aspect of continuing faithfulness.

A friend is not made by a single gift but from complete tranquility and long association. [We are not saved] by showing faith, love, or perseverance for only a day, but "the one who endures to the end will be saved" [Matt 10:22].

—Clement of Alexandria, *Who Is the Rich Man Who Is Saved?* 32

How is it that a woman or man—the most faithful, most prudent, and most approved in the church—goes over to the other faction? . . . And is it surprising that someone who was approved might afterward fall away and return to his former condition? . . . Only the Son of God persevered and was preserved without fault. What then? If a bishop, deacon, widow, virgin, teacher, or even a martyr falls from the rule of faith, does this mean that heresies possess the truth? Do we prove the faith by persons, or persons by the faith? No one is wise unless he is faithful; no one is eminent unless a Christian; and no one is a Christian except the one who perseveres even to the end. . . . Are we surprised that some persons forsake the churches of Christ when the things that we suffer in accordance with the example of Christ prove that we are Christians?

—Tertullian, *Prescription against Heretics* 3

An old man was asked, "What can keep a diligent brother from stumbling when he sees others returning to the world?" And he replied, "One ought to observe the way dogs chase after rabbits. When one of them sees a rabbit, he pursues it until he catches it, not letting anything hinder his pursuit. The other dogs see only the dog in pursuit and they run with him for a time, but then after a while they reconsider and turn back. Only the one who has seen the rabbit pursues it until he catches it, and he is not hindered from his goal by those who turned back. He does not think about cliffs, undergrowth, or thorns. So it is with the one who seeks Christ the Master: always focusing his attention always on the cross, he jumps over every occasion for stumbling until he reaches the Crucified One.

—*Apophthegmata Patrum*, Anonymous Collection, # 203 Nau

Righteousness

What is the meaning of "Offer a sacrifice of righteousness" [Ps 4:5]? Seek after righteousness, bring an offering of righteousness. This—not the sacrifice of sheep and calves but the practice of righteousness—is the greatest gift one can bring to God; this is an acceptable sacrifice, an offering that is pleasing. Behold the life of the church described in advance; and in place of material things behold the rational things that should be sought. As I said before, in this verse he is not speaking about righteousness as being a particular virtue but as being virtue in general; so we call persons righteous who have all virtue in themselves. This sacrifice does not require money, a sword, an altar, or fire; it does not dissolve into smoke, ashes, and odor. Rather, this sacrifice is fulfilled through the intentions of the one who makes the offering. Indigence does not hinder it—poverty is not an obstacle; nor is place, nor any other such thing. Instead, wherever you are you can sacrifice righteousness; you yourself are the priest, the altar, the sword, and the sacrificial animal. Intellectual and spiritual qualities are like this: they have greater ease and they are not bothered with externals.

—John Chrysostom, *Commentary on the Psalms* 4.9, on Ps 4:5

Epiphanius [Bishop of Salamis] said, "God sells righteousness at a very low price to those who are eager to buy it: a little piece of bread, an inexpensive garment, a cup of cold water, a small coin."

—*Apophthegmata Patrum*, Alphabetical Collection, Epiphanius # 16

See also the passages in this chapter under Justice.

Saying and Doing

Speech is not as persuasive as practice, that silent exhortation.

—Gregory of Nazianzus, *Letters* 77

Poemen again said, "Teach your heart to keep those things that your tongue teaches."

—*Apophthegmata Patrum*, Alphabetical Collection, Poemen # 188

One of the fathers said, "We need spiritual work; we have come [to the desert] for this. It is laborious to teach with the mouth when not doing bodily work."

— *Apophthegmata Patrum,* Anonymous
Collection, # 240 Nau

Abba Isidore of Pelusia said, "Life without a word is naturally more beneficial than a word without a life. For the former is beneficial even when silent, but the latter is a nuisance even when calling out. But if word and life coincide, then they produce one image of the whole of philosophy."

— *Apophthegmata Patrum,* Alphabetical
Collection, Isidore of Pelusium # 1

Sexual Morality

Above all, I admonish you to maintain the boundary of sexual purity, knowing—as you do—that you are a temple of the Lord, members of Christ, a habitation of the Holy Spirit, chosen for hope, consecrated to faith, destined for salvation, children of God, brothers and sisters of Christ, companions of the Holy Spirit, owing nothing any longer to the flesh as reborn from the water. And indeed on account of redemption sexual purity is preferable even to free will, which we should always desire to have in our power, so that what has been consecrated by Christ might not be corrupted. . . .

Sexual purity is the dignity of the body, the ornament of morality, the sanctity of the sexes, the bond of those who are married, the pledge of offspring, the protection of modesty, the source of chastity, the peace of the home, the summit of concord. . . . Sexual purity is always seemly, as the mother of innocence. Sexual purity is always adorned with modesty alone, rightly conscious of its own beauty even if it is displeasing to the wicked. Sexual purity seeks nothing in the way of adornments, being its own glory. Sexual purity commends us to the Lord, unites us with Christ, drives from our members the illicit conflicts of our desires, instills peace in our bodies. . . . This virtue is always approved in men and to be sought after by women, just as sexual immorality—which is its enemy—is always detestable. . . . [The continuation of this passage is quoted below, under Sexual Immorality.]

Sexual purity holds the first place in virgins, the second in those who are chaste, the third in those who are married, and is truly glorious in all according to their rank.

— Novatian, *On Chastity* 2.1–2; 3.1–3; 4.1

IN THE following passage, after quoting Jesus' sayings on chastity, adultery, and divorce, Justin Martyr continues with these words:

Thus all who enter into second marriages that are permitted by human law are sinners according to our Teacher, and so are those who look upon a woman with lust. For he rejects not only the man who commits adultery in deed but also the one who desires to commit adultery, since not only our deeds but also our thoughts are manifest to God. There are many men and women who are sixty and seventy years old who have been disciples of Christ from childhood and have remained (sexually) pure. And I vow to show such from every race of humanity.

—Justin Martyr, *1 Apology* 15

THE FOLLOWING comments are based on Prov 6:27–28.

So that you may not ask, "What harm is there in the eyes, since surely one who looks need not be overcome?" the writer shows you how lust is a fire. The flesh is a garment, an easy victim, and lust is a tyrant. . . . For he who looks upon a woman, even though he escapes, does not withdraw pure from lust. What need is there for troubles when self-control and freedom from trouble are readily available? . . . According to the spiritual meaning, the one who allows an impure thought to continue in his heart "keeps a fire in his bosom." And the one who destroys his own soul by sinful acts "walks upon coals."

—Hippolytus, *On Proverbs*

THE NEXT selection, concerning sexually suggestive speech, followed citation of several Scriptures about shameful speech.

One must keep altogether away from shameful things that are heard, both words and things seen; and even more must one keep pure from shameful deeds, from either exhibiting or exposing parts of the body that need not be shown and looking at parts that are forbidden. . . . The Instructor does not permit us to utter anything shameful and keeps us far away from licentiousness. For he always skillfully cuts off the roots of sin; for example, "You shall not commit adultery" is cut off by the command "You shall not lust." For adultery is the fruit of lust, which is the evil root. Similarly, the Instructor attacks the impure use of names in order to cut off impure and licentious sexual intercourse. The disorderly use of names also induces interest in offensive conduct; but the modest use of words trains a person to be temperate with regard to lustful acts. . . . For neither the knee, the leg, nor any such member— nor the names we have for them, nor their activity—is shameful. Even a person's private parts have been deemed worthy of respect and not shame. Their unlawful activity is shameful, deserving of shame and reproach and—because of this—punishment. In reality the only thing shameful is wickedness and those actions that are in accord with wickedness. Thus stories about deeds of wickedness, such as talk about adultery, pederasty, and similar things, should be considered obscenities.

—Clement of Alexandria, *Instructor* 2.6.52

TERTULLIAN responded to the pagan slander that Christian meetings were occasions for incestuous unions.

A most scrupulous and faithful chastity keeps us [Christians] from [incest], and to an equal extent from illicit sexual intercourse and excess after marriage, so we are protected from any occurrence of incest. To make matters even more secure, some of us drive away the power of sexual sin entirely by the continence of virginity, still being boys when old men.

—Tertullian, *Apology* 9.19

Another time, when Ephraim was on the road, a prostitute attempted by her suggestiveness to flatter him into shameful intercourse and, if not successful at that, to move him to anger, for no one had ever seen him angry. He said to her, "Follow me." When they had reached a very crowded place, he said to her, "In this place, come, do as you desire." But she, seeing the crowd, said to him, "How can we do this and not be ashamed when such a great crowd is present?" He said to her, "If we are ashamed before people, how much more should we be ashamed before God, who reproves the hidden things of darkness?" Having been put to shame, she went away unsuccessful.

—*Apophthegmata Patrum,* Alphabetical
Collection, Ephraim, # 3

Wisdom

COMPARE the following to Origen's threefold division—the wisdom of the world, the wisdom of the rulers of the world, and the wisdom of God—found in *First Principles* 3.3.1.

⊄here is divine wisdom, and there is human wisdom. We call human wisdom "the wisdom of the world," which is "foolishness with God." Divine wisdom is different. Because it is divine, it comes to those who have prepared themselves for its reception. . . . We say that human wisdom is a school for the soul, but divine wisdom is the goal. . . . Divine wisdom is the first of the so-called charismata [grace gifts] of God [1 Cor 12:8–9]. . . .

At the present time the churches have, in proportion to their numbers, a few wise men who have come over from the wisdom we call "according to the flesh," and they have some who have crossed over from that to divine wisdom.

—Origen, *Against Celsus* 6.13, 14

Religion cannot be separated from wisdom nor wisdom from religion, for it is the same God who is known (this is the role of wisdom) and honored (this is the role of religion) by both. But wisdom precedes and religion follows, for knowing God comes first and worshiping him is the result. . . . The source of wisdom and religion is God; and if these two streams flow away from him, they must of necessity dry up. Those who are ignorant of him can be neither wise nor religious.

—Lactantius, *Divine Institutes* 4.4.2–4

⊄he principal wisdom is a life worthy of praise and purified for God—that is, being cleansed for God—who is most pure and most radiant and who asks that our only sacrifice be purification, which is a contrite heart, a sacrifice of praise, a new creation in Christ, a new person, and those things that Scripture tells us are objects of his love. The best wisdom despises wisdom that consists of words, turns of phrase, and deceitful and elaborate antitheses. . . . I do not consider wise the person who is wise in speech and has a ready tongue but is unstable and undisciplined in his soul, like the tombs that are outwardly attractive and beautiful but within are full of decaying corpses and bad odors. I consider wise the person who speaks little about virtue but whose deeds provide many examples of it, and his life adds to the trustworthiness of his words.

—Gregory of Nazianzus, *Oration* 16.2

Negative Attitudes and Actions

Anger

Beware of anger. If it is not possible to avoid it, then let it be controlled. For indignation is an evil enticement to sin. It disturbs the mind, leaving no place for reason. Therefore, if possible, the first thing one should do is to train one's nature in tranquility through practice, inner sentiment, and intention. Next, realizing that this emotion is to some extent implanted in our nature and habits—so that it cannot be rooted out and avoided—it must be restrained by reason, if it can be foreseen. Or, if the mind becomes filled with indignation before it can be purposefully attended to or prevented, consider how you might conquer the passion of your mind, how you might temper anger, lest it take possession of you. Resist anger, if you are able; if not, withdraw. . . .

The first thing to do then is to calm your mind. If you cannot do this, then put a bridle on your tongue. Next, do not pass up any opportunity for reconciliation. . . .

Thus, prepare yourself to be like a child who never retains an injury in his thoughts or occupies himself with malice, but let all things be undertaken blamelessly. . . . Guard the simplicity and purity of your heart. Do not respond to anyone who is angry with anger, nor with folly to one who is foolish [Prov 26:4]. One fault quickly causes another fault. If you rub stones together, does not fire break out?

—Ambrose, *Duties* 1.21.90, 92, 93

A demon, you see, does not tremble so much at the one who expels him from a person as he does at those who control their anger and have superiority over their temper, because anger is also a demon that is hard to deal with, and an angry person should be considered worse off than one who is possessed. After all, being possessed does not cast one into hell, but being angry and harboring malice casts one out of the kingdom of heaven.

—John Chrysostom, *Commentary on the Psalms* 4.5, on Ps 4:1

Freedom from anger begins with the silence of our lips when our heart is stirred. The middle stage is silence of our thoughts at the mere stirring of our soul. The last stage is maintaining secure calm when impure winds are blowing.

—John Climacus, *Ladder of Paradise* 8

Abba Isaiah was asked, "What is anger?" And he answered, "Strife, a lie, and ignorance."

— *Apophthegmata Patrum,* Alphabetical
Collection, Isaiah # 11

SEE THE section Sin and Sinners for more selections.

Covetousness

Abba Isaiah was asked, "What is avarice?" He replied, "Not believing in God and that he cares for you, despair over God's promises, and arrogance."

— *Apophthegmata Patrum,* Alphabetical
Collection, Isaiah # 9

We should not think that "covetousness" [1 Tim 6:10] consists simply in the desire for what belongs to someone else. Indeed even what seems to be ours belongs to another, for nothing—including ourselves—is ours but all things belong to God. And so when we feel impatience over a loss, grieving for the loss of something that was not our own, then we are shown to be entangled in covetousness. When we reluctantly endure being parted from what belongs to someone else, we are in fact seeking what really belongs to God. He who is impatient over a loss is properly said to sin against God by preferring earthly things over heavenly things. He distresses the Spirit, which he received from the Lord, over a mundane matter. Freely, therefore, let us let go of earthly things so that we may preserve heavenly things. . . . We should not lay down our soul for money but money for our soul, whether voluntarily giving it or patiently losing it.

— Tertullian, *On Patience* 7

Robbery and covetousness—whether for gold or silver—are the same thing, for they are born from the same intention. The one who steals a little would not refuse stealing much. If the latter does not occur, it is not because of the person's choice but because there was no opportunity. A poor person who acts unjustly toward a poorer person would not, if he were able, spare a richer person. The outcome results from weakness, not from the person's choice.

— John Chrysostom, *Homilies on 2 Timothy*
3.3, on 2 Tim 1:16–18

Even as one whose feet are bound cannot easily walk, so those who store up material treasures are not able to ascend to heaven.

—John Climacus, *Ladder of Paradise* 26

Division

Children of the devil] know how to cut us off from God, for they know that a person who loves his neighbor loves God. For this cause, as enemies of virtue, they sow in our hearts pretense about what is our own, and this becomes like kindling wood, filling us with great enmity against one another so that we do not speak with our neighbor even from a distance.

—Anthony, *Letter* 2[6].11

GREGORY of Nazianzus' discussion of religious divisions during his time sounds similar to the denominational conflicts we experience today. This is also true of the other things he thought divide believers, including the use of party (denominational) names to distinguish people. A similar statement is recorded in Chapter V, under The Name Christian.

East and West are separated into opposing parties and are in danger of becoming divided as much in opinion as in location. How long [are we to be divided]—mine and yours, the old and the new, the more rational and the more spiritual, the nobler born and the less well born, the majority and the minority? I am ashamed in my old age, after being saved by Christ, to be called by any other name.

—Gregory of Nazianzus, *Oration* 42.21

IN GREEK, the word *hairesis*, from which we derive our English word "heresy," designated a division, a party, or a school of thought. In the following passage I have translated the word as "division," but the reader should also keep in mind that the word can also refer to a school of thought. The criticism that Christianity is internally divided is an old one. In the following selection, Origen responds to Celsus's accusation that there are divisions (heresies) among Christians.

In reply to this we say that different divisions occur only with regard to those subjects whose first principle and usefulness for life merits serious attention. [Medicine is useful and necessary and so there are various schools of medicine.] . . . Yet no one who is reasonable avoids medicine because it is divided [into different schools of thought], nor would one whose goal is proper conduct hate philosophy, excusing his hatred on the grounds that it has many divisions. Thus one should not condemn the sacred books of Moses and the prophets because there are divisions in Judaism. . . .

Just as one who is qualified in medicine chooses the best after experiencing and prudently examining various schools of thought, and as one who is truly advanced in philosophy has made the effort to know as much as possible about the various schools and to identify himself with the teaching that he finds most convincing, so also the wisest Christian is the one who looks carefully into the divisions within Judaism and Christianity.

—Origen, *Against Celsus* 3.12, 13

Envy and Jealousy

Beloved brothers and sisters, some people think that jealousy over what seems good and envy of those who are better is a small and ordinary fault; and since it is thought to be small and ordinary, it is not feared; since it is not feared, it is treated as unimportant; since it is treated as unimportant, it is not easily avoided; and thus it becomes a dark and hidden occasion for destruction. . . .

Jealousy's occasions for destruction—so manifold and fruitful—extend widely. Jealousy is a root of all kinds of evil, a source of disasters, a nursery of misdeeds, an occasion for wrongdoing. Hatred arises from it; animosity proceeds from it. Jealousy inflames covetousness, since one who observes that another is more wealthy cannot be content with what he has. When one sees another receive honors, jealousy excites ambition. When jealousy blinds our perception and diminishes the secret condition of our mind, the fear of God is disregarded, the teachings of Christ are neglected, and the day of judgment is forgotten.

—Cyprian, *On Jealousy and Envy* 1; 6

GREGORY of Nyssa—like Cyprian in the treatise just cited—attributed the devil's effort to deceive humanity to his envy of the high status possessed by human beings (based on Wis 2:24).

Envy is the passion that causes evil; it is the father of death, sin's first entrance, the root of wickedness, the birth of sorrow, the mother of misfortune, the basis of disobedience, the beginning of shame. . . .

Envy is the death-dealing sting, the hidden weapon, the sickness of nature, the bitter poison, the self-willed emaciation, the bitter dart, the nail of the soul, the fire in the heart, the flame burning on the inside.

With envy, it is not its own misfortune but the good fortune of another that is unfortunate. Again, inversely, success is not one's own good fortune but the misfortune of a neighbor. Envy both is grieved at the good deeds people do and takes advantage of their misfortunes.

— Gregory of Nyssa, *Life of Moses* 2.256–258

It seems to me that the passions of envy and hypocrisy are much more serious than anger, inasmuch as hidden evil is more dangerous than manifest evil. . . . Envy and hypocrisy are passions that cause hatred to smolder like a hidden fire within the depths of the heart, while hypocrisy's outward appearance takes the form of friendship. . . . I would like to say to the envious person, What have you suffered, you poor wretch? For what are you wasting away when you look upon the success of your neighbor vindictively? What charge would you bring against him? That he is well favored in body, eloquent in speech, comes from a better family? That having entered into some office he is splendidly honored? That an abundance of possessions has come to him? That he is honored in public meetings because of his prudence? That he is admired by the crowds for his good works? That he rejoices in his children, delights in his wife, is distinguished by those who visit his house? Why do these things pierce your heart like arrows?

— Gregory of Nyssa, *On the Beatitudes* 7

Of all the vices, therefore, envy is surely more destructive and more difficult to heal, because it is aroused by the very remedies that extinguish the others. For example, a person who grieves over a loss imposed on him is cured by generous compensation, and a person who is angered by injuries imposed on him is placated by humble satisfaction. But what can be done for a person who is offended by the very fact that he thinks you are humbler and kinder, a person whose wrath is aroused not by avarice, which is soothed by money, nor by hurtful injury nor love of revenge, which is overcome by favors, a person who is annoyed by the success of someone else's happiness? What person would want to fall from his good character, or be separated from his prosperity, or be overcome by any misfortune in order to satisfy someone else's envy? . . . For the poison of serpents—that is, carnal sins and vices . . . leave the mark of their wounds in the flesh. . . . But the poison of envy . . . destroys the very life of religion and faith before the body feels a wound. A blasphemer clearly exalts himself not against a human being but against God. And a person who criticizes his brother for nothing other than his happiness censures the judgments of God, not the faults of human beings.

—John Cassian, *Conferences* 18.16.11–14

Fear

WRITERS in the early church expressed the thought that "the fear of God knows no other fear."

Fear is experiencing a danger in advance; or, again, it is a trembling of one's heart when agitated and distressed over undisclosed events. It is the loss of assurance. A proud soul is a slave of fear because it trusts only in itself and is frightened by sounds and shadows. . . . The slave of the Lord fears only his own Master, but the one who does not yet fear him is often afraid of his own shadow.

—John Climacus, *Ladder of Paradise* 21

Flattery and Worldly Honor

Amma Syncleitica also said, "Just as something cannot be both a plant and a seed at the same time, so it is impossible while surrounded with worldly glory to produce heavenly fruit."

—*Apophthegmata Patrum,* Alphabetical
Collection, Syncleitica # 22
(Guy, supp. 4)

My head does not swell from flattery. Flattery is false praise. The false praise of a flatterer is "the sinner's oil." Consequently, when people mock someone by rendering false praise they say of him, "I anointed his head." Therefore, love to be "mercifully reproved by the just," but never to be praised by a sinner in derision. . . . Oil is glory—it shines and rests on the surface; but glory that is true glory ought to be the good.

—Augustine, *Expositions on the Psalms*
141.13, on Ps 141:5

Gambling

ALTHOUGH the Scriptures do not specifically prohibit gambling, early Christians observed that gambling violates many biblical principles.

The game of dice is an obvious snare of the devil. He presides over the game in person, bringing to it the deadly venom of the serpent and even inducing ruin, which when it is seen to be nothing, a great let-down is brought about in the players. . . . This hand is accustomed to the unbridled passion of gambling because gambling is like the devil's hunting spear and those who play the dice are wounded with an irresistible allurement.

It is at the gambling table, I tell you, where the devil slyly watches for the moment when he shall surprise the players and immediately rejoice in his triumph over his victims. It is at the gambling table where one finds disloyalty and deception. I tell you, it is at the gambling table where insane frenzy and dishonest transactions transpire, and where language is as poisonous as a serpent's venom. At the gambling table, friends become bitter enemies, and one finds the ultimate excess of the most frightful crimes, and brotherly love is changed into discord. At the gambling table, one finds only outrage, a most cruel boldness, a mad fury, and a wild impatience. I tell you, it is at the gambling table where one loses his possessions and enormous sums of money. . . . You damn yourselves by your sin, yet after having committed it, you do not stop! . . . Gambling's temptation is obvious to everyone, but its punishment is hidden. The gambling board is the devil's snare and the enemy's trap that entices greed but [in actuality brings] utter ruin. By gambling, men become poor, squandering their own riches. Then, after all of their own fortunes have been wasted, they overwhelm themselves with borrowed money. . . .

Stop being a dice player and start being a Christian. Before Christ, beneath the gaze of the angels, and in the presence of the martyrs, cast your money upon the altar of the Lord. Distribute your money to the poor before you allow it to be squandered by your unruly passions. Entrust your stakes to Christ, who is always victorious! Servant, find your recreation in the Lord and obey his divine impulse.[2]

—Pseudo-Cyprian, *Concerning the Dice-Players* 5; 6; 11

If I let you go and dismiss this assembly, some will run to the dice. There they will find swearing, harsh quarreling, and the pangs of avarice. There the devil stands, inflaming the fury of the players with the dotted bones, transferring the same sums of money from one player to another, now exalting this one with victory and making the other feel dejected, again exhibiting the former as boastful and the latter as ashamed. . . . Leisure without the fear of the Lord is a teacher of evil to those who do not know how to use their time.

—Basil of Caesarea, *Hexaemeron* 8.8

Idolatry

The principal crime committed by the human race—the highest charge against the world, the whole cause of judgment—is idolatry. For even though each individual misdeed has its own specific aspect and is destined for judgment in its own name, nevertheless it is also described as the crime of idolatry. . . . In idolatry all crimes are discovered, and in all crimes there is idolatry. . . .

Most people simply assume that idolatry is to be understood only as burning incense, sacrificing a victim, serving a sacrificial banquet, or as something bound to sacred functions or priesthoods. . . . If idolatry is the head of unrighteousness, then our first objective is to be fortified in advance against its multiplicity, while we recognize it in more than its obvious manifestations.
—Tertullian, *On Idolatry* 1; 2

SOME Christians justified their participation in certain aspects of pagan society on the grounds that the component elements in these activities were part of God's good creation. Tertullian responded by pointing out that good things can be put to evil use and any association with idolatry was especially serious.

All the profane pleasures of worldly shows . . . and even idolatry itself are dependent on the things of God. Yet a Christian ought not be involved in the wild behavior that takes place at the racetrack [the Roman circus], or the atrocities of the arena, or the indecencies of the stage on the ground that the horse, the panther, and the voice were given to human beings by God. Even so, a Christian may not commit idolatry with impunity because the incense, the wine, the fire that devours them, and the animals that are the victims are God's creation. . . . Even so, therefore, with regard to what one wears, material wealth is incorrectly excused as coming from God if its use is foreign to God and one is guilty of the charge of worldly glory.
—Tertullian, *On the Apparel of Women* 1

FURTHER observations on idolatry by Tertullian are quoted below, under Sin and Sinners.

Judging

If you cancel someone else's physical debt, then whatever holds your own soul in bondage will be canceled. If you pardon, you will be pardoned.

You will be your own judge, your own legislator. By your attitude toward the person who is subject to you, you pronounce the sentence from above upon yourself.

— Gregory of Nyssa, *On the Lord's Prayer* 5

The justice of the divine judgment reveals that the governing factor is the intention of a person with regard to those in need. In a sense each person is his own judge, pronouncing sentence upon himself by means of his judgment toward those who are subject to him.

— Gregory of Nyssa, *On the Beatitudes* 5

Passions

A brother asked [Poemen]: "What does it mean, 'Do not repay evil for evil'?" [1 Thess 5:15]. The old man replied, "This condition is expressed in four ways: first, from the heart; second, from the countenance; third, from the tongue; and the fourth is not to return evil for evil. If you can purify your heart, evil will not come into your countenance; but if it comes into your countenance, take care not to speak; but if you do speak, quickly cut the evil off so as not to do evil in return for evil."

— *Apophthegmata Patrum*, Alphabetical Collection, Poemen # 34

Abba Pityrion, the disciple of Abba Anthony, said, "If anyone wants to drive out demons, he must first subdue the passions; for he will banish the demon of the passion that he has mastered. For example, the devil accompanies anger; so if you control your anger, the devil of anger will be banished. And so it is with each of the passions."[3]

— *Apophthegmata Patrum*, Alphabetical Collection, Pityrion # 1

Pride and Fame

IN THE next selection Gregory of Nyssa comments on Matt 5:3.

How then can a person be lord of another's life if he is not lord of his own? If a person is poor in spirit, looking to the One who willingly became poor on account of us, observing the equality of our nature, and not being insolent toward those of the same humanity because of the deceptive pomp that goes with holding an office, then this person is truly blessed and exchanges the temporary humility of this life for the kingdom of heaven.

—Gregory of Nyssa, *On the Beatitudes* 1

Abba Elias, the minister, said, "What strength does sin have where there is repentance? And what profit does love have where there is pride?"

—*Apophthegmata Patrum*, Alphabetical Collection, Elias # 3

Abba Isidore of Pelusia said, "Prize the virtues and do not serve glory, for the virtues are immortal, but glory quickly disappears."

—*Apophthegmata Patrum*, Alphabetical Collection, Isidore of Pelusium # 2

Abba James said, "One who receives praise must remember his sins and understand that he is not worthy of the things said."

—*Apophthegmata Patrum*, Alphabetical Collection, James # 2

Abba Poemen said, "A brother who lived with some other brothers asked Abba Bessarion, 'What should I do?' The old man said to him, 'Keep quiet, and do not esteem yourself highly.'"

—*Apophthegmata Patrum*, Alphabetical Collection, Poemen # 79

Abba Sylvanus said, "Woe to the person whose reputation is greater than his work."

—*Apophthegmata Patrum*, Alphabetical Collection, Silvanus # 10

One old man approached another old man one day, and while they were talking, one of them said, "I am dead to the world." The other old man said, "Do not be so confident in yourself, brother, before you leave the body, for even if you say you are dead, Satan is not yet dead."

—*Apophthegmata Patrum*, Anonymous Collection, # 266 Nau

A person who rejects correction shows the passion of pride, but one who welcomes correction has been released from its bondage. . . .

An old man, most distinguished in spirituality, admonished a proud brother who in his blindness said, "Forgive me, father, for I am not proud." The very wise old man said to him, "What clearer proof of your passion of pride do you offer us than to say, 'I am not proud'?"

Pride causes us to forget our faults, for the remembrance of them is a protector of humility.

—John Climacus, *Ladder of Paradise* 23

As fire does not give birth to snow, so those who seek honor here will not enjoy it in heaven. . . . As those who climb a rotten ladder are in danger, so all honor, glory, and power are opposed to humility.

—John Climacus, *Ladder of Paradise* 26

If you desire enduring remembrance, do not put your name on buildings; instead, erect monuments of virtuous deeds, which will both preserve your name during your present life and prepare eternal rest for you in the life to come. If you desire and long for remembrance, this is the true and clearest way: practice virtue, for nothing makes a name so immortal as virtue.

—John Chrysostom, *Commentary on the Psalms* 49.6, on Ps 49:10–11

Sexual Immorality

CLEMENT of Alexandria's comments on sexual immorality sound quite contemporary.

A man who wishes to be beautiful must adorn what is most beautiful in human beings, namely, the mind, which must be exhibited in the most suitable manner every day. He should pluck out lusts, not hairs. . . .

In our day the life of wicked pleasure has reached a state of great licentiousness, and lust is poured out upon the cities and has become law. Women stand at the brothels and sell their own flesh for wanton pleasure, and boys who have been taught to deny their nature act the part of women. . . . Men take the role of women, and women act like men, contrary to nature. . . . No opening of the body is closed to licentiousness. Sexual intercourse is made public and pleasure is domesticated.

—Clement of Alexandria, *Instructor* 3.3.20, 21

Sexual immorality is always detestable, handing over its servants to obscene behavior, sparing neither bodies nor souls. For, when the proper character of body and soul is subdued, immorality subjects the entire person under the triumphal standard of lust. By seduction at first, so that as much as it pleases the more it may harm, this enemy of continence exhausts both possessions and modesty. . . . Often, a man is not restrained within permitted limits and becomes passionate beyond the boundaries of his sex, being insufficiently satisfied unless he seeks even in the bodies of men not a new pleasure but searches out in an unnatural way extraordinary and abnormal pleasures of men with men, which is contrary to nature itself.

—Novatian, *On Chastity* 3.3–5

Fornication is not marriage, nor even the beginning of marriage. If those joined by fornication can be separated, this is best. But if they are satisfied in every way to live together, let them acknowledge the penalty of fornication [which in Basil's church was exclusion from communion for seven years] and stay together so that something worse does not result.

—Basil of Caesarea, *Letters* 199 [*Canonical Epistle* 2].26

It is impossible to enter the kingdom of heaven bearing the guilt of fornication. If this is true of fornication, then it is even more true of adultery. Just as a woman who is bound to her husband commits adultery if she has intercourse with another man, so also a man who is bound to his wife commits adultery if he takes another woman. . . . If sexual intercourse creates one body [1 Cor 6:16], then the man who comes together with a harlot necessarily becomes one body with her.

—John Chrysostom, *Homilies on John* 63.4

Sin and Sinners

Human beings received knowledge of good and evil. The good is to obey God, to believe in him, and to keep his commandment; this is a human being's life. Similarly, not to obey God is evil; this is a human being's death.

—Irenaeus, *Against Heresies* 4.39.1

A mistake is unintended sin; an involuntary sin is injustice; voluntary injustice is evil. Sin, therefore, is within my control. . . . Again, the Lord

shows clearly that transgressions and trespasses are within our power by setting forth various cures that correspond to the different passions.

—Clement of Alexandria, *Miscellanies*
2.15.64.3 and 69.2

Although there are ten thousand things that human beings do, one
might say that all sin derives from two sources: ignorance and weakness. Both
are within our power, whether we do not desire to learn or do not control our
desire. On account of the first, people do not judge well; on account of the
second, they cannot follow right judgments.

—Clement of Alexandria, *Miscellanies* 7.16

The one who has received forgiveness of sins ought to sin no more.
For in addition to the first and only repentance of sins (this would be repentance from those sins committed in the first and heathen life—I mean sin
committed in ignorance), there is proposed for the moment, for those who
have been called, a [second] repentance, which cleanses the soul from trespasses so that faith may be established. Since the Lord knows our hearts and
foreknows what will happen, he foresaw from the beginning humanity's
fickleness and the devil's craft and cunning. . . . Therefore, being full of
mercy, he gave a second repentance to those who are believers but who fall
into some kind of trespass, so that if anyone is tempted by force or deceit
after his calling he might still receive one repentance that is not to be repented of. . . . I do not know which is worse—to sin knowingly or, having
repented of these sins, to transgress again.

—Clement of Alexandria, *Miscellanies*
2.13.56.1–57.3

Just as a mirror is not bad because it shows an ugly person what he
looks like, and just as a physician is not bad because he tells a sick person he has
a fever—for the physician is not the cause of the fever but is only the one who
exposes it—so the one who exposes the soul [in this context, this is God] is not
ill-disposed to the one who is sick in his soul. For he does not put trespasses into
a person, but he exposes the sins that are present so that they may be corrected.

—Clement of Alexandria, *Instructor* 1.9.88

FOR THE historical circumstances of the following passage, where Tertullian
specifies various types of sins, see his passage from *On the Apparel of Women*,
cited above under Idolatry.

God is the Creator of the universe; it is good, and it is given as a free gift to humankind by its Maker. . . . We must consider not only by whom all things were made but also by whom they were perverted. . . . Because there is a vast difference between the Creator and the perverter, there is a vast difference between a corrupted condition and a pure condition. . . . The highest offense with respect to God is idolatry. What is there that offends God that is not God's? But when it offends him, it ceases to be his; and when it ceases to be his, it offends him. Human beings, who are the authors of every iniquity, are the work of God—we are indeed created in his image—but in body and spirit we have fallen away from our Maker. For we did not receive eyes so that we might lust, a tongue for speaking evil, ears so that we might listen to evil speech, a throat for the sin of gluttony and a stomach as an ally of gluttony, genitals for unchaste excesses, hands for violence, and feet for a wandering life; nor was the spirit placed in our bodies so that we might think about treachery, fraud, and iniquity.

—Tertullian, *On Shows* 2

There are then three emotions that rashly lead human beings into all misdeeds: anger, the desire for wealth, and the sexual drive. . . . Anger desires revenge; desire for wealth seeks riches; and sexual drive seeks pleasure. God appointed certain limits for all of these. If these emotions transgress their limits and become too great, then they necessarily pervert their nature and are transformed into defects and vices. . . . A desire for wealth was given to us so that we may acquire whatever is necessary for life; the sexual drive, for propagating offspring; the emotion of anger, for restraining the sins of those who are subject to us. [The author then proceeds to elaborate that these desires were given for a good purpose but are misused through avarice, sexual immorality, and violence.]

—Lactantius, *Divine Institutes* 6.19

Doctors say that when a plague is caught by one person or animal, it spreads by contagion to all those who are nearby. Such is the nature of illness that from one person it infects everyone with sickness. This is also the way it is with workers of iniquity; sharing sickness one with another, they are sick together and they die together. . . . When fire touches something that is highly flammable, it is impossible for all of it not to burn, especially if a favorable wind happens to carry the flame. When the winds of evil kindle sin, it is impossible for the sin that touches one not to cross over to all.

—Basil of Caesarea, *Homilies on the
Psalms* 1.6, on Ps 1

Sin is alienation from God, who is the true and only life. Although the first man lived many hundreds of years after his disobedience, God did not lie when he said, "In the day you eat thereof you shall surely die." For by reason of his alienation from true life, the sentence of death was confirmed against him that same day. Adam's bodily death followed at a much later time.

— Gregory of Nyssa, *Against Eunomius*
2.13 [175]

It is impossible to conceive of the origin of evil as anything other than the absence of virtue. . . . God is not the author of our present evils, and he established our nature so that we are our own master and are free; evils are caused when we refuse to take advice and choose what is worse instead of what is better.

— Gregory of Nyssa, *Catechetical Oration* 5

You observe the feasting of the sinner, but interrogate his conscience. Does it not stink worse than any sepulcher? You observe his joy, you admire the bodily health of his children and his abundant wealth; but look within, at the ulcers and wounds of his soul, the sadness of his heart. . . . Thus a wicked person punishes himself and a righteous person graces himself; and each one finds in his own person the rewards for his deeds, whether good or bad. . . .

[The author then offers another response to the inequities in this life that he observes between good and bad people.] Why do sinners possess abundant wealth and riches, dine continually, and neither grieve nor sorrow, while the righteous live in want and suffer the loss of mates and children? . . . Is it not evident that the rewards and punishments we deserve are received after death?

— Ambrose, *Duties* 1.12.46; 1.15.57

Whoever sins against his neighbor sins against himself, and whoever does evil to his neighbor does evil to himself; and the one who does good to his neighbor does good to himself. Indeed if it were otherwise, who would ever be able to sin against God, or who could hurt or refresh him, or—indeed—who could ever serve or bless him?

— Anthony, *Letter* 2[6].7

Abba Anthony said to Abba Poemen, "This is a human being's great work: to take responsibility for his own sins before God and to expect temptation until his last breath."

— *Apophthegmata Patrum*, Alphabetical
Collection, Anthony # 4

If the monk does not think in his heart that he is a sinner, God will not hear him. The brother said, "What does that mean, to think in his heart that he is a sinner?" Then the old man [the monk Moses] said, "When someone is occupied with his own faults, he does not see those of his neighbor."4

— *Apophthegmata Patrum*, Alphabetical
Collection, Seven Instructions of
Abba Moses to Abba Poemen # 3

The leaders of the people must be people who are not proud and who also hate pride. That is, they should be without fault themselves and also hate faults in others. I am not saying that they should hate persons, but that they should hate faults.

— Origen, *Homilies on Exodus* 11.6,
on Exod 18:21

IN HER comments on anger, Syncleitica draws the same distinction that Origen drew between the sin and the sinner.

Syncleitica also said, "It is good not to become angry, but if this should happen, the apostle does not permit the passion to continue for the length of even one day: 'Let not the sun go down' [Eph 4:26]. But you wait until all your time expires. Why do you hate the person who grieves you? This person is not the one who did the wrong, but the devil. Hate the sickness, not the sick person."

— *Apophthegmata Patrum*, Alphabetical
Collection, Syncleitica # 13

When you sense a little movement of passion, do not consider it as little, but remember that it gives birth to the greatest abuses. When we see a little fiber catch fire at home, we become alarmed and terrified; we do not think about the beginning but the end result of this beginning. We become alarmed and run around in an effort to quench the blaze completely. Evil consumes the soul even more thoroughly than this fire. Hence we must take preventive measures. If we are negligent, then correction becomes more difficult. . . . Accordingly, let us not be negligent about little sins but zealously suppress them, so that we may be free of the worst sins.

— John Chrysostom, *Commentary on
the Psalms 6*

GOD PROMISED through the preaching of Jonah that he would destroy the city of Nineveh (Jonah 3:4), but he did not destroy the city, since the people repented (Jonah 3:7–10). Augustine explains that the prediction came true, since there are two ways for God to destroy sinners.

Indeed, who can deny that what the Lord predicted in the case of the Ninevites was fulfilled, unless he pays too little attention to the way God overthrows sinners, not only in wrath but also truly in mercy? For sinners are overthrown in two ways—either as the people of Sodom, so that the people themselves are punished for their own sins, or as the people of Nineveh, so that the actual sins of the people are destroyed by repentance. What God predicted, therefore, came to pass: the evil Nineveh was overthrown and a good Nineveh was built.

—Augustine, *City of God* 21.24.4

God deemed it more in accordance with his power and goodness to bring about good from evil than not to allow evil to exist. Evil would never have existed if our changeable nature—which is good and brought into existence by God, who is the highest and unchangeable Good and created all things as good—had not made itself so by sinning. For by its sin our nature convicts itself on its own testimony that it was created good. For unless it was itself a great good—although not equal to the Creator—without question the falling away from God would not have been considered by it as evil. So the nature that once enjoyed God teaches by its very fault that it was created to be the very best, inasmuch as it is miserable because it does not enjoy God.

—Augustine, *City of God* 22.1.2

GREGORY of Nazianzus gave expression to the wishes of many to be free from sin.

Tell me of my wrongs, so that I may either cease from being evil or be put to shame. Oh, how I especially pray that I not sin! But if I do, to be converted from my wrongs, for this is the second best portion for those who think properly. For even if I do not assume the role of prosecutor and become my own accuser—as the just man did [Prov 18:17, LXX]—I rejoice in being healed by another.

—Gregory of Nazianzus, *Oration* 33.6

Slavery

SLAVERY was such an integral part of Greco-Roman society that few authors went beyond attacking its abuses to attack the institution itself; one who did was Gregory of Nyssa.

When someone claims God's property as his own and assigns dominion to his own race, so as to consider himself the lord of men and women, is he not through pride overstepping his own nature and imagining that he is different from those who are under him? . . .

You condemn human beings—whose nature is free and who possess free will—to slavery and you make laws in opposition to God, overturning his law for human nature. As though resisting and fighting against divine decrees, you bring under the yoke of slavery one who was made specifically to be the lord of the earth and appointed for rule by the Creator [Gen 1:28]. . . . Irrational animals are the only slaves of human beings. . . . But in dividing human nature into slaves and lords you have caused it to be enslaved to itself and to own itself. . . .

He who knew human nature rightly said that the whole world was not worth being given in exchange for a human soul [Matt 16:26]. Therefore, whenever a human being is for sale, nothing less than the lord of the earth is led to the marketplace.

—Gregory of Nyssa, *Homilies on*
Ecclesiastes 4, on Eccl 2:7

Misuse of the Tongue

We ourselves must refrain altogether from shameful language and stop the mouths of those who use it—by a stern look, by turning away our face, by turning up our nose in derision, and often by a very harsh word. "For it is what proceeds out of the mouth," he says, "that defiles a person" [Matt 15:18], shows one to be profane, pagan, uncultured, and licentious, and not appropriate, well behaved, or self-controlled.

—Clement of Alexandria, *Instructor* 2.6.49

Blessed are those whose mouth God opens. God opened the mouth of the prophets and filled it with his eloquence. . . . I fear, however, that there are those whose mouth is opened by the devil. When one speaks a lie, it is certainly the devil who has opened the mouth and enabled the person to utter it. The devil opens the mouth of those who give false witness and who speak foolishly, uttering obscenities and the like. I also fear that it may be the devil who opens the mouth not only of those who speak slanders and calumnies [Rom 1:29–30] but also those who utter careless words for which they shall give account on the day of judgment [Matt 12:36].

—Origen, *Homilies on Exodus* 3.2, on
Exod 4:10–17

IN THE next selection, Basil is not addressing sinful speech but social correctness. His positive instructions also indicate what should be avoided.

First of all, it is good to be diligent about speech. One should not employ incorrect usage, but ask questions without contentiousness and answer without ostentation, not interrupting the speaker when he has something profitable to say, nor desiring to interject one's own words for display, being moderate in speaking and hearing. One should not be ashamed to learn, and should teach ungrudgingly. And if one has been taught by another, he should not hide that fact. . . . One should first reflect upon what he desires to say and then make it public. One should be courteous in manners and agreeable in conversation, not aiming at agreeableness through wit but showing gentleness through kind encouragement. Harshness should always be put aside, even when it is necessary to rebuke.

—Basil of Caesarea, *Letters* 2.5

WHILE Ambrose urged silence as a way of avoiding improper speech, he acknowledged that there are appropriate times for speech.

Above all else we should learn to be silent so that we can speak. . . . I have seen many people fall into sin through speech, but hardly anyone through silence; and so it is more difficult to know how to keep silent than how to speak. . . . "There is a time to be silent and a time to speak" [Eccl 3:7]. If then we will give account for every idle word [Matt 12:36], let us watch lest we also be held accountable for our idle silence. . . . So, let us guard our hearts and our mouths. . . . Let there be a door to your mouth that can be shut when necessary and let it be carefully barred, lest anyone cause your voice to rise in anger and you respond to insults with insults.

—Ambrose, *Duties* 1.2.5; 1.3.9, 10, 13

Gossip and Slander

Be sincere and without guile, and you will be as little children who do not know the evil that destroys the life of human beings. First, do not slander anyone, and do not listen gladly to one who slanders. Otherwise, if you believe the slander that you hear, you who listen become guilty of the slanderer's sin. For since you believed it, you yourself have something against your brother. Thus you are guilty of the slanderer's sin. Slander is evil; it is an unruly demon, never keeping peace but always living in dissension. Therefore, abstain from it, and you will always have peace with all."
—Hermas, *Mandates* 2.1–3 [27.1–3]

Everyone recognizes the nature of rumor. One of your own said, "Rumor is an evil and no other evil is swifter" [Virgil, *Aeneid* 4.174]. Why is rumor evil? Because it is swift? Because it is an informer? Or because most often it is a liar? Even when it brings some truth, is it without the fault of lying, either subtracting from, adding to, or changing the simple truth? What then? It is evil because the condition of rumor is such that it cannot continue without lying, and it lives only as long as there is no proof. For where there is proof, rumor ceases, and—as if it accomplished its task of spreading a report—when it delivers a fact, it is henceforth held to be a fact and is called a fact. . . . Rumor—a word for what is uncertain—has no place where there is certainty.
—Tertullian, *Apology* 7

BASIL was a victim of slander before the Christians in Neocaesarea, to whom he made the following comments.

A slanderer injures three persons at once: the one whom he unjustly accuses, his hearer, and himself. . . . I see that of the three who are injured, I [the victim] am the one who loses the least. I am deprived of you, but you are robbed of the truth. The person who is the cause of this separates me from you, but he is alienating himself from the Lord, because it is not possible to be kin to God by doing what is forbidden. . . . For what greater evil can one experience than the loss of the truth, the most precious thing of all?
—Basil of Caesarea, *Letters* 204.3

One of the old men used to say, "When we came together with one another at the beginning, we spoke for one another's benefit, we had the

harmony of a chorus, and we ascended to heaven. Now when we come to-
gether, we come for slander and we drag one another into the pit below."
— *Apophthegmata Patrum,* Anonymous
Collection, # 238 Nau

Lying

There are three different kinds of liars: those whose thoughts are a
lie, those whose words are a lie, and those whose life itself is a lie. One whose
thoughts are a lie is suspicious. If he sees someone speaking with another person, he supposes, "They are talking about me." . . . If someone says something, he supposes that he is being attacked. . . . Everything he says is based
not on reality but on suspicion. From this come curiosity, slander, eavesdrop-
ping, quarrels, and harsh judgments. . . .

An example of one whose words are a lie is one who gets up late for
his vigil and does not say, "Forgive me because I am late getting up," but says,
"I had a fever, I felt dizzy, I was not able to get up, I was weak." He speaks ten
lying words instead of one word of repentance that would humiliate him. . . .
Again, if he desires something, he is not content to say, "I want this," but he
keeps turning out words, saying, "I am ill," "I need this," or "I was prescribed
this." . . .

Finally, there is the one whose life itself is a lie: the profligate who
pretends self-control, the miser who talks about alms and praises compassion, and the proud person who marvels at humility (he *marvels* at it because
he does not wish to *praise* the virtue). . . . The person whose life is a lie is not
single-minded but two-faced. He is one thing within and another on the outside. His whole life is duplicitous and a joke. . . .
— Dorotheus of Gaza, *Teachings* 9.97, 101, 103

A lie is the destruction of love, and perjury is the denial of God. No
sensible person imagines that lying is a small sin. . . . Hypocrisy is often the
mother and cause of lying. . . . One who possesses the fear of the Lord rejects
lies, since his own conscience is an impartial judge.
— John Climacus, *Ladder of Paradise* 12

The Power of the Good

RESPONDING to evil with evil does not eliminate evil.

Poemen said, "Wickedness never destroys wickedness. If someone does something bad to you, do good to that person so that the doing of good may destroy the evil."

— *Apophthegmata Patrum,* Alphabetical
Collection, Poemen # 177

Evil is not strong enough to prevail over the power of good, nor is the thoughtlessness of our nature stronger or more enduring than the wisdom of God. For what is changeable and mutable cannot be superior to or more enduring than the nature that always remains the same and is firmly fixed in goodness. Divine counsel is always unchangeable; our mutable nature, however, does not remain fixed in evil. Our nature, if it advances toward the good, will always be in motion, because the goodness through which it travels is infinite and the motion toward the things ahead will never reach completion. What is sought is unlimited, thus we never lay hold of the object and cease moving. . . . [Evil, on the other hand, is limited.] When [our nature] has passed through the extent of wickedness, by necessity it turns its motion toward the good.

— Gregory of Nyssa, *On the Making
of Man* 21.1–2

Virtue

ACCOUNTABILITY to God produces virtuous living, which is based on piety.

Just let someone be so bold as to deny what the source and origin of every benefit is: it is belief in the God of the universe, doing everything to please him, and not even thinking anything that is displeasing to him—since not only our words and deeds but also thoughts will be judged. Is there any other doctrine that would more effectively lead human nature toward living well than the belief and conviction that the God who is over all observes all things—everything that is said, done, and even thought by us? Let the one who wishes to do so point out another way that simultaneously converts and so influentially improves not just one or two people but so many. An accurate comparison of both ways will help him understand which doctrine leads toward the good life.

— Origen, *Against Celsus* 4.53

On account of his own virtue God created in us a love for the beauty of righteousness, . . . prudence, . . . true wisdom, . . . temperance, . . .

courage, . . . patience, and—above all—godliness, which is rightly said to be the mother of all virtues. For godliness is the beginning and end of all the virtues, and from it all the other virtues, when they are pursued, come to us most readily.

—Gregory Thaumaturgus, *Panegyric to Origen* 12

Let not the desire for possessions gain control over anyone, for what is the benefit of acquiring those things that we cannot take with us? Instead, why not obtain those things that we can take with us: prudence, justice, temperance, courage, understanding, love, kindness to the poor, faith in Christ, freedom from wrath, hospitality? If we possess these qualities, we shall find that they prepare for us in advance a welcome in the land of the meek.

—Athanasius, *Life of Anthony* 17

Religious virtue is divided into two parts: those things that pertain to the divine and those things that pertain to right conduct (for purity of life is a part of religion). Moses learned first the things that must be known about God, namely that none of those things known by human comprehension is to be ascribed to him. Then he was taught the other side of virtue, learning what pursuits perfect a virtuous life.

—Gregory of Nyssa, *Life of Moses* 2.166

A virtuous life is perfected when we become like God. Because of this, those who are virtuous are greatly attentive to successfully accomplishing purification of the soul and a disposition that is unmixed with any evil. The result is that the mark of the transcendent nature is stamped in them through the good qualities of their lives. The life of virtue is not uniform and of one kind. . . . [Just as many threads are woven into a garment,] so also an excellent life of virtue comes about through the weaving together of many elements.

—Gregory of Nyssa, *Commentary on Canticles* 9

A pure life that is straightened by virtue is purified from all defilements of sin; it is free of any suspicion of the bad, shines with temperance, and is dignified by prudence. Such a person is courageous when faced with the assaults of the passions, not being at all weakened by bodily luxuries, and is separated especially from fastidiousness, indolence, and empty vanity, . . .

surpassing all the deceits that come by way of the senses. This person strives for the angelic life even while living in the flesh, believing that the one true wealth is the possession of virtue, the one true nobility is kinship with God, and the one true dignity and political power is control over oneself so as not to be enslaved to human passions.

—Gregory of Nyssa, *On the Lord's Prayer* 3

COMMENTING on Matt 5:6, Gregory of Nyssa affirmed that virtues endure while passions are transitory. The same idea with regard to human glory is presented above, in the section Pride and Fame.

To me, this saying [Matt 5:6] seems to mean that none of the things pursued for the sake of pleasure in this life satisfies those who pursue them. . . . Are not all pleasures that are accomplished through the body fleeting, since they do not remain for long with those who have attained them? Therefore, we learn from the Lord this sublime teaching: only the pursuit of virtue that is planted within us is firm and lasting. For a person who aims his life straight at the higher things—such as prudence, temperance, piety toward the divine, or any other of the higher gospel teachings—does not in these virtuous actions obtain transitory and unstable enjoyment but enjoyment that is firm, enduring, and extends to all of one's life.

Why is this so? Because one can always do these things and there is no time throughout our lives that produces a satiety of doing good. For prudence, purity, unchangeableness in every good, and avoidance of the bad can be done at all times. As long as one longs for virtue, one's enjoyment grows through its practice. For those who give themselves over to improper desires, even if their soul is always attentive to licentiousness, the pleasure does not last indefinitely. Satiety puts a stop to the gluttonous enjoyment of food, and when thirst is quenched, so is the pleasure of drink. It is the same with other things; once the desire for pleasure has been quenched by its satisfaction, a certain interval of time must pass before the desire for pleasure is again called forth.

On the other hand, when the possession of virtue is firmly established within someone, it is not limited by time or satiety. It always provides those who live by it a pure, ever-new, and flourishing experience of its own good things. . . . The possession of virtue follows the desire for virtue, and this ingrained goodness brings unceasing enjoyment to the soul. Such is the nature of this goodness that it not only sweetens the one enjoying it in the present but also brings active enjoyment to every moment of time. For remembrance of those who have lived correctly causes those who are upright to rejoice; so too this present life when it is conducted according to virtue and the expectation of reward, which is—I suppose—again nothing other than virtue itself. Virtue is both the work of those who live uprightly and the reward for virtuous deeds.

—Gregory of Nyssa, *On the Beatitudes* 4

CHRISTIANS accepted the four cardinal virtues that were expressed in Greek philosophy.

What duty connected with the cardinal virtues was lacking in these men [Old Testament heroes: Abraham, Jacob, Joseph, Job, David]? In the first place, they established prudence, which is concerned with the search for truth and creates a desire for fuller knowledge. Second, they established justice, which assigns to all their due, does not claim what belongs to someone else, and disregards one's own advantage. In the third place, they established courage, which in war excels in greatness of mind and at home is eminent, being superior to bodily strength. And fourth, they established temperance, which maintains the manner and order of all things that should be done or spoken. . . .

Temperance consists in scorning pleasure; courage, in facing labors and dangers; prudence, in the desire for good things and knowing how to distinguish what is beneficial from its opposite. Justice is the good guardian of another's rights and the protector of what belongs to oneself, preserving what belongs to each.

—Ambrose, *Duties* 1.24.115; 2.9.49

VIRTUE is useful.

Whatever is disgraceful cannot be useful, nor—on the other hand—can something honorable be useless. Usefulness always accompanies integrity, and integrity, usefulness.

—Ambrose, *Duties* 3.14.90

VIRTUE is powerful; on account of virtue, God and one person make a majority.

David took his stand not with the multitude but with virtue as his ally, and because of this he drew God to his side. I say these things so that we might be attentive to the affairs of the righteous, even if they are weak. And even if the unrighteous are strong, let us flee from their alliance. Nothing is weaker than evil, even if it has the whole world in alliance with it. And nothing is stronger than virtue, even if it happens to be alone, for God stands with it. Who can deliver a person whom God fights against? Who can destroy a person who is helped by God?

—John Chrysostom, *Commentary on the Psalms* 7.2, on Ps 7:1

CHAPTER III

Conversion
and Salvation

> Christians are made, not born.
> —Tertullian, *Apology* 18.4; *Testimony of the Soul* 1

*T*HE STARTING POINT for the early Christian perspective on human life and morality was conversion and the experience of salvation in Christ. The selections in this chapter were chosen not so much to present a theoretical view of conversion and what was involved in salvation as to convey their practical implications. Conversion means change, and a change in life was involved in becoming a Christian. In the early centuries the norm was not to grow up in a Christian family but to come to Christ and the church by conversion, as expressed in the quotation from Tertullian that heads this chapter.

Salvation was grounded in God's initiative for human salvation, what Christians know as God's grace. The need for grace is made evident in the inability of human beings to save themselves. An act of God's grace, the incarnation, is the foundation of salvation. The preaching and teaching of the gospel provides the connecting link between God's grace and the human response. The persuasive power of the gospel is expressed in the literature of the Christian apologists, who also paid tribute to the gospel's good effects through contrasting the miracles of Moses, Christ, and Christ's disciples with the works of magicians.

According to the early church writers, salvation depends on grace but is received according to free will. Although early Christian authors recognized that many factors influence human conduct, they emphasized the fundamental and central role played by human freedom of choice. Indeed, there is no subject on which Christian writers of the first four centuries speak with more unanimity than free will. While they especially opposed the determinism associated with ancient astrology, they also rejected both philosophical determinism and the assignment to human beings of predetermined natures that they ascribed to gnostic thought. Human freedom was part of being created in the image of God. Because this freedom is the basis of virtue and the occasion for sin to arise, it is also the basis of just rewards and punishments. Sin cannot be blamed on God; it results from the choices made by rational beings. Indeed, for God to intervene in human choices would be for God to cancel the liberty that is intrinsic to human beings. Although free will offers the occasion for sin, free will itself is good. Much of scripture is meaningless—as are our human attitudes—if there is not free will.

Free will carries with it the ability to change one's life. The theological word for this change is repentance—the change of heart or mind that results in a change in one's conduct. Several writers offer definitions for the words that are used for repentance; some urge that there are limits to the time of repentance, which must be made sincerely and in full.

For Christians, the theological basis for repentance is faith. It is often thought that the writings of early Christian authors represent a decline from the robust doctrine of salvation by faith taught by the Apostle Paul. Although our selections are not designed to address the issues involved in this theological question, perhaps enough is included to allow readers some appreciation of what is said on the subject of faith. Faith comes by accepting the gospel message. As in the New Testament, salvation by faith was contrasted with salvation under the Jewish law. Faith for the Christian was the basis for good works and for the right exercise of reason.

Repentance and faith were both closely related to confession. Confession itself took two forms: confession of sin and confession of faith, both verbally and in one's actions. Although verbal confession might be made on a number of occasions, the principal occasion referred to in our sources is baptism. It was understood that baptism expressed both repentance and faith. At baptism, repentance took the form of renouncing the devil; faith was confessed in God, Christ, and the Holy Spirit. Baptism was the decisive moment that separated an individual's life from the world and identified him with Christ and the church. For those who fell into serious post-baptismal sin, a public ceremony of humiliation was devised as part of the procedure for returning to the fellowship of the church. In our selections we have included the fullest extant description of this activity as it took place in the early period of the church.

The end result of conversion is salvation. In Christian faith, salvation is in Christ alone. Early Christian writers fleshed out the notion of salvation in different ways, and we include several of these among our selections. Irenaeus provides an early formulation of what became in the Greek church a characteristic way of describing salvation: Christ became like us so that he might restore us to the image and likeness of God. Irenaeus's teaching combined the traditional idea of Christ as the revealer of God with the equally traditional language of salvation through the self-giving of Christ's blood; he integrated these into the concept of establishing communion with God. Along with these descriptions of salvation, Irenaeus also spoke of salvation as a victory over the forces of evil.

According to pagans and some heretics, the idea of incarnation was degrading to deity. Orthodox Christians replied that incarnation was necessary for salvation, and they frequently affirmed that the great work of God is the salvation of his human creation.

Grace

ONE OF the many fine rhetorical passages in the *Epistle to Diognetus* is this rapturous praise of God's grace:

We who were reproved by our works and are unworthy of life are now counted worthy through the kindness of God. And we who made it clear that we could not enter into the kingdom of God by ourselves are enabled through the power of God. . . . God's appointed time for revealing his own kindness and power finally came. Oh, the surpassing kindness and love of God! He did not hate us, nor reject us, nor bear malice toward us; but he was long-suffering, he put up with us, and, being merciful, he himself took our sins. He gave his own Son as a ransom for us—the holy for the impious, the innocent for the wicked, the righteous for the unrighteous, the incorruptible for the corruptible, the immortal for the mortal. For what could cover our sins except his righteousness? In whom could we who are lawless and impious be justified, except in the Son of God alone? Oh, the sweet exchange! Oh, the inexpressible creation! Oh, the unexpected benefits! The lawlessness of many was hidden in the one Righteous Person; the righteousness of One justified the many lawless ones.

— *Epistle to Diognetus* 9

The Lord himself was the one who saved them [human beings], because by themselves they did not have the power to be saved. [He cites

Rom 7:18, 24–25; Isa 35:4.] Because we cannot do it by ourselves, we must be
saved by the help of God.

— Irenaeus, *Against Heresies* 3.20.3

The Lord did not set us free so that we might depart from him; for
it is impossible for anyone placed outside the good things of the Lord to acquire the means of salvation by himself. But the more we obtain his grace, the
more we should love him.

— Irenaeus, *Against Heresies* 4.13.3

If a human being had not conquered the antagonist of humanity,
the enemy would not have been justly conquered. Again, if God did not give
salvation, we would not possess it securely. And unless humanity were united
to God, it could not share in incorruptibility.

— Irenaeus, *Against Heresies* 3.18.7

Because some do not believe and some are contentious, not everyone attains perfection of the good. For it cannot be attained without freedom
of choice, nor does everything lie within our purpose, such as what may suc-
ceed. For "we are saved by grace" [Eph 2:5], not without good works, but
having been disposed toward the good, we must acquire the desire for it. We
must also possess a healthy purpose that does not change its mind regarding
the eager pursuit of the good. For this we especially need divine grace, correct
teaching, sincere readiness to obey, and the Father drawing us to himself.

— Clement of Alexandria, *Miscellanies* 5.1

It is good for each one to perceive his own particular nature and the
grace of God. If a person who does not perceive his own weakness and the divine grace receives a blessing without having examined and condemned himself, he will suppose that what has been bestowed on him by heaven's grace is
his own virtuous deed. . . . Divine things have been revealed to babes [Luke
10:21] who come into better things after their childhood. They remember
that they did not come to such a condition because of themselves, but God's
inexpressible goodness brought them to the greatest possible blessedness.

— Origen, *First Principles* 3.1.12

We ourselves hold the view that our human nature is in no way
sufficient to seek after God and find him clearly without the help of the One
whom we seek. God is found by those who—after doing all that is within

their power—confess that they are in need of him. God makes himself known to whomever he judges it suitable to manifest himself—to the extent that God can be known by a human being and to the extent that the soul of a human being, while still living in the body, is able to know God. . . .

The word of God makes clear [Matt 11:27] that the soul does not acquire knowledge of God apart from God. Rather, knowledge comes only through divine grace and with a particular kind of inspiration. Indeed it is reasonable that knowledge of God is greater than human nature and not in accord with it, hence so many errors exist among human beings with regard to God. Knowledge of God is brought about through God's kindness, his love for humanity, and his marvelous divine grace. It comes to those whom God, in his foreknowledge, perceives will live in a way that is worthy of the One who makes himself known, never perverting piety toward him.

— Origen, *Against Celsus* 7.42, 44

The one peaceful and trustworthy tranquility, the one solid and strong security, is deliverance from the disturbances of a turbulent world, to be secured to the dock in the harbor of safety. Such persons lift their eyes from earth toward heaven. Being admitted to the favor of the Lord and already near God in mind, they may boast that whatever others consider exalted and great in human affairs does not appeal to their consciousness. . . . One will understand that previously the enemy who damaged us saw to it that deceitful injury made some progress against us. The more we are granted to know and to condemn what we were, the more we are compelled to love what we shall be in the future. One does not attain this by seeking after rewards, nor by the work of our hands, as though the highest human dignity and power were produced by elaborate exertion. Rather, it is a free gift of God and is easily obtained. Just as the sun shines naturally, as the day gives light, as the fountain flows, and as the rain gives moisture, so the heavenly Spirit himself pours down upon us.

— Cyprian, *To Donatus* [*Letter* 1] 14

THE FOLLOWING selection is part of an appeal to conversion.

As long as a person still remains in this world, it is never too late to repent. The approach to God's favor is open, and there is easy access to those who seek truth and understand its value. It is permissible at the very close of life and end of your time to entreat God on behalf of your sins and implore him, the one and true God, in confession and in faith that acknowledges him. Pardon is granted to the one who confesses, saving favor is given to the believer out of divine piety, and a transition to immortality comes at death itself. Christ imparts this grace. He bestows this gift of mercy by conquering death on the cross, his victory monument; he redeems the believer with the recompense of his blood, reconciles humanity to God the Father, and gives life to our mortal nature through heavenly regeneration.

—Cyprian, *To Demetrianus* 25–26

Gospel

When we observe that the message immediately persuades the multitude from a life of licentiousness to one of stable good order, from a life of injustice to one of greater goodness, from a life of misery and cowardice to one of such great vigor that they even despise death because of the godliness manifested in them, is it not appropriate for us to marvel at the power of the word? For at the beginning, the discourse of those who were ambassadors of Christian teachings and those who worked to organize the churches of God (indeed their message itself) came with persuasiveness, a persuasiveness that is unlike that of people who promise the wisdom of Plato—or any of the other philosophers—who are men and who possess mere human nature. The demonstration presented by Jesus' apostles was from God and its persuasiveness came from the "Spirit and power" [1 Thess 1:5]. Thus their word—or rather the word of God through them—ran swiftly and quickly, transforming many of those who were sinners by nature and habit. These were people whom no one could change by punishment, but the word shaped, molded, and transformed them according to its will.

—Origen, *Against Celsus* 3.68

The fruit of the signs and wonders performed by Christ and his disciples was not deceit but the salvation of souls. Who could claim that a better life, one that daily reduces the number of evil deeds, comes about through deceit?

—Origen, *Against Celsus* 2.50

Free Will

We [Christians] do not say that fate causes human beings to act or experience the things that happen but, according to freedom of choice, each person either acts properly or sins; and good people are persecuted and imprisoned through the working of wicked demons.

—Justin Martyr, *2 Apology* 7.3

At all times God has preserved in human beings their free will and their free choice.

—Irenaeus, *Against Heresies* 4.15.2

Matthew 23:37] declared the ancient law of human freedom by which God made human beings free from the beginning, in possession of free choice, even as they possess their own souls, to be used as God intended—voluntarily, and not under compulsion from him. For compulsion is not an attribute of God, but good intention is always present with him. Therefore he gives good advice to all. For he placed the power of choice within human beings, just as he did the angels—for angels are rational beings—so that whoever obeys might justly possess the good. Indeed the good is given by God but truly preserved by human beings, and whoever does not obey is justly not found with the good, and he will receive deserved punishment. . . .

Because human beings have possessed free will from the beginning, and God, in whose likeness human beings were created, possesses free will, human beings are advised always to maintain the good, which is done through obedience to God. . . .

And the Lord preserved in human beings free will and the power of free choice not only in works but also in faith.

—Irenaeus, *Against Heresies* 4.37.1, 4, 5

Those who chose to belong to him are the ones who are perfected by faith. . . . This is the law from above: that virtue be chosen by the one who wills it. . . . Now everything virtuous changes for the better, and in order to change it chooses knowledge, which lies within the soul's own power. . . .

To believe and to obey are within our own power.

—Clement of Alexandria, *Miscellanies* 7.2, 3

COMPARE the following passage with the one quoted in Chapter V, under Evil in the World.

Reason without goodness is not reason, and goodness without reason is not goodness. . . . It was necessary for the image and likeness of God to be

created with free will and power, which define this very image and likeness. . . .
The rewards of good and evil could not be assigned to one who was either good
or evil by necessity rather than by choice. . . . Human liberty will, on reflection,
show itself more guilty because it was responsible for what it committed.

—Tertullian, *Against Marcion* 2.6.2, 3, 7, 8

ALTHOUGH all early Christian thinkers affirmed freedom of the will, Origen
made it the foundational principle of his thought, listing it among the "First
Principles" accepted in the church's teaching.

This also is defined in the preaching of the church: every rational
soul has free will and choice. The soul is in a battle against the devil, his angels, and opposing powers, because they endeavor to oppress our souls with
sins. If we live rightly and prudently, we should make every effort to rid ourselves of such things. It also follows that we are not subject to necessity nor in
any way compelled to do what we do not want to do, whether good or evil.
For if we have free will, some forces might be able to motivate us to sin and
others to help us toward salvation; but we are not compelled by any necessity
to act either rightly or wrongly.

—Origen, *First Principles* preface 5

BOOK 3, chapter 1 of Origen's *First Principles* is devoted to the subject of free will.
His conclusion reconciles 2 Tim 2:20–21 and Rom 9:21, by affirming that both
free will and the working of God are necessary for making progress in virtue.

Neither that which lies within our own power apart from the
knowledge of God, nor mere knowledge of God—if we have not also
brought something to the good—compels us to make progress. We do not
become vessels for honor or dishonor solely through that which lies within
our power apart from the knowledge of God, nor does this occur apart from
making full use of what is worthily placed within our power. By itself, God's
fashioning does not make someone honorable or dishonorable, as if he did
not consider our free will that inclines us toward what is the better or what is
worse to be a matter for distinction.

—Origen, *First Principles* 3.1.24

Our nature is not the cause of evil; instead, evil is caused by a free
will that is voluntarily inclined toward evil. By the same token, our nature is

not the cause of righteousness, as if it were incapable of unrighteousness, but the word that we receive [cf. Mark 4:20] makes us righteous.

—Origen, *Commentary on Matthew* 10.11

Before it came into this world, the soul committed no sin, but we who came into the world sinless now sin of our own free will. . . . The soul is self-governing; and although the devil can make suggestions, he does not have the power to compel us to act against our will.

—Cyril of Jerusalem, *Catechetical
Lectures* 4.19, 21

People ask, "Why does God allow evil in our world?" The blame lies with human beings, not with God. Neither God nor our nature is the cause of evil, but the exercise of our free will.] Since free will is characterized by the power to choose according to one's own mind, the author of our present evils is not God, since he created our nature to be its own master and unrestricted. Rather, evils result from recklessness that chooses what is worse instead of what is better.

—Gregory of Nyssa, *Catechetical Oration* 5

Nothing evil can come into existence apart from our free choice.

—Gregory of Nyssa, *Life of Moses* 2.88

God's good gift—free choice of action—became an instrument for sin through humanity's sinful use of it. For free will that is not enslaved is by nature good, and no one would reckon among the good things anything that was subjugated to necessity. But the free impulse of the mind, rushing undisciplined to choose evil, distracted the soul, as it was dragged down from what is exalted and honorable toward the passionate urges of nature. This is what "he gave" means—not that he himself caused the evil in human life but that human recklessness used God's good gifts in the service of evil.

—Gregory of Nyssa, *Homilies on
Ecclesiastes* 1.13–14

IN THE following passage, Gregory of Nyssa puts forth the striking image that we each become our own parents through the choices we make.

Now it is certainly required that what is subject to change be—in a sense—always coming to birth. . . . Such a birth occurs by choice. We are in some way our own parents, giving birth to ourselves by our own free choice in accordance with whatever we wish to be, . . . molding ourselves according to the teachings of either virtue or vice.

—Gregory of Nyssa, *Life of Moses* 2.3

We are governed by free will and are not subjected—as some say—to the necessity of fate. That is why God promised his kingdom and threatened punishment. He would not have done that to people bound by necessity. He would not have laid down laws and given exhortations if we are prisoners of fate. Since we are free and masters of our choices—becoming either evil through a lack of effort or good through our striving—because of this he appointed these medicines, correcting us through both the fear of punishment and the expectation of the kingdom. Thus he instructs us to live a life of wisdom. From these considerations and from the way we ourselves act, it is clear that neither fate, chance, birth, nor the course of the stars administers our affairs. For if everything that happens depends on these things rather than on our free will, then why whip a slave who is a thief? If your wife has committed adultery, why do you take her to court? Why are you ashamed of bad deeds? Why do you not endure reproaches? Instead, when someone calls you an adulterer, a fornicator, a drunkard, or such like, you regard it as an insult. . . . The myth of fate is demolished. Our lives are subject to no compelling necessity. Everything—as I have said—is compensation for freedom of the will.

—John Chrysostom, *Homily on Perfect Love* 3

Change

Do not be sad when you see that your nature is subject to change, but let the change be for the better, "being transformed from glory into glory" [2 Cor 3:18]. Always strive to become better and more nearly perfect through daily growth, even if you never attain the end of perfection. For perfection is truly this: never to stop growing toward the better, since perfection is not circumscribed by any limits.

—Gregory of Nyssa, *On Perfection,* conclusion

For the one who has done the greatest good deeds but at the end shipwrecks his life in evil, all the former labors are profitless, . . . and for the one who at first lived badly and carelessly but afterward repented, it is possible during the time after repentance to overcome the evil conduct that endured for a long time. . . . Does the thief wish forgiveness? Then let him steal no more. The adulterer? Let him burn with passion no longer. The fornicator? Let him henceforth live purely. The robber? Make recompense and give back more. The false witness? Make a practice of telling the truth. The perjurer? Swear no more. Cut off the other passions—anger, desire, grief, fear—as well, so that at your departure from this life you will have been reconciled with your adversary here. It is probably impossible to eradicate habitual passions all at once. But with God's power, human intercession, the help of brothers and sisters, sincere repentance, and constant care, they are corrected.

—Clement of Alexandria, *Who Is the Rich
Man Who Is Saved?* 40

After being persuaded by the word, we keep far away from demons and follow the only unbegotten God through his Son. We who formerly rejoiced in fornication now embrace self-control alone. We who employed magical arts have now dedicated ourselves to the good and unbegotten God. We who loved more than anything else to acquire wealth and possessions now bring what we have into a common treasury and share with all those who are in need. We who hated and murdered one another and would not show hospitality to those of a different tribe—on account of different customs—now, after the coming of Christ, eat with others, pray for our enemies, and attempt to persuade those who hate us unjustly, so that those who live according to the good counsels of Christ may share with us the things hoped for from God, who is the Lord of all.

—Justin Martyr, *1 Apology* 14

Repentance

IN THE same context as above on Change, here Clement of Alexandria offers a succinct statement of the result or purpose of repentance.

True repentance consists in no longer being guilty of the same things but in rooting out completely from our souls the sins by which we condemn ourselves to death.

—Clement of Alexandria, *Who Is the Rich
Man Who is Saved?* 39

ELSEWHERE Clement speaks about what causes repentance.

There are two kinds of persons who are repentant. The more common is the person who has fear because of what has been done; the more appropriate kind is the person whose conscience causes the soul to be ashamed of itself.

—Clement of Alexandria, *Miscellanies* 4.6

CLEMENT recognized that the profession of repentance might be superficial rather than deep seated.

Repentance consists in not submitting again to the same fault. Frequent repentance and the propensity to adopt easy change—which results from a lack of training—are really the practice of sinning. Repeatedly asking for pardon for frequent trespasses is not repentance but only the appearance of repentance.

—Clement of Alexandria, *Miscellanies* 2.13.58.3–59.1

THE PRECEDING quotations have as their primary context the sins that are committed after one becomes a Christian. But "repentance" was also a term used for the conversion involved in becoming a Christian. In the following selection Clement of Alexandria exhorts pagans to convert to Christianity, spelling out some of the changes this would bring.

Therefore let us repent and pass from ignorance to knowledge, from foolishness to wisdom, from licentiousness to self-control, from injustice to righteousness, from godlessness to God.

—Clement of Alexandria, *Exhortation* 10

CONVERSION repentance is also the context of the following quotation by Cyril of Jerusalem. For those preparing for baptism, Cyril first offered biblical examples of sinners who repented and were saved, and then drew the following conclusion:

Therefore, brothers and sisters, since we have many examples of those who sinned, repented, and were saved, you also must heartily make confession to the Lord, so that you may receive forgiveness of your former sins, be counted worthy of the heavenly gift, and inherit the heavenly kingdom with all the saints.

—Cyril of Jerusalem, *Catechetical Lectures* 2.20

IN ANOTHER reflection on repentance—as both an inner decision and an outward act—Clement of Alexandria considers both the literal meaning of one of the words used for repentance and the theological basis of repentance in faith.

To will is the work of the soul, but to do is not without the body. For deeds are not measured by their outcome alone but are also judged according to free will—whether or not the deed was readily chosen, whether one repented of his sin, whether one gained knowledge from stumbling and came to another mind, which is what the word [repentance] means ("after these things he knew"). The first knowledge was innocence, but repentance is knowledge that comes later. Therefore repentance is the achievement of faith. For if one does not believe that what he engaged in was sin, he will not change. And if he does not believe that punishment awaits the transgressor and salvation the one who lives according to the commandments, he will accordingly not reform.

—Clement of Alexandria, *Miscellanies*
2.6.26.4–27.1

While then we are on the earth, let us repent. For we are clay in the hands of the workman. A potter who makes a vessel shapes it again if it becomes misshapen or crushed in his hands; but if it has already been placed in the fiery furnace, he cannot rescue it. It is the same way with us. As long as we are in this world, let us repent with our whole heart of the evil deeds that we have done in the flesh, so that the Lord may save us while we still have time for repentance. For after we depart from the world, we can no longer make confession or repent. . . .

While we have opportunity to be healed, let us give ourselves to the healing God and offer recompense to him. What kind of recompense? To repent from a sincere heart.

—*2 Clement* 8.1–3; 9.7–8

MORAL teachers continued to stress the urgency of repenting today.

It was said about an old man that when his thoughts said to him, "Let things be today, and repent tomorrow," he responded, "No! I will repent today, and may the will of God be done tomorrow."

—*Apophthegmata Patrum*, Anonymous
Collection, # 271 Nau

In the following two selections Lactantius offers two definitions of repentance. The first compares repentance to the circumcision of the heart spoken of by the prophets. His second defines it as a rejection of sin.

In circumcision of the heart, God] set repentance before us. That is, if we confess our sins and make satisfaction to God, we will obtain from God the pardon that is refused to those who are obstinate and hide their offenses. God does not look on outward appearances—as human beings do—but on the most intimate and secret things of the heart.

—Lactantius, *Divine Institutes* 4.17.17

Repentance is nothing other than professing and affirming that we will sin no more.

—Lactantius, *Divine Institutes* 6.13

John Climacus speaks of repentance by Christians, but his descriptions apply as well to becoming a Christian.

Repentance is the restoration of baptism. It is a covenant made with God for a second life. Repentance is the purchasing of humility. Repentance is always distrustful of bodily enchantment. It is self-critical reasoning and solicitude for one's carelessness. Repentance is the daughter of hope and the denial of hopelessness. Repentance is being guilty but not put to shame. Repentance is reconciliation with the Lord through the performance of good works that are the opposite of one's faults. Repentance is the purification of conscience. It is the willing endurance of afflictions. The penitent creates his own punishments, for repentance is the strong affliction of the stomach [fasting] and the flogging of the soul with grievous sensations.

—John Climacus, *Ladder of Paradise* 5

Confession of sin (see further below) was closely related to repentance, and indeed the Greek word for "confession" *(exomologesis)* became the common word used for the discipline imposed on those who were guilty of post-baptismal sins so that they could be restored to the fellowship of the church. Tertullian distinguished the meaning of the two words.

> Now in the Greek language the word for "repentance" [*metanoia*] is not formed from the confession of a sin, but from a change of mind.
> —Tertullian, *Against Marcion* 2.24.8

TERTULLIAN spoke of two repentances. The first is repentance that accompanies conversion and baptism; the second is repentance by those who fall into sin after their baptism.

> God commanded that baptismal repentance lead the way, as if disposing and arranging beforehand by the solemn pledge of repentance those whom he called through grace to the promise firmly established for the seed of Abraham. . . .
> Having discovered the truth, repent of errors; repent of having loved what God does not love . . . , for voluntary obedience consists in similarity of minds. . . .
> Baptismal washing is an act that seals one's faith, a faith which begins and is commended by faithful penitence. We are not washed in order to cease sinning but because we have quit sinning, since in heart we are already washed [repentance being a renunciation of sin]. . . .
> The second kind of repentance is *exomologesis* and is most often expressed and described by this Greek term [described in our next unit]. . . .
> Since you know that after the first bulwarks of the baptism commanded by the Lord there still remains for you in *exomologesis* a second safeguard against hell, why do you desert your salvation?
> —Tertullian, *On Repentance* 2.4; 4.4;
> 6.16–17; 9.2; 12.5

Confession of Sin

WHEN Cyril of Jerusalem addressed candidates for baptism, he included in his discussion of repentance the confession of sins. After referring to Hezekiah's prayer in 2 Kgs 20 and Isa 38, he continues:

> Hezekiah prevailed in canceling God's decree [of death against him]; and does not Jesus grant forgiveness of sins? Turn and groan for yourself, close the door and pray that you may be forgiven, that he may remove

the burning flames from you. For confession has power even to quench fire, power even to tame lions.

—Cyril of Jerusalem, *Catechetical Lectures* 2.15

Most often, when early Christian writers spoke of the confession of sin, they were referring to sins committed by Christians. But because confession was closely associated with repentance, we have included passages about confession here rather than in Chapter V. In the following selection Tertullian describes the formal, public confession made by Christians who had fallen into serious sin, so that they might be reconciled with the church.

The second repentance], which is most often expressed and described by the Greek term *exomologesis,* is the confession of our transgressions to the Lord. Not that he is ignorant of them, but inasmuch as confession gives birth to repentance and God is appeased by repentance, confession arranges for satisfaction. Thus *exomologesis* is a discipline for human abasement and humiliation, enjoining behavior that brings mercy. With regard to clothing and dress, it requires that one lie in sackcloth and ashes, cover the body with soiled clothing, lay the soul low with lamentations, and exchange severe treatment for those sins that were committed; it also allows only plain food and drink, not—to be sure—for the stomach's sake but for the soul's. And for the most part it commands that prayers be strengthened through fasting: it commands to heave sighs, to weep, to groan unto the Lord God day and night, to fall prostrate before the elders, to kneel before God's dear ones, and to enjoin all the brothers to be ambassadors on behalf of your supplications. All these things *exomologesis* performs, in order to make repentance acceptable, so that it may honor God through the fear of danger, so that its pronouncement of judgment on the sinner may act in place of God's wrath and the temporal afflictions may—I will not say frustrate but—expunge eternal punishments.

—Tertullian, *On Repentance* 9

Confession [*exomologesis*] is a petition for pardon, because the person who petitions for pardon confesses guilt; penitence, too, is acceptable to God, who desires it rather than the death of the sinner [compare Ezek 18:32; 33:11].

—Tertullian, *On Prayer* 7

To err is human; to confess one's error, wise.

—Jerome, *Letters* 57.12

Faith

AFTER referring to the priests and kings of Israel, the author of *1 Clement* writes:

> All of these were glorified and magnified not by themselves, their works, or the righteous deeds they accomplished but by God's will. Therefore we also, who have been called through his will in Christ Jesus, are justified not by ourselves, our wisdom, our understanding, our piety, or the works that we accomplish in holiness of heart, but by faith, through which Almighty God has justified all from eternity.
>
> — *1 Clement* 32.3–4

> None of my instructions is hidden from you, if you hold completely faith and love in Jesus, which are the beginning and goal of life. For faith is the beginning and love is the goal. Where these two are in unity God is, and everything else that leads to nobleness and goodness follows. No one who professes faith practices sin, nor does anyone who possesses love practice hatred. "A tree is known by its fruit" [Matt 12:33]; so also those who profess that they belong to Christ are manifested by the deeds they do. For the deed does not belong to the profession made now but to being found in the power of faith until the end.
>
> — Ignatius, *Ephesians* 14

> Do you disbelieve that the dead are raised? When the resurrection occurs, then you will believe, whether willingly or not, but your belief will be considered unbelief if you do not believe now. Why do you disbelieve? Or, do you not know that faith precedes all things? What farmer is able to harvest if he does not first entrust the seed to the earth? Who is able to cross the sea if he does not first entrust himself to the ship and the pilot? What sick person is able to be healed if he does not first entrust himself to the physician? Who is able to learn a craft or profession if he does not first commit and entrust himself to a teacher? If then the farmer trusts the earth, the sailor the ship, and the sick person the physician, do you not want to entrust yourself to God, who has given so many of his pledges?
>
> — Theophilus, *To Autolycus* 1.8

> For the law [of Moses] did not prohibit them from believing in the Son of God, but rather it exhorted them, saying that human beings are saved

from the wound of the old serpent only through belief in him who in the likeness of sinful flesh was lifted up from the earth on the martyr's tree, who draws all things to himself, and who gives life to the dead [John 3:14–15; 12:32].

—Irenaeus, *Against Heresies* 4.2.7

Quoting Gal 3:6, 11, Irenaeus writes:

Abraham was justified by faith. . . . So too are we justified not through the law, but through the faith of Him to whom witness was borne by the law and prophets, whom the Word of God brought to us.[1]

—Irenaeus, *Demonstration of the Apostolic Preaching* 35

For Clement of Alexandria, who was a learned man, simple faith without learned demonstration was nonetheless equal to demonstrated faith. This simple faith comes from the Scriptures, which contain the first principles of spiritual knowledge. Like the first principles of mathematics or logic, these principles are not established by reasoning but are the basis on which reasoning proceeds.

Thus, a person who with sure judgment places trusts in the divine Scriptures receives an incontrovertible demonstration in the voice of God, who gave the Scriptures. Faith does not receive confirmation through demonstration.

—Clement of Alexandria, *Miscellanies* 2.2.9.6

Clement of Alexandria wrote extended reflections on the nature of faith and its relationship to philosophical thought. Below are a few brief observations that represent his thought. After quoting Rom 10:17, 14–15, Clement writes:

Do you see how he restores faith in the word of the Lord and the Son of God through hearing and through the preaching of the apostles? . . . Thus, just as playing ball does not depend only on one person throwing the ball skillfully but also requires another person to catch it gracefully, . . . so also it follows that teaching is worthy of belief when the faith of the hearers— as a kind of natural art, so to speak—contributes to the learning. . . . We proclaim that faith is the first inclination toward salvation, after which fear, hope, and repentance, progressing together with self-control and patience, lead us to love and knowledge. . . . Just as it is impossible to live without the four elements [earth, air, fire, and water], so it is impossible to have knowledge without faith. Faith is the foundation of truth.

—Clement of Alexandria, *Miscellanies*
2.6.25.1–4; 2.6.31.1–3

Since faith is the voluntary assent of the soul, it is also the doer of good works and the foundation of just conduct.

—Clement of Alexandria, *Miscellanies* 5.13.86

We need the eyes of the mind in order to understand intellectual matters. Just as the perception of visible things requires the eyes of the body, we need faith for the contemplation of divine things. What the eye is for the body, faith is for reason. We can say even more: as the eye needs light to display visible things, so the mind needs faith to display divine things and keep firm the viewpoint concerning them.

—Theodoret, *Cure of Pagan Diseases* 1.78–79

Truly, faith is a firm and unshakeable conviction regarding divine things. Reason has the ability to believe, according to prudence, but afterward faith is demonstrated by virtuous activity, because it is manifested through works. For it is written, "Faith without works is dead" [Jas 2:20]. A right-thinking person would not dare count anything dead and inactive among the good things. Through faith, reason receives its goal, which is the good. . . . Faith is an implanted and unchanging stability in prudence, action, and virtue; . . . the final goal of faith is the good.

—Maximus the Confessor, *Mystagogy* 5

Confession of Faith

When we enter the water, we profess the Christian faith in the words of its law; our mouths bear witness that we have renounced the devil, his pomp, and his angels.

—Tertullian, *On Shows* 4

Each of you was asked whether you believe in the name of the Father, the Son, and the Holy Spirit. And you acknowledged that saving confession and went down into the water three times, and rose up again. By this symbol you shadowed forth the three-day burial of Christ.

—Cyril of Jerusalem, *Catechetical Lectures*
20.4 [*Mysteries* 2.4]

Baptism

In baptism, we are illuminated; being illuminated, we are made children; being made children, we are perfected; being perfected, we are made immortal. . . . This work is variously called a gift of grace, illumination, perfection, or washing. It is the washing through which we are cleansed of our sins, the gift of grace by which the penalties of our sins are removed, the illumination through which the holy light of salvation is beheld, that through which the divine is clearly seen. . . . Instruction leads to faith, and faith together with baptism is trained by the Holy Spirit. . . . We who have repented of our sins, renounced our faults, and been purified by baptism run back to the eternal light, children running to their Father.

—Clement of Alexandria, *Instructor*
1.6.26.1–2; 30.2; 32.1

TERTULLIAN wrote the first surviving treatise on baptism.

It will not be superfluous to give this summary concerning our sacrament [vow] of water, by which we are set at liberty for eternal life through washing away the sins of our early blindness [Acts 22:16]. . . .

Is it not wonderful that by bathing death is washed away? . . .

After the world's elements were set in order, when inhabitants were given to it, the command to produce living beings came first to the waters [Gen 1:20]. The liquid element was the first to bring forth life, so there might be no cause for wondering whether in baptism the waters know how to give life. . . .

The ruling principle of baptism . . . [is] that the spirit of God who was carried upon the waters from the beginning [Gen 1:2] remains upon the waters as the one who administers baptism.

—Tertullian, *On Baptism* 1; 2; 3; 4

IN THE next selection, Cyril of Jerusalem addresses candidates who were beginning the forty-day period of preparation for baptism.

Let your mind be refined as by fire for reverence; let your soul be forged as metal; let the stubbornness of unbelief be hammered out; let the superfluous flakes of iron fall off and what is pure remain; let the rust from the iron fall off and the genuine metal remain. . . . Then may the gate of paradise be opened to each man and woman among you. Then may you enjoy the fragrance of the Christ-bearing waters. Then may you receive the name of Christ and the power of things divine. . . .

Great is the baptism that lies before you: the ransom of captives, the forgiveness of sins, the death of sin, the regeneration of the soul, the garment of light, the holy perpetual seal, a chariot to heaven, the delight of paradise, a welcome into the kingdom, the gift of adoption. But a serpent along the way keeps watch on those who walk by. Beware, lest he bite you with unbelief. He sees so many receiving salvation, and he seeks whomever he may devour [1 Pet 5:8]. Come to the "Father of spirits" [Heb 12:9] and pass by that serpent. How then do you pass him by? "Shod your feet with the preparation of the gospel of peace" [Eph 6:15] so that even if he bites, he cannot harm you. Have an indwelling faith, a mighty hope—a stout boot—that you may pass by the enemy and enter the presence of your Lord. Prepare your own heart for the reception of teaching, for participation in the holy mysteries. Pray more frequently that God may make you worthy of the heavenly and immortal mysteries. . . . And if you notice any shameful thought rising up in your mind, then contemplate the judgment and remember salvation. Give your mind wholly to learning so that it may forget base things. . . .

May God "erase the record that is against you" [Col 2:14] and grant you amnesty for your former trespasses. May he plant you in his church, enlist you in his army, and put "the armor of righteousness" [2 Cor 6:7] on you. May he fill you with the heavenly things of the new covenant and give you the indelible seal of the Holy Spirit throughout all ages, in Christ Jesus our Lord.

— Cyril of Jerusalem, *Procatachesis* 15; 16; 17

Salvation

In love, the Master took us to himself. Because of the love he had for us, Jesus Christ our Lord gave his blood for us—his flesh for our flesh, his soul for our souls.

— *1 Clement* 49.6

Christ, being the firstborn of all creation [Col 1:15], became also the beginning of another race who are begotten by him through water, faith, and wood (containing the mystery of the cross), just as Noah was saved by the wood when he with his family floated upon the waters. . . . As was demonstrated by all of the symbols at the flood—I mean water, faith, and wood—those who prepare themselves and repent of the sins they have committed will escape the coming judgment of God.

—Justin Martyr, *Dialogue* 138

Therefore, we have rightly shown that the Father is known by no one except the Son and those to whom the Son revealed him [Luke 10:22]. The Son reveals the Father to whomever he wishes. No one knows God without the good will of the Father and the working of the Son.

—Irenaeus, *Against Heresies* 4.7.3

First of all, believe not only in the Father but also in his Son, who is now manifested. He is the one who leads human beings into fellowship and unity with God.

—Irenaeus, *Against Heresies* 4.13.1

When the Son of God became flesh and was made a human being, he summed up in himself the long history of human beings, offering salvation to us in a summary manner; thus what we lost in Adam—that is, being in the image and likeness of God—we might recover in Christ Jesus.

—Irenaeus, *Against Heresies* 3.18.1

The Word of God became man, and he who is the Son of God was made the Son of Man, so that human beings might become children of God making room for the Word and receiving adoption. For we would not be able to receive incorruptibility and immortality in any way other than by being united with incorruptibility and immortality. How could we be united with incorruptibility and immortality unless incorruptibility and immortality were first made what we are? Thus what was corruptible was absorbed by incorruptibility and what was mortal by immortality, so that we might receive adoption as sons.

—Irenaeus, *Against Heresies* 3.19.1

For we could not learn the things of God unless our Teacher became man, while still existing as the Word. For no one else could reveal to us the things of the Father except his very own Word. . . . The Word is perfect in all things, since he is both the powerful Word and true man. Redeeming us in a rational manner by his blood, he gave himself as the redemption for those who had been led into captivity. . . . The Lord redeemed us by his own blood and gave his soul for our souls, his flesh in the place of our flesh. He poured out the Spirit of the Father for the sake of union and communion between God and human beings, imparting God to human beings with certainty through the Spirit and attaching human beings once again to God through his incarnation. His coming gave us incorruption surely and truly through communion with God.

—Irenaeus, *Against Heresies* 5.1.1

The Word of God who was made the Son of Man fought and conquered, for he was a human being contending for his forebears, and his obedience put an end to disobedience. He bound the strong man [Matt 12:20], set the weak free, and gave salvation to his creation by destroying sin. For he who loves the human race is a most holy and merciful Lord.

[The continuation of the passage presents a thought more familiar to Western theology from its formulation in the Middle Ages by Anselm.]

Therefore, as we have said, he united a human person with God. For if a human being had not conquered humanity's opponent, the enemy would not have been justly conquered. Furthermore, if God had not given salvation we would not possess it securely. And if a human being were not united to God we could not share in incorruption. For it was necessary that the Mediator between God and human beings, through his kinship to both, bring both into friendship and harmony, presenting human beings to God and revealing God to human beings.

—Irenaeus, *Against Heresies* 3.18.6–7

AN EXHORTATION to pagans to become Christians describes what the Lord does for his followers.

What then does this instrument—the Word of God, the Lord, the New Song—desire? To open the eyes of the blind, to open the ears of the deaf, to lead by the hand the lame or the straying to righteousness, to show God to foolish human beings, to put an end to corruption, to conquer death, to reconcile disobedient children to their father. The instrument of God loves humanity. The Lord shows mercy; he disciplines, exhorts, admonishes, saves, guards, and out of his abundance promises the kingdom of heaven as the reward for our learning. The only benefit he gains from us is our salvation.

—Clement of Alexandria, *Exhortation* 1

⊂he Lord's work consists only in this—to save humankind.
—Clement of Alexandria, *Exhortation* 9

Ӏ propose a simple and definite reason: God would not have been able to enter into association with human beings if he had not taken into himself the experiences and emotions of a human being. In doing this, he tempered the strength of his majesty, which human limitations would have found unbearable, by humility that was indeed unworthy of him but—at the same time—necessary for humanity. Yet this act was worthy of God, for nothing is so worthy of God as humanity's salvation.
—Tertullian, *Against Marcion* 2.27.1

⊂he unique Son of God, who was the Word and Wisdom of the Father and in glory with the Father before the world was, emptied himself of glory, took the form of a servant, and was made obedient even unto death [Phil 2:6–8]. He did this so that he might teach obedience to those who could obtain salvation in no other way except by obedience. . . . Thus, since he came to restore the discipline not only of ruling but also of being ruled by obedience—as we have said—he first accomplished in himself what he wanted others to accomplish. He was made obedient to the Father, and this not only in death on the cross but indeed at the end of the world he will also embrace in himself all those whom he subjects to the Father and who come to salvation through him. At that time he himself—with them and in them—will also be subject to the Father [Origen then quotes 1 Cor 15:28].
—Origen, *First Principles* 3.5.6

Someone asks, "What then? We have been deceived and we are lost." I respond, "Does not salvation remain?" "We have fallen." "Can we not rise again?" "We have been blinded." "Can we not recover our sight?" "We have been crippled." "Can we not walk upright?" To speak briefly, "We died." "Then can we not rise again?" Oh, human! Cannot he who raised Lazarus on the fourth day when he already stank raise you who are alive much more easily? He who poured out his precious blood for us will himself deliver us from our sin. Let us not despair for ourselves, brothers and sisters; let us not abandon ourselves to a hopeless condition. For it is a fearful thing not to believe in the hope of repentance. . . . A robber who does not expect pardon grows desperate, but if he has hope for forgiveness, he often finds a place for repentance. . . . Our nature is capable of salvation but our free choice is also required.
—Cyril of Jerusalem, *Catechetical Lectures* 2.5

A CLASSIC formulation of salvation as divinization, which Irenaeus had only intimated, is found in Athanasius.

If a person wishes to see God, who by nature is invisible and in no way can be seen, he may know and comprehend him through his works. Even so, let the one who does not see Christ with his understanding at least comprehend him through his bodily works, and let him test whether they are human or divine. . . . Let him marvel that divine things have been revealed to us through such ordinary means, that by death immortality came to everyone, and that by the Word becoming a human being universal providence and its Giver and Creator—the very Word of God—have been made known. For he was made a human being that we might be made a god [that is, immortal]. He revealed himself in a body that we might receive an idea of the invisible Father, and he endured the insolence of people that we might inherit immortality.

—Athanasius, *The Incarnation of the Word* 54.1–3

EARLY Christian writers often used rhetorical paradoxes to express the nature of Christ and his salvation (see *Epistle to Diognetus* 9, quoted above under Grace). No one was better at this than Gregory of Nazianzus.

Let us become like Christ, since Christ became like us. Let us become gods on account of him, since he became a human being on account of us. He assumed the worse [nature] that he might give us the better [nature]. He became poor that we through his poverty might become rich [2 Cor 8:9]. He took the form of a servant [Phil 2:7] that we might receive freedom. He descended that we might be exalted. He was tempted that we might conquer. He was dishonored that he might give glory. He died that he might save. He ascended that he might draw to himself those who were lying below in the calamity of sin. One should give all—offer all—to him who gave himself as a ransom and substitute for us. One will give nothing less than oneself when one understands the mystery; on account of him, one will become everything that he became on account of us.

—Gregory of Nazianzus, *Oration* 1.5

IN THE selection below, Gregory of Nyssa replies to "an objection that has been brought against us" by unbelievers.

If there is such power in Christ as the word sets forth, so that both the destruction of death and the introduction of life reside in him, why does he not effect his purpose by the mere exercise of his will alone, instead of working out our salvation in such a roundabout way—being born, growing up, and saving human beings by the experience of death—when it was possible for us to have been saved without his subjecting himself to such conditions? With regard to such reasoning, it is sufficient to say to those with a reasonable disposition that the sick do not dictate the means of treatment to their physicians nor dispute the method of their healing with their benefactors.

—Gregory of Nyssa, *Catechetical Oration* 17

CHAPTER IV

Life-Nourishing Doctrines

God needs no one; the believer needs God alone.
— *Sentences of Sextus* 49

AS IS EVIDENT FROM THE READINGS in the first two chapters, Christian thought about human life, society, conduct, and morality is based on deeply held doctrinal beliefs. It was impossible to select very many passages on even the most common human experiences that did not reference the system of faith out of which the reflections were made. In this chapter we look at some of the explicit theological statements made by early Christian writers. We did not, however, select passages that are the most important for doctrinal history, although a few of these may be included. Rather, our purpose was to select passages in which the practical implications of those beliefs are drawn out or are implicit, or that have devotional value.

The passages are grouped according to an order that is conventional for theological study: God (theology in its more limited sense of the doctrine about God), Christ (Christology), the Holy Spirit (pneumatology), spiritual beings (angelology), human nature (anthropology), church (ecclesiology), revelation, and the last things (eschatology)—each with appropriate subdivisions. Thus general descriptions of God are followed by passages on his trinitarian nature, his infinity, his work as Creator and Judge; and then on the knowledge of God, his gifts and providential care for his creatures, and his promises. Because it is God's nature to care for human beings, and because of what he has done for them, there is a particular conduct that is the appropriate response to him.

The selections concerning Christ cover his nature and his career, but more attention is given to his titles, his functional roles as teacher and example, and his effects in changing lives. The moral argument that was made from reformed lives was one of the more effective approaches used by Christian apologists in support of their teachings and their Teacher.

Our selections on the Holy Spirit and spiritual beings also concentrate on functional aspects, since this was the approach taken by early writers. Only at a later stage in Christian thought was attention given to the Spirit's divine nature. Although they noted special spiritual gifts, the writers' emphasis was more on what the Holy Spirit does—the Spirit's sanctifying work and moral influence on human life. Angels are spiritual beings who remained obedient to God; the devil and demons are spiritual beings that were created by God but rebelled against him, and they now seek to lead human beings astray.

Human beings are made in the image of God—an image that is spiritual, not bodily. The soul is a mirror that reflects God and allows human beings to see the true image of God, which is Christ; but sin mars the image and must be removed for one to see clearly. Against Plato's teaching that the soul possesses natural immortality, some Christian writers affirmed the biblical teaching of creation and granted only conditional future immortality. Many, on the other hand, freely used the word "immortal" with reference to the soul (albeit created), but combined this with a strong affirmation of the resurrection of the flesh. The soul is rational, and reason is a distinctive quality that characterizes human beings. Reason and freedom are to be used for learning and choosing the good.

The doctrine of revelation was important, because knowledge of God comes about only when he makes himself known. God's principal revelation was through Christ. Part of God's plan of salvation included the church, where one receives spiritual leadership, pastoral care, and teaching. God's revelation was preserved for the church in the Scriptures, which serve as the foundation for doctrine, spirituality, and church life. Belief in revelation through the prophets, the Lord, and the apostles brought conviction about the truth of Christianity. This truth was confirmed by the transformed lives of those who were being saved by Christ. The promised second coming of Christ and the resurrection of human bodies brought the certainty of future rewards and punishments, according to deeds in this life.

God

Dear, whoever you are: God's form is unutterable and inexpressible, since it cannot be seen with fleshly eyes. In glory, he is unlimited; in greatness, incomprehensible; in grandeur, inconceivable; in strength, incomparable; in wisdom, without equal; in goodness, inimitable; in beneficence, indescribable. For if I call him Light, I speak of his creature; if I call him Word, I speak of his beginning; if I call him Mind, I speak of his prudence; if I call him Spirit, I speak of his life; if I call him Wisdom, I speak of his offspring; if I call him Strength, I speak of his might; if I call him Power, I speak of his activity; if I call him Providence, I speak of his goodness; if I call him Kingship, I speak of his glory; if I call him Lord, I speak of him as judge; if I call him Judge, I speak of him as just; if I call him Father, I speak of him as all things; if I call him Fire, I speak of his wrath.

You say to me, "Does God show wrath?" Certainly. He shows wrath to those who practice evil; but he is good, kind, and compassionate to those who love and fear him. For to the godly he is Teacher and to the just he is Father, but to the ungodly he is both Judge and Punisher.

He is without beginning because he is uncreated. He is immutable because he is immortal. He is called God because he established all things on his own steadfastness [Ps 104:5, LXX]. . . . He is Lord because he rules the universe; Father because he is before the universe; Demiurge and Maker because he is the creator and maker of the universe. He is Most High because he is above all things; Almighty because he controls and encompasses all things. . . .

"God made all things exist out of things that did not exist" [2 Macc 7:28], so that through his works his greatness might be known and understood.

— Theophilus, *To Autolycus* 1.3–4

GOD KNOWS all things; human achievements have their origin in God and are according to his providence.

Nothing would exist in the first place without the will of God. . . . For God knows all things, not only the things that are but also the things that will be, and how each thing is. Foreseeing each individual movement, "he observes all things and hears all things," looking upon the naked soul within and eternally understanding each thing individually. Just as in theaters one sees each individual part and also glances around to take in the whole, so it is with God. For he looks on all things and at each part in one glance, although he does not give all things his primary attention. Many things in life originate in human reasoning, but they received their stimulus from God. For instance, health through medical skill, good bodily condition through exercise, and wealth through business originate and exist according to divine providence that is coupled with human cooperation. The understanding is indeed from God; then immediately good persons freely indeed choose to obey the will of God.

—Clement of Alexandria, *Miscellanies* 6.17

The object of our worship is the one God, who for the glory of his majesty produced out of nothing all this huge mass with all its component elements, bodies, and spirits. He did this by the word with which he commanded, by the reason with which he gave order, by the power with which he could do it. Hence the Greeks have applied the name *kosmos* [order] to the world. He is invisible, yet he can be seen [spiritually]. He is incomprehensible, yet by grace he is manifested. He is beyond human calculation, yet human senses have a conception of him.

—Tertullian, *Apology* 17.1–2

Christian truth declares without reserve that "if God is not one, he is not." . . . In so far as our human condition can define God, I give the definition that is recognized by everyone's conscience: God is the Highest and Greatest, established in eternity, unbegotten, uncreated, without beginning, without end.

—Tertullian, *Against Marcion* 1.3.1–2

TERTULLIAN opposed Marcion's two gods—one wholly good and the other wholly just.

Since the close association and agreement between goodness and justice is such that it is impossible to conceive of their separation, how can you establish from these that there are two different gods? . . . God's goodness created the world; his justice regulated it. . . .

Justice is the fullness of the Deity himself, manifesting God as both perfect Father and perfect Lord: a Father in his mercy, a Lord in his discipline; a Father in gentle power, a Lord in severity; a Father to be loved with dutiful reverence, a Lord necessarily to be feared; to be loved because he prefers mercy to sacrifice [Hos 6:6]; to be feared because he does not want sin; to be loved because he prefers a sinner's repentance to his death [Ezek 23:11]; to be feared because he does not want sinners who do not repent now. Accordingly, the law commands both: "You shall love God" [Deut 6:5] and "You shall fear God" [Deut 5:29]. It proposed one for obedient persons, the other for transgressors.

—Tertullian, *Against Marcion* 2.12–13

THE CONTEXT of the following passage is an argument in favor of the resurrection of the flesh and against a resurrection of the soul only.

Those who do not think that God can do anything that does not lie within their suppositions have poor knowledge of God. . . . I, for my part, prefer to believe that God is unable to deceive. . . .

—Tertullian, *On the Resurrection of the Flesh* 38

God is greater than mind itself. Nor is it possible to imagine how great God is, for if it were possible to imagine him, he would be less than the human mind that conceives him. . . . For whatever can be thought about him is less than he is. And whatever might be declared about him is less than he is, when compared with him. . . . Anything that can be unfolded about God explains something about his greatness and power rather than God himself. . . . For if the keenness of our eyes becomes dim upon looking at the sun, because our gaze is overcome by the brightness of the rays that meet it and cannot look upon the orb itself, then the keenness of our mind experiences the same thing with regard to every thought about God. The more the mind is attentive to God, the more it is blinded by the light of its own thought. For—I repeat once more—what can one say that is worthy of him who is more sublime than all sublimity, higher than all height, deeper than all depth, clearer than all light, brighter than all brightness, more splendid than all splendor, stronger than all strength, more powerful than all power, more beautiful than all beauty, truer than all truth, mightier than all might, more majestic than all majesty, more potent than all potency, richer than all riches, wiser than all wisdom, kinder than all kindness, better than all goodness, more just than all justice, and more merciful than all clemency? For every virtue must necessarily be less than the One who is both God and Parent of all virtues.

—Novatian, *On the Trinity* 2

CYRIL of Jerusalem, in explaining God to candidates for baptism, answers an objection: "If we cannot comprehend God, how can we talk about him at all?"

For we do not say what ought to be said about God, for that is known only to him. We say only what human nature is capable of saying and what our weakness is able to bear. For we do not explain what God is but confess frankly that we do not have exact knowledge about him. For when it comes to God, to confess our ignorance is great knowledge. . . .

But someone will say, "If the divine substance is incomprehensible, then why do you talk about these things?" Since I cannot drink up all of the river, should I not even take in moderation what is beneficial to me? . . . Or again, if I enter a large garden and cannot eat all of the accumulated fruits, do you wish me to go away altogether hungry? I praise and glorify our Creator, for a divine command says, "Let all that has breath praise the Lord" [Ps 150:6]. I am attempting now to glorify the Lord, not to interpret him. Even though I know that I shall fall short of glorifying him worthily, I consider it a work of piety to attempt it at all.

— Cyril of Jerusalem, *Catechetical Lectures* 6.2; 6.5

THE GREEK Fathers asserted that human beings may know the attributes but not the essence of God.

The word "to know" has many meanings. We say that we know the greatness of God, his power, his wisdom, his goodness, his providence that cares for us, and the justice of his judgment, but not his very essence. . . . He who says that he does not know the essence is not confessing that he does not know God, because our idea of God is gathered from the many attributes we have enumerated. . . . The activities [of God] are various, but God's essence is simple. We say that we know our God from his activities, but we do not undertake to draw near to his essence. His activities come down to us, but his essence remains unapproachable. . . .

How then am I saved? Through faith. Faith is sufficient if it knows that God is, not what he is, and that "he is a rewarder of those who seek him" [Heb 11:6]. Therefore, knowledge of the divine essence involves perception of his incomprehensibility. He is to be worshiped because his essence exists, not because we comprehend what that essence is.

— Basil of Caesarea, *Letters* 234.1–2

The divine nature in and of itself is goodness, holiness, joy, power, glory, purity, and eternity; and it is always exactly the same in these qualities. When we think such things about the divine nature and whatever we have learned from the divine Scriptures and our own meditations, do we then dare to call such a being our own Father? [Father implies likeness.] . . . He whose essence is good does not have the nature to become the father of any evil will, nor does the Holy One have the nature to be the father of a person whose life is defiled. . . . When we say "Father," the unjust addressing the Just and the impure the Pure, this is the height of pride and abuse, since we are naming God as the father of our own wickedness. For the word "Father" signifies the cause of what exists from him. . . .

Those who say that the Incorruptible, the Just, and the Good is their Father must prove the right of kinship by the life they live. Do you see what preparation we need, what sort of life we must live, how much zeal is needed to attain such boldness of speech, our conscience being so lifted up as to dare to say to God, "Father"?

— Gregory of Nyssa, *On the Lord's Prayer* 2

THE FOLLOWING passage contains one of Gregory of Nyssa's definitions of God, along with his own statement about all things—past, present, and future—being seen by God at once (compare his comments with those of Clement of Alexandria above).

The Nature that is all-sufficient and everlasting, encompassing the universe, exists neither in space nor in time, but is both before these and above these in an ineffable way—self-contained, perceived by faith alone, immeasurable in ages, without the accompaniment of time. . . . Within that transcendent and blessed Power all things are always equally present as in an instant—past and present are controlled and seen by its comprehensive power over all things.

— Gregory of Nyssa, *Against Eunomius* 1.372 [26]

IN ORATION and in poetry Gregory of Nazianzus provided a spiritual and devotional perspective on the nature of God.

Of the many and great things that we both have and shall have from God—one cannot say how many and how great—the greatest and kindest of all is our inclination toward him and our relationship with him. For what the sun is to beings who possess the sense of sight, God is to beings who possess intellect. One gives light to the world that is visible, the other to the world that is invisible. One enlightens our bodily eyes like the sun, the other causes our intellectual nature to be godlike. And just as the sun supplies to those things that see and those things that are seen the power to see and to be seen—and is itself the most beautiful of the things seen—so God is the Creator of the ability to think and to be thought of, both in those beings who are capable of thought and in those who are thought about; and he himself is the highest of the highest objects of thought, at whom every desire is brought to a standstill and beyond whom it can go no further. The most philosophic, the most penetrating, the most inquiring mind does not have—nor will ever have—a more exalted object. For God is the ultimate of things to be desired. When we arrive at him, we rest from all speculation.

—Gregory of Nazianzus, *Oration* 21.1

O God, you are above all that is!
How will a word praise you?
For no word can describe you.
How will the mind consider you?
For no mind can apprehend you.
You are too wonderful for words,
Since you originate whatever is spoken.
You only are unknowable,
Since you originate whatever is thought.
All beings speak of you,
And those that do not speak cry out in praise.
All beings think of you,
And those that do not think honor you.
The desires of all are common;
The pains of all are common.
All beings make prayer to you.
To you every thinking creature speaks a song of silent praise.
Everything abides in you alone;
Everything that moves moves together with you.
You are the goal of everything;
The One, the All, yet Nothing.
You are not one among many nor the totality of all beings;
You have all names; how shall I call you?
You alone are unenclosed;
You are hidden above the clouds.
What heavenly mind will enter in?
Have mercy!

O God, you are above all that is!
What else can be done than to celebrate you in song?
— Gregory of Nazianzus, *Poems* 1.1.29

In God, justice and love are combined. Thus John Chrysostom comments on Ps 111:7.

€verything done by God is truth and judgment. Judgment is righteousness, and Scripture often knows that truth means his loving-kindness. . . . Everything done by him is full of both qualities. If he had demanded righteousness only, then everything would have been destroyed; but if he had employed only loving-kindness, then the majority of people would have become indifferent. Varying his approach to the salvation of human beings, he employed both of these for their correction.
— John Chrysostom, *Commentary on the Psalms* 111.5–6, on Ps 111:7

The Trinity

Christians were charged with being "atheists" because they did not worship the state gods of Rome. In this section we offer some of the early formulations of the Trinity that were given in response to this charge, before the great creedal definitions of the fourth century were adopted.

We are not atheists since we hold that God is one, uncreated, eternal, invisible, without passions, incomprehensible, unlimited, apprehended by the mind and reason alone, surrounded by light, beauty, spirit, and indescribable power, by whom the universe came into being, is set in order, and is controlled by his Word. . . . We understand also a Son of God. . . . The Son of God is the Word of the Father in idea and activity. For by him and through him all things came to be, since the Father and the Son are one. Since the Son is in the Father and the Father is in the Son in the unity and power of the Spirit, the Son of God is the Mind and Word of the Father. . . . He is the first offspring of the Father not as coming into being—for God, being eternal Mind, had the Word [Reason] within him from the beginning, being eternally in possession of reason—but he came forth to be the idea and activity of all material things. . . . Moreover, we say that there is a Holy Spirit who is at work in the prophets and who flows forth from God, flowing forth and returning back again as the rays of the sun. Who then would not be puzzled upon hearing that those who hold to God as Father, and the Son as God, and to a Holy Spirit—showing their power in unity and their difference in order—are called atheists? . . .

[Christians] know the true God and the Word from him, the unity of the Son with the Father, the fellowship of the Father with the Son, the Spirit, the unity of these and the distinction of these who are united—the Spirit, the Son, and the Father.

—Athenagoras, *Plea for the Christians* 10; 12

TERTULLIAN opposed the view of Praxeas, who made Father, Son, and Holy Spirit three subsequent modes of manifestation of a God who is singular in being. In opposition to this view, Tertullian offered analogies from nature of things that are simultaneously one and three. The inherent limitation in these comparisons is that the natural world does not fully correspond to the spiritual world. Tertullian's analogies do, however, have the virtue of beginning with unity and explaining how something that is one in substance can be three, unlike some modern, popular explanations that begin at the opposite end, seeking to explain how something that is plural can be one.

For God sent forth the Word . . . just as a root puts forth a plant, a fountain flows forth into a stream, and the sun sends out its ray. . . . Now both the root and the plant are two things, yet they are closely connected; a fountain and a stream are two objects, but indivisible; the sun and its ray are two forms, yet they hold together. Everything that is produced from something else must necessarily be second from the thing that produces it, even though—at the same time—it is not separate from it. Where there is a second, there are two; and where there is a third, there are three. For the Spirit is third from God and the Son, just as the fruit of the plant is third from the root, or the channel of a stream is third from the fountain, or the apex of the ray is third from the sun. Nothing, however, is alien from its original source, from which its own properties derive.

—Tertullian, *Against Praxeas* 8

ONE APPROACH to distinguishing the three individuations within the one God appealed to their respective operations, the ways by which each is known. Thus Origen distinguished between the Father who imparts existence to all things, the Son (the Word or Reason) who lives in rational beings,

and the Holy Spirit who lives in those who are holy or sanctified. In developing his approach, Origen used language of subordination, which the church
as a whole later rejected.

⟨he God and Father who holds together all things extends to each
thing that exists, since he gives existence to each—whatever it is—from his
own being. The Son in a lesser way than the Father (since he is second to the
Father) extends only to rational beings. In a still lesser way, the Holy Spirit
penetrates only to holy persons. According to this, the power of the Father is
greater than the Son and the Holy Spirit, the power of the Son is more than
the Holy Spirit, and again the power of the Holy Spirit exceeds all other holy
things. . . .

The paramount work of God the Father is to make it possible for all
things to exist according to their nature. The paramount ministry of the Lord
Jesus Christ is conferring the gift of reason, making it possible for those who
receive it to act well. There is also the other grace of the Holy Spirit, which is
given to the worthy, ministered by Christ, and worked by the Father according to the merits of those who are made capable of it. . . .

God the Father makes existence possible for all things. Participation
in Christ, according to his Word (or Reason), causes rational beings to exist.
As a consequence of this, they become worthy of either praise or blame, since
they are capable of both virtue and vice. Consequently, the grace of the Holy
Spirit is present so that those beings whose essence is not holy may be made
holy through participation in the Spirit. First, existence comes from God the
Father; second, rational nature comes from the Word; and third, holiness
comes from the Holy Spirit.

—Origen, *First Principles* 1.3.5, 7–8

WE NOW offer a later, classic formulation of the Trinity that is expressed in
terms of the relationships between the One-in-Three God (not Three-in-
One). The selection comes from Gregory of Nazianzus, a fourth-century
thinker who was influential in the final clarification of the Christian doctrine
of the Trinity.

⟨⟨e honor Monarchy, but a Monarchy that is not limited to one
Person. . . . Therefore Unity, having from the beginning been moved to Du-
ality, brought about a Trinity. For us, this is Father, Son, and Holy Spirit. The
Father is the Begetter and the Producer, but in a manner without reference to
passion, time, or a body. I do not know how someone could describe the

things pertaining to the One Begotten and the One Produced by altogether avoiding visible things.

—Gregory of Nazianzus, *Oration* 29.2

1 hold this position . . . to worship God the Father, God the Son, and God the Holy Spirit—three individuals, one Godhead that is inseparable in glory, honor, substance, and kingship.

—Gregory of Nazianzus, *Oration* 31.28

The Infinity of God

GREGORY of Nyssa, if not the first to formulate the infinity of God, was the first to make it a central part of his metaphysics and spirituality.

Since the First Good is infinite in its nature, participation in the enjoyment of it will necessarily also be infinite. For always, as more is being grasped, even more is always being discovered; and this participation is never able to equal the Good, because there is no limit to the participation, nor does growth through participation ever cease.

—Gregory of Nyssa, *Against Eunomius*
1.291 [22]

The Divine One himself is the Good—in the primary and proper sense of the word—whose very nature is goodness. . . . Therefore, since it has not been demonstrated that there is any limit to virtue except evil, and since the Divine does not admit any opposite, we hold that the divine nature is unlimited and infinite. Certainly whoever pursues true virtue participates in nothing other than God, because he himself is absolute virtue. Since, then, it is the nature of those who know what is good to desire participation in it, and since this good has no limit, then a participant's desire has no stopping point but stretches out with the limitless.

—Gregory of Nyssa, *Life of Moses* 1.7

God as Creator

How can I speak about what God creates? Behold the entire world—that is his work! Heaven, sun, angels, and human beings are the "works of his fingers" [Ps 8:3]. Such is the power of God! His volition alone effected the creation of the world. For God alone created it, since he alone is truly God. He created by his bare volition; what came into existence is the result of his will alone.

—Clement of Alexandria, *Exhortation* 4

God is the Creator of the universe; the universe is good; and it has been given to human beings.

—Tertullian, *On Shows* 2

Remember that God manifests his creative greatness quite as much in small objects as in the very largest.

—Tertullian, *On the Soul* 10

Deceived by their inherent atheism, [some philosophers] think that the universe has no governor or administrator, as if it were carried along by chance. In order that we might not be subject to such influences, the writer of the creation account immediately enlightens our understanding with the name of God in the very first words: "In the beginning God created" [Gen 1:1]. . . .

These [scientists] have discovered all things except one: the fact that God is the Creator of the universe and the just Judge who brings worthy recompense to every action in life. . . .

Intelligent reason presided in the arrangement of visible things, just as the word "beginning" suggests. You will discover that the world was not conceived by chance or in vain, but for a useful end and for the great advantage of all beings, since it is truly the school for reasonable souls and the training ground for the knowledge of God, since through visible and sensible things the mind is led—as by the hand—to the contemplation of invisible things [Rom 1:20].

—Basil of Caesarea, *Hexaemeron* 1.2, 4, 6

JOHN Cassian affirmed that God created nothing evil—even the devil and his angels were not created evil.

Far be it from me to assert that God created anything that is essentially evil. As Scripture says, "Everything that God made was very good" [Gen 1:31]. For if we say that God created these beings evil and made them so as to occupy the ranks of evil and be always ready to deceive and destroy human beings, then we defame God by calling him the creator and author of evil, contrary to the teaching of the Scripture we cited. That is, we would be saying that he himself established wills and natures that are wicked, creating them so that they would always persevere in iniquity and never be able to change their disposition into a good will. . . .

None of the faithful doubts that before the founding of this visible creation God made the spiritual and heavenly powers. Since these powers knew—through the kindness of the Creator and for the sake of this glorious blessedness—that they came into existence out of nothing, they rendered perpetual thanks to him and ceaselessly fixed their attention on praising him. For we ought not to think that God initiated his creation and his work at the first establishment of this world, as if during those innumerable previous ages his providence and divine superintendence were altogether idle, and as if we believe that he was alone and a stranger to munificence, having no one upon whom to bestow the benefits of his kindness. It is too ignoble and inconsistent to think such about that immeasurable, eternal, and incomprehensible majesty. . . .

I say that there is no doubt that God created all the heavenly powers and forces before the temporal beginning in Genesis.

—John Cassian, *Conferences* 8.6–7

The use of thoughts in accord with reason produces self-control, love, and knowledge; but the use of thoughts contrary to reason produces licentiousness, hatred, and ignorance.

Evils gain entrance into the powers of the soul—which are desire, emotion, and reason—by their misuse. The misuse of the rational faculty produces ignorance and folly. The misuse of the faculties of emotion and desire produces hatred and licentiousness. Their proper use produces knowledge and prudence, love and self-control. If this is the case, nothing created and made by God is evil.

Food is not evil, but gluttony is. Procreation is not evil, but fornication is. Possessions are not bad, but the love of money is. Glory is not bad, but vainglory is. If this is the case, then nothing is evil in and of itself but only its misuse, which occurs when we neglect the natural cultivation of the mind.

—Maximus the Confessor, *Charity* 3.1, 3–4

God as Judge and His Punishments

It would be more unworthy of God to spare an evildoer than to punish him, especially the supremely good God, who cannot be fully good unless he is the enemy of evil, so that his love for good is exercised though his hatred of evil and his defense of the good is fulfilled through the overthrow of evil.

—Tertullian, *Against Marcion* 1.26

CHRISTIAN apologists argued for belief in God on the grounds that it produces a virtuous life.

Let someone be so bold as to say that the source and beginning of everything beneficial is something other than faith in the God of the universe, doing everything with reference to pleasing him in every respect, and not thinking about anything displeasing to him, since not only words and actions but also thoughts will be judged. [I answer,] What teaching so moves human nature earnestly to live well as does the faith or the opinion that God looks upon everything that is said, done, and even thought by everyone?

—Origen, *Against Celsus* 4.53

THE FOLLOWING words were written with reference to the fall of Adam and Eve.

The first thing that humans learned was their own shame, and they hid themselves from God. Yet even here human beings gained something, namely death and the cutting off of sin so that evil might not be immortal. Thus their punishment became a kindness. For I am persuaded that it is in kindness that God punishes.

—Gregory of Nazianzus, *Oration* 38.12 [45.8]

Knowledge of God

Those who see God shall share in life. For this purpose he who is unlimited, incomprehensible, and invisible made himself visible, comprehensible, and accessible to believers, so that those who receive him and see him through faith might be made alive. For as his greatness is past discovery, so also his goodness is inexpressible. Beholding it bestows life on those who see him. Since it is not possible to live without life, the existence of life results from sharing in God. Sharing in God consists in knowing God and enjoying his goodness.

—Irenaeus, *Against Heresies* 4.20.5

Apart from the knowledge of God, what solid basis for happiness can there be, since death is present? Like a dream, happiness slips away before it is grasped.

— Minucius Felix, *Octavius* 37

Believing—not doubting—with reference to God is the foundation of knowledge.

— Clement of Alexandria, *Miscellanies* 7.10

To know the truth is to share in divine wisdom. But the unaided human being cannot arrive at this knowledge, but only as taught by God.

— Lactantius, *Divine Institutes* 2.3.23

It is better and more profitable to be a common person with little learning and through love come near to God than to be among those who have much learning and appear to be experienced but blaspheme against their own Master.

— Irenaeus, *Against Heresies* 2.26.1

Which comes first, knowledge or faith? In the case of learning, we say in general that faith precedes knowledge. But in our teaching, if someone says that knowledge comes before faith we do not object, for we understand that knowledge is what accords with human comprehension. . . . In our faith about God, the idea that God exists leads the way. We infer this from the things he made. For by understanding his wisdom, his power, his goodness, and all his invisible qualities from the creation of the world [Rom 1:20], we come to recognize him. So, too, we accept him as our Lord. For since God is the Creator of the whole world and we are a part of the world, God is also our Creator. Faith follows this knowledge, and worship follows such faith. . . .

Knowledge is manifold. It is the perception of the one who created us, the apprehension of his wonderful works, the keeping of his commandments, and intimate communion with him. . . . God will be known to his worshipers . . . and through their good works he receives them into intimate communion with himself.

— Basil of Caesarea, *Letters* 235.1, 3

A rational capacity that comes from God is implanted in every person; it is the first law in us, is common to all, and leads us from visible things up to God. . . .

No human being has ever found God—that is, what he is in nature and essence—nor can anyone find him. As to whether or not he will ever be found, this is a question for those who wish to inquire and philosophize. In my own thinking he will be found when that which is godlike and divine within us—I am speaking about our mind and reason—grows increasingly similar to its original, and the image ascends to the Archetype it now longs for. It seems to me that this is the meaning of "We shall know as we are known" [1 Cor 13:12].

—Gregory of Nazianzus, *Oration* 28.16–17

We say these things . . . so that [our adversaries] may see that they do not have complete wisdom and that their superfluous arguments that void the gospel are not invincible. For whenever we, abandoning faith, put forward the power of reason and in our inquiries leave out the trustworthiness of the Spirit, and then reason is found inferior to the greatness of the subject [the divinity of the Son] (and assuredly it will remain inferior since its starting point is the weak instrument of the human mind), what happens then? The weakness of reason is revealed by the mystery, and the subtlety of reason makes the cross empty—or so it seemed to Paul [1 Cor 1:17]. For in our view faith brings fullness to reason.

—Gregory of Nazianzus, *Oration* 29.21

THE FOLLOWING passage discusses knowledge and faith, and also affirms the value of education.

Even as we say that one can be a believer without possessing an education, we also affirm that such an unlearned person cannot have full knowledge of the faith. An informed faith, and not simply faith by itself, causes one to accept things that are stated correctly and not to accept the contrary. If ignorance is both a lack of training and a lack of learning, teaching imparts the understanding of things divine and human. Just as it is possible to live life uprightly in poverty—this is also possible in abundance—similarly we affirm that someone who has the benefit of a basic education would more readily and easily pursue virtue. Although virtue is not unattainable without a preliminary education, nevertheless it comes to those who have learned and "who have trained their faculties by exercise" [Heb 5:14].

—Clement of Alexandria, *Miscellanies*
1.6.35.2–4

Faith needs knowledge, even as knowledge needs faith. For faith cannot exist without knowledge, nor can knowledge exist apart from faith. . . . For it is necessary first to believe and then to learn. When something is known it must be desired, and when desired it must be done. Not even the letters of the alphabet can be known unless one has faith in the teacher, because one must call the first letter by a certain name, the second by its name, and the others in the same way. If a student contradicts the teacher, saying it is not necessary to name the first letter alpha but gives it another name, he will never learn the truth but will necessarily remain in error and receive what is false in place of the truth. But if a student believes the teacher and accepts the lessons according to the teacher's rules, knowledge quickly follows this faith.

—Theodoret, *Cure of Pagan Diseases* 1.92–94

SEE ALSO Chapter III, under Grace, and below, under Revelation.

Gifts of God

Beloved, how blessed and marvelous are the gifts of God! Life in immortality, splendor in righteousness, truth in boldness, faith in confidence, self-control in holiness; and all these things fall within our understanding. What things are being prepared for those who endure? The Creator and Father of the ages, the All-holy himself, knows their greatness and beauty. Let us then strive to be among those who endure for him so that we may share in the promised gifts.

—*1 Clement* 35.1–4

In the beginning God created Adam, not as if God were in need of a human being, but so that he might have one on whom to bestow his favors. . . . He did not command that we follow him because he was in need of our services, but because he was offering us salvation. To follow the Savior is to share in salvation, and to follow the light is to receive the light. For those who are in the light do not illuminate the light but are illuminated and enlightened by it. They offer nothing to the light, but receiving its benefit, they are illuminated by it. Service toward God is similar in that we offer nothing to God, nor does God need human service. But to those who follow and serve him God assigns life, incorruption, and eternal glory. He offers a benefit to those who serve him because they serve and to those who follow because they follow; but he receives no benefit from them, for he is rich, perfect, and without any needs. On account of this, God seeks service from human beings so that he might benefit those who persevere in his service, because he is good and merciful. To the same degree that God needs nothing, human beings need fellowship with God.

—Irenaeus, *Against Heresies* 4.14.1

The Providence of God

THE GOD who created the world continues to sustain and control the world, and to exercise providential care for each individual.

This God, . . . whom the church knows and worships, is the God to whom all nature—both things visible and things invisible—always bears witness, whom angels adore, stars wonder at, seas bless, lands revere, and all things under the earth look up to. The mind of all human beings is conscious of him, even if this is not expressed. At his command all things are set in motion: springs gush forth, rivers flow, waves arise, all creatures bring forth their young, winds are compelled to blow, showers fall, seas are stirred up, all things everywhere spread their fruitfulness. . . . If he embraces all things and contains all things—and all things, as well as the whole, consist of individuals—then his care extends even to each individual thing, since his providence extends to the whole, whatever it is.

—Novatian, *On the Trinity* 8

PERSECUTION seemed to contradict the providence of God. Pagans stressed this point, and Christians raised it up as a question.

The Lord did not suffer on account of the will of the Father, nor do those who suffer persecution do so because of God's intention, since one of two things is the case: either persecution is a good thing because it is willed by God, or those who command and those who oppress are innocent. But nothing occurs outside the will of the Lord of the universe. Briefly, it remains to be said that such things happen because God does not prevent them, since this alone preserves both the providence and the goodness of God. We should not think that God effects tribulations—this should not even be considered—but it is proper to be persuaded that God does not prevent those who effect tribulations from doing so, and he uses the reckless deeds of adversaries for good.

—Clement of Alexandria, *Miscellanies* 4.12

GOD CAN overrule evil with good, but the fact that God brings good out of bad does not relieve human beings of their responsibility and guilt for wrong actions.

Let no one excuse evil conduct on the grounds that one's evil happens to be useful to the world, or perhaps could be useful. So that no one misunderstands what is meant here, I point out that God preserves free will in each person, and even though he uses the evil committed by wicked persons in his administration of all things and arranges them for the benefit of all, the person who does evil is no less blameworthy. As one who is blameworthy, the evil person functions in a way that is repulsive to every individual yet useful to all. It is as if—to borrow an illustration from cities—a person who committed crimes and was condemned to perform public works that are useful to all were doing something useful for the whole city; he himself exists in a repulsive situation, one in which no one with even moderate understanding would wish to find himself. . . . No one should find an excuse to sin because of the things said on this topic—that is, on the grounds that his sin makes him useful to the whole community.

—Origen, *Against Celsus* 4.70

THE FOLLOWING passage warns against referring everything that happens to "the will of God."

Good, solid faith does not refer all things to the will of God. . . . Saying that "nothing is done without God's assent" is as if we did not acknowledge that some things lie within our own power. And if we contend that nothing is done by us without the will of God, then every sin will be excused. . . . Accordingly, we ought not to refer to the Lord's will those things that are clearly done by our own choice.

—Tertullian, *Exhortation to Chastity* 2

THE OTHER side of belief in providence is trust in God's care.

One of the fathers asked Abba Sisoes, "If I am sitting in the desert and a barbarian comes and tries to kill me, and I am stronger than he is, shall I kill him?" The old man said, "No, leave him to God. In fact, regardless of the trial that comes to a person, that person should say, 'This happened because of my sins,' and if something good comes, say, 'It is the providence of God.'"

—*Apophthegmata Patrum*, Alphabetical
Collection, Sisoes # 34

We can compare the incomparable mercy of our Creator to something mortal, not because they are equal with regard to piety but because they are similar with respect to kindness. A dutiful and careful nurse carries for some time a small child in her bosom, so that in time she might teach the child to begin walking. First, she lets him crawl, and then she holds him up so that he is supported at each step, sustained by the strength of her hands. Next, she leaves him for a little while. If she sees him tottering, she grabs him at once, catching him when he wobbles, picking him up when he falls, and either preventing him from falling or letting him fall lightly and lifting him up after a tumble. When she has brought him to boyhood or to the strength of adolescence and young manhood, she lays upon him some burdens and labors by which he will be exercised but not overwhelmed, and she lets him contend with his equals. How much more does the heavenly Father of all know whom to carry in the bosom of his grace and whom within his oversight to exercise for the attainment of virtue through the choice of free will, helping him as he struggles, hearing him when he calls, never abandoning him when he seeks after him, and from time to time snatching him from danger even when he does not know it.

—John Cassian, *Conferences* 13.14.9

In the next selection, Gregory of Nyssa comments on Matt 6:11.

These words contain further meaning, so that you might learn through your own words that human life is short. Only the present belongs to us. The hope of the future is uncertain, for we do not know what tomorrow will bring [Prov 27:1]. Why do we suffer beforehand over what is uncertain? Why do we distress ourselves with thoughts about the future? [He quotes Matt 6:34.] Here "evil" refers to the suffering of evil. Why are we anxious about tomorrow? Because of this, he gives us commands for today that prevent us from worrying about tomorrow. In effect, he is saying that "he who gives you the day also gives the things pertaining to the day."

—Gregory of Nyssa, *On the Lord's Prayer* 4

The extent of God's providence is such that all his actions and institutions serve his purposes.

To me, in this verse [Ps 50:6] the writer seems to refer to God's righteousness, his abundant providence, his loving-kindness toward all, his varied and manifold plan for all human beings—through creation, through the law, through grace, through things seen, through things unseen, through the prophets, through the angels, through the apostles, through punishments, through blessings, through threats, through promises, through the pattern of history.

—John Chrysostom, *Commentary on the Psalms* 50.4, on Ps 50:6

THE QUESTION is often asked, "Why does a God who is good allow bad things and bad people to exist?"

We say that these occasions of stumbling are permitted so that the rewards of the noble might not be diminished. [He quotes Job 40:8; 1 Cor 11:19.] He spoke these words to predict the future and indicate beforehand the reward of those who are sober. For he says that this reveals more clearly the virtue of those who are not deceived.

Evils are permitted for another reason: so that some people might not be denied the benefit of conversion by being removed too soon. Just as Paul was saved, so also the robber, the prostitute, the tax collector, and many others. If these people were removed from this life before being changed, not one of them would have been saved.

—John Chrysostom, *On Providence* 12.3–5

ONE SHOULD look to the future in order to see the unfolding providence of God.

When an inexperienced person sees the seed that has been kept hidden behind bolted doors—where there was no moisture—carried off in a sack by the farmer and scattered, cast, and lying upon the ground unnoticed by everyone who passes by, not only exposed to moisture but also delivered to the soil and water without any protection, does he not think that the seed will be destroyed? And does he not condemn the farmer who did these things? But the criticism would be inappropriate in this case; it betrays the inexperience and ignorance of a person who does not judge rightly and expresses an opinion prematurely. If that person waits for the summer, when he sees the grown crop standing tall and the sharpened scythe—the scattered and unprotected grain that had been left lying in the field and delivered to the soil, where it decayed and decomposed, now rising and multiplying, appearing more beautiful, putting off the old and restored with great vigor, standing like spearmen and guards, a reed rising to the top, pleasing to the eye, nourishing and offering much gain—then he will be greatly amazed that the fruit was brought to such abundance and beauty.

—John Chrysostom, *On Providence* 9.2–4

The Promises of God

[For the true believer] the future is already present through love. For he has believed—on account of prophecy and the coming [of the Lord]—in God, who does not lie. And what a person believes he possesses and holds on to the promise (for he who promised is the Truth). And on account of his knowledge, this person securely receives the goal of the promise through the trustworthiness of the One who promised it. A person who knows the certainty of the future in the circumstances of the present goes forth in love to meet the future.

—Clement of Alexandria, *Miscellanies* 6.9

Christ

As I said, Christians received no earthly discovery, nor do they give such careful attention to preserving mortal thought, nor are they entrusted with the administration of human mysteries. But he who is truly God, the Almighty, the Creator of all, the Invisible One, founded among humankind and implanted in their hearts the truth, the holy and incomprehensible word. He did not send to humankind—as one might suppose—a servant, angel, ruler, one of those who manages earthly affairs, or one of those who is entrusted with administration in heaven, but him who is the Maker and Creator of the universe, by whom he created the heavens, by whom he shut up the sea within its own boundaries, whose mysteries all the elements faithfully keep, from whom the sun received the measure of the course of the days to keep, the one whose command the moon obeys and shines at night, the one whom the stars obey, following in the course of the moon. By him all things have been arranged, defined, and placed in subjection—the heavens and the things in the heavens, the earth and the things on the earth, the sea and the things in the sea, fire, air, the deep, things in the heights, things in the depths, and things in between. He sent this one to human beings. Did he send him—as we human beings might suppose—in tyranny, fear, and amazement? Not at all! He sent him in gentleness and meekness. As a king sends his son, he sent a king. He sent him as a god. He sent him as a human being to human beings. He sent him as one who saves, as one who persuades but does not compel, for compulsion is not an attribute of God. He sent him as one who does not pursue but calls. He sent him as one who does not judge but loves. For he will send him in judgment, and then who will resist his coming?

—*Epistle to Diognetus* 7

There is one Physician, who is both flesh and spirit, both begotten and not begotten, God who became flesh, true life in death, both from Mary and from God, first passible and then impassible—Jesus Christ our Lord.

—Ignatius, *Ephesians* 7.2

Be deaf, therefore, whenever someone speaks to you apart from Jesus Christ, who was of the family of David, who was from Mary, who was truly born, who both ate and drank, who was truly persecuted under Pontius Pilate, and who was truly crucified and died as things in heaven, on earth, and under the earth looked on. He was also truly raised from the dead, since his Father raised him. And in his likeness his Father will also raise in Christ Jesus those of us who believe in him and apart from whom we do not truly live.

—Ignatius, *Trallians* 9

Being fully persuaded concerning our Lord that he was truly of the family of David according to the flesh, the Son of God according to the will and power of God, truly born from the virgin, baptized by John in order that all righteousness might be fulfilled by him, truly nailed [to a tree] in the flesh on our behalf—we are his fruit from his passion—blessed by God!—under Pontius Pilate and Herod the tetrarch, so that through the resurrection he might erect a sign forever for his saints and believers, both among the Jews and the nations, in the one body of his church.

He suffered all these things for us so that we might be saved. And he truly suffered, just as he also truly raised himself.

—Ignatius, *Smyrnaeans* 1–2

Therefore, there is one God, the Father. And there is one Christ Jesus our Lord, who came in accordance with the entire dispensation [of God] and summed up all things in himself. For in every respect he is also man, made by God, and therefore he summed up man in himself: the invisible made visible, the incomprehensible made comprehensible, the impassible made passible, and the Word made man, summing up all things in himself.

This occurred so that, just as the Word of God is the head in things above the heavens—things spiritual and things invisible—so also he might be preeminent in things visible and corporeal; and, assuming supremacy and appointing himself the head of the church, he draws all things to himself at the proper time. . . .

For he devoted himself to the precious and abundant will of God, seeing that he himself is the Savior of those who are saved, the Lord of those who are under authority, the God of everything that has been made, the only-begotten of the Father, the Christ who was proclaimed, and the incarnate Word of God when the fullness of time arrived for the Son of God to become the Son of Man.

—Irenaeus, *Against Heresies* 3.16.6, 7

Our Savior surpasses all human nature. He is Beauty and alone is to be loved by those of us who long for true beauty, for "he was the true light" [John 1:9]. He was shown to be "King," hailed as such by inexperienced children and unbelieving and ignorant Jews [Matt 21:1–16] and proclaimed as such by the prophets themselves. He is so rich that he disdained all the earth and all the gold that is both above and below the earth in all its glory, when the adversary offered it to him [Matt 4:8–10]. What should we say about how he alone is High Priest, the only one who knows the worship of God, "Melchizedek king of peace" [Heb 7:2], the most qualified of all to lead the race of humanity? He is also the Lawgiver, since he gives the law through the mouths of the prophets, commanding and teaching most clearly both the things that are to be done and those that are not to be done. Who is more noble-born than this one, whose only Father is God?

—Clement of Alexandria, *Miscellanies* 2.5.21.1–22.1

GREGORY of Nazianzus's rhetorical paradoxes cover many events in the life of Jesus.

In his human nature he had no father, and in his divine nature no mother. All this is from his deity. He was carried in the womb of his mother but was recognized by the prophet, who was himself still in the womb and leaped before the Word on account of whom he came into being [Luke 1:41]. He was wrapped in swaddling clothes, but when he rose again he took off the grave clothes. He was laid in a manger but was glorified by angels, revealed by a star, and worshiped by the Magi. . . . He had no form or beauty to the Jews

[Isa 53:2], but to David his beauty was the fairest among human beings [Ps 45:2], and on the mountain he flashed like lightning and became brighter than the sun, foreshadowing the future.

He was baptized as a human being but remitted sins as God; he had no need of purification himself but was baptized that he might sanctify the waters. He was tempted as a human being, but he conquered as God; he bids us take courage, since he has overcome the world [John 16:33]. He was hungry but fed thousands, and he himself is the living and heavenly bread [John 6:33, 35]. He was thirsty but called out, "If anyone is thirsty, come to me and drink" [John 7:37], and he promised those who believe that they would be fountains of water [John 7:38]. He was weary, but he is rest for those who are weary and burdened [Matt 11:28]. He was heavy with sleep, but he walked lightly on the sea [Matt 8:24]. . . .

He prayed, but he hears prayer. He wept, but he causes tears to cease. He asked where Lazarus was laid, for he was a human being; but he raised Lazarus, for he was God. He was sold, and very cheaply (thirty pieces of silver), but he redeems the world, and that at a great price (his own blood). As a sheep he was led to the slaughter, but he shepherds Israel and now also the whole world. As a lamb he was silent, yet he is the Word, proclaimed by the voice of one crying in the wilderness [John 1:23]. He was bruised and wounded, but he heals every disease and every infirmity [Matt 9:35]. He was lifted up and nailed to the tree, but by the tree of life he brings restoration, he saved even the robber crucified with him, and he darkened the visible world. Who is this who was given vinegar to drink and gall to eat? He who turned the water into wine, who is the destroyer of the bitter taste, who is Sweetness and altogether desirable [Song 5:16]. He delivered up his life, but he has power to take it again. . . . He died, but he gives life, and by his death he destroyed death. He was buried, but he rose again. He descended into Hades, but he brought up souls and he ascended to heaven; and he shall come to judge the living and the dead.

—Gregory of Nazianzus, *Oration* 29.19–20

THE SAME evidence for Jesus' birth and death testifies to the virgin birth and resurrection.

Then let this very fact—that the gospel proclamation did not accord with nature—be proof to you of the manifestation of his deity. For if the narratives concerning Christ were within the bounds of nature, where is the Godhead? . . . He who recorded that he was born also related how he was born. If therefore on the evidence stated it is trustworthy that he was born, then it is altogether incredible—on the same evidence—that he was not born in the way described. For the author who speaks of his birth also adds that it was of a virgin; and the one who mentions his death bears further testimony to his resurrection from the dead. If therefore, from what you have heard, you grant that he was born and he died, then on the same grounds you will grant that both his birth and his death were outside human experience.

—Gregory of Nyssa, *Catechetical Oration* 13

THERE were many summaries of Jesus' career.

He himself manifested conception without intercourse, birth without impurity, motherhood from virginity, voices of the unseen testifying from above to his extraordinary worth, the healing of natural diseases simply and without the use of means—occurring by the mere speaking of a word and the exercise of his will—the return of the dead to life, the fear of the demons, his power over tempests, his walking on the sea . . . his disregard for food as long as he wished, his abundant banquets in the wilderness. . . . But how can we narrate one by one the gospel miracles?

—Gregory of Nyssa, *Catechetical Oration* 23

As many as are led by the Spirit of God are children of God" [Rom 8:14], but by grace, not by nature. For there is only one Son of God by nature, who in his compassion became the Son of Man for our sakes, so that we who are by nature children of men might become children of God through his grace. He who remains unchangeable received our nature, whereby he took us to himself and, holding on to his divinity, he participated in our infirmities. This was so that we who are mortal sinners, by being changed into something better, might participate in his immortality and righteousness, and preserve what he made good in our nature, which through his natural goodness is now filled with the supreme good.

—Augustine, *City of God* 21.15

Titles Applied to Christ

EARLY Christian authors delighted in playing on the various titles and names that they found applied to Christ in Scripture (as in Clement of Alexandria above).

When the good things in the gospel narratives are considered, it becomes clear that the apostles preached Jesus as the good news. Of course they are said to preach in the gospel that the resurrection is one good thing but in a way the resurrection is Jesus, for Jesus says, "I am the resurrection" [John 11:25]. . . .

Let no one marvel if we understand that Jesus is preached in the gospel under a plural name of good things. When we understand what all is involved in the names ascribed to the Son of God, then we perceive how many good things Jesus, who is preached in the gospel by those whose feet are beautiful [Isa 52:7], is. One good is life, and Jesus is "Life." Another good is "Light of the World" [John 8:12], which is "the true light" and the "light of human beings" [John 1:9]. The Son of God is said to be all of these things. In addition to Life and Light, another good according to this conception is the "Truth." And a fourth beyond these is "the Way" that leads to the truth. Our Savior teaches us that he himself is all these things when he says, "I am the way, the truth, and the life" [John 14:6]. Is it not good to rise again and shake off the dust of mortality, attaining this from the Lord who is the Resurrection, for he said, "I am the resurrection" [John 11:25]?

Another good is "the Door" through which one enters into highest blessedness, and Christ says, "I am the door" [John 10:9]. Why must one speak of "Wisdom," of which it is said, "God created me at the beginning of his ways for his work" [Prov 8:22]? . . . The eighth good that is catalogued by us is "the Power of God," which is the Christ. Let us not be silent about "the Word," who is God after the Father of the universe. . . . Blessed are those who make progress and receive these good things from those whose feet are beautiful, namely those who preach them in the gospel. [After continuing in a similar vein, the remainder of the book (chapters 16–39 [42]) elaborates on Jesus as the Beginning, the Word, Light, Resurrection, the Way, the Truth, the Life, the Door, the Shepherd, the Anointed, the King, the Teacher, the Master, the Son, the Vine, the Bread, the First and Last, the Sword, the Servant, the Lamb, the Paraclete, the Expiation, Wisdom, Sanctification, Redemption, Righteousness, Demiurge, High Priest, the Rod, the Flower, the Stone, and the Logos.]

— Origen, *Commentary on John* 1.8–9 [10–11]

He is called "the Door" [John 10:7, 9], but do not take this name literally—as a wooden door—but as a spiritual, living Door who distinguishes among those who enter in. He is called "the Way" [John 14:6], not in the sense of a way that is walked on by feet but as one leads to the Father in heaven. He is called "the Sheep" [John 1:29], not an irrational sheep but one that cleanses the world of its sins through his precious blood, one that is led before the shearers and knows that he must be silent [Isa 53:7]. This Sheep is again called "the Shepherd" and says, "I am the Good Shepherd" [John 10:11]: a Sheep because of his humanity, a Shepherd because of the loving-kindness of his Godhead. . . . Again, he is called "a Lion" [Rev 5:5], not as a devourer of people but as indicating his royal, steadfast, and bold nature; he is called a Lion in opposition to the lion who is our adversary, who roars and seeks to devour those who have been deceived [1 Pet 5:8]. . . . He is called "the Stone," not a lifeless stone cut out by human hands but "a chief cornerstone," about whom it is said, "whoever believes shall not be put to shame" [1 Pet 2:4–6].

He is called "the Christ" [anointed], not in the sense of having been anointed by human hands but anointed from eternity to his high priesthood by the Father on behalf of humanity. He is called "the Dead," not as one who remains among the dead—as all in Hades do—but as the only one who is "free among the dead" [Greek, Ps 87 [88]:5]. He is called "Son of Man," not as each of us who is born from the earth but as the one who comes upon the clouds to "judge both the living and the dead" [Matt 24:30; John 5:27; 2 Tim 4:1]. He is called "Lord," not improperly as those who are so called among people but as one who possesses natural and eternal lordship. He is called "Jesus," being well named because of his salutary healing [Matt 1:21]. He is called "Son," not as one who is advanced by adoption but as one who has been begotten by nature. . . . The faith provides you protection beforehand, rightly saying, "In one Lord, Jesus Christ," for even if the titles are many they have but one subject.

—Cyril of Jerusalem, *Catechetical Lectures* 10.3–4

Christ's authority over all things is made evident by the title of kingship. His purity and freedom from all passion and evil is signified by the names for virtue, each being understood as referring to what is morally the best. Christ is—and is said to be—"righteousness" itself [Heb 7:2], "wisdom and power" [1 Cor 1:24], "truth" [John 14:6], "goodness" [cf. John 7:12], "life" [John 14:6], "salvation" [Acts 4:12], "incorruptibility," "unchangeableness," and "immutability."

—Gregory of Nyssa, *On the Christian Profession*

Christ as Teacher and Example

The preexistent Savior recently appeared; he who is in the One who exists, because "The Word was with God" [John 1:1], has appeared. The

Word in whom all things were created appeared as Teacher. As Creator, he gave life at the beginning, in the act of creation. As Teacher, he appeared and taught us to live well so that, as God, he might afterward lead us to live eternally.

—Clement of Alexandria, *Exhortation* 1

Human beings who become famous rarely attain fame for many things at the same time. . . . But Jesus is amazing—in addition to other things—for his wisdom, his works of power, and his ability to rule. For he persuaded people not as a tyrant persuades—that is, to withdraw with him from their laws—nor as a robber arms his followers against others, nor as a rich person gives to his clients, nor as one of those who are known as blameworthy. Rather, as a teacher of the word, he persuaded us about the God of the universe and how to worship him, and about all moral conduct, which can make anyone who lives according to the God who is over all become like him.

—Origen, *Against Celsus* 1.30

Nothing out of place was ever undertaken by Jesus, who is exhibited to human beings as the example of how they must live and how they must die for godliness, even if we do not consider the benefit to the whole world that came when he died on behalf of humanity.

—Origen, *Against Celsus* 2.16

The Christ Who Changes Lives

ON THE claim that Christ and his teachings change the conduct of human beings see Chapter III under Change and below, under the Truth of Christianity.

We ourselves say that the whole inhabited world of human beings contains the work of Jesus. In it dwell the churches of God through Jesus, churches made up of those who have changed from innumerable evils. And indeed the name of Jesus still removes disturbances, demons, and diseases from people's minds. It produces marvelous gentleness, dignified character, love for humanity, and the greatest goodness and clemency—that is, in those whose Christianity is not a pretense in order to obtain food or other human needs but who genuinely accept the word concerning God, Christ, and the coming judgment.

—Origen, *Against Celsus* 1.67

CELSUS claimed that Jesus worked his miracles by magic. Origen's reply appealed to Jesus' conduct as a teacher and example, as well as to the reformation of life he effected.

There would be a likeness [between magicians and Jesus] if Celsus had demonstrated Jesus' similarity to those who use the magical arts. But there is not a single magician who, through the things he does, calls on those who watch him to reform their character and trains in the fear of God those who are amazed at what they see, or who attempts to persuade those who are looking on to live as people who will be judged by God. The magicians do none of these things, because they are not able. Neither do they desire to be engaged in the correction of human beings, inasmuch as they themselves are full of the most shameful and notorious sins. Since Jesus, through the wonders he did, called on those who witnessed his deeds to reform their characters, is it not reasonable that he offered himself as an example of the most excellent life, not only to his genuine disciples but also to others? He did this so that his disciples might be influenced to teach people according to the will of God, and so that the others—after they were more fully taught from the word, from his character, and from his wonders how they must live—might do everything with an eye toward pleasing God, who is over all. If the life of Jesus was like this, how can anyone reasonably compare him to magicians and not believe in accordance with the proclamation that he is God manifest in a human body, in order to do good to the human race?

—Origen, *Against Celsus* 1.68

The power to command the winds and calm the force of the sea with a word lay within the power of no one except the One through whom all things came into existence [1 Cor 8:6], including the sea itself and the winds. Also, the teaching that calls for the love of the Creator, which is in agreement with the law and the prophets [Matt 23:37], restrains human impulses and transforms character according to godliness. To those who are able to see, what else can this mean except that the One who accomplished such things was "truly the Son of God" [Matt 14:33]?

—Origen, *Commentary on Matthew* 12.2

The Holy Spirit

The Activities of the Holy Spirit

The third article [of our faith] is the Holy Spirit, through whom the prophets prophesied and the patriarchs were taught about God, and the just were led in the path of justice, and who "in the end of times" [Acts 2:16–17] has been poured forth in a new manner upon humanity over all the earth, renewing man to God.[1]

—Irenaeus, *Demonstration of the Apostolic Preaching* 6

What then are the Paraclete's [John 14:16–17] administrative functions? Are they not these: the direction of discipline, the revelation of the Scriptures, the reformation of the intellect, the promotion of better things?

—Tertullian, *On the Veiling of Virgins* 1.5

In the following passage, Origen uses language that reflects a functional view of the Holy Spirit, but also language which later orthodoxy found unacceptable; the passage leads into a quotation of 1 Cor 12:4–6.

We who are persuaded that there are three hypostases—the Father, the Son, and the Holy Spirit—and believe that nothing is unbegotten except the Father, accept as more godly and true that all things came into being through the Word, and that the Holy Spirit is more worthy of honor and is first in order of all the things that the Father brought into existence through Christ. . . . I think the Holy Spirit—if I may speak in this way—supplies the material content for the gifts from God, which those who are called holy because of the Spirit and their participation in him receive; for the material content of the gifts we have named is worked from God and is ministered by Christ, but exists according to the Holy Spirit.

—Origen, *Commentary on John* 10 [6]

The following passage is the most elaborate description of the Holy Spirit's work that we have from the first three centuries.

He who was in the prophets and apostles is therefore one and the same Spirit, except that in the prophets he was occasionally present and in the apostles was always present. . . . It is the Spirit who places prophets in the church, instructs teachers, directs tongues, grants powers and healings, does wonderful works, offers discernment of spirits, affords powers of government, suggests counsels, and orders and arranges whatever other gifts there are of charismata, thus bringing the Lord's church everywhere and in all things to perfection and completion. . . . The Spirit is the one who effects from water the second birth as a kind of seed of divine generation and a consecration of a heavenly nativity, the pledge of a promised inheritance, and—as it were—a kind of written certificate of eternal salvation; he makes us a temple of God and builds us as his house. . . . He is an inhabitant who is given to our bodies to effect their holiness. He is the one who, working in us for eternity, leads our bodies to the resurrection of immortality, accustoming them to union with heavenly power and association with his divine eternity. . . . It is he who restrains insatiable desires, controls immoderate lusts, quenches unlawful fires, overcomes reckless impulses, rejects drunkenness, repels avarice, drives away luxurious wild partying, binds with love, joins affections together, repels sects, expounds the rule of truth, overthrows heretics, drives out the wicked, and guards the Gospels.

—Novatian, *On the Trinity* 29

The Holy Spirit's coming is gentle; the perception of him is fragrant; his burden most easy; flashing rays of light and knowledge precede his coming. . . . He comes to save, to heal, to teach, to admonish, to strengthen, to exhort, to enlighten the mind: first he enlightens the mind of the one who receives him, then others also through that one. . . .

He works in each person in a way that is suitable. Being present in our midst, he observes the habits of each of us, our reasoning, conscience, and what we say and think. . . . If anyone proves to be unworthy of his grace on account of blindness, we should not blame the Spirit but our own unbelief.

—Cyril of Jerusalem, *Catechetical*
Lectures 16.16, 22

The Holy Spirit was present with all things at the creation; those things were not brought to completion by their own achievement but were complete at the creation itself, since the Holy Spirit introduced his own grace for the completion and perfection of their substance.

Who will deny that it was through the grace of the Spirit that the dispensations in regard to humanity came about, according to the goodness of God and through our great God and Savior Jesus Christ? If we examine older times, there are the blessings of the patriarchs, the help provided through the giving of the Law, the types, the prophecies, the courageous acts in war, the signs wrought by righteous people. If we consider the dispensations pertaining to the coming of the Lord in the flesh, all of these things were through the Spirit. First, he was present within the very flesh of the Lord, becoming his anointing and inseparably present with him. . . . Is not the ordering of the church clearly and incontestably effected by the Spirit? . . . [1 Cor 12:28]. This ordering is in accordance with the distribution of gifts from the Spirit.

—Basil of Caesarea, On the Holy
Spirit 16.38–39

The Indwelling of the Holy Spirit

God always imparts his own Spirit to those who are capable of participating in him. The Spirit comes into those who are worthy, but not by way of division and separation.

—Origen, Against Celsus 6.70

THE PRECEDING selection by Origen states a principle. In fact, there is a difference, he affirmed, between the time before Christ, when the Spirit was given only to certain persons, and after Christ's ascension, when the gift of the Spirit became available to all. Compare the following statement to the citation from *First Principles* 1.3.5, quoted above under The Trinity.

Before that time [Christ's ascension] the gift of the Holy Spirit was bestowed only on prophets and a few others who happened to be deserving. But after the coming of salvation, it was written that the Scripture was fulfilled that was spoken by the prophet Joel: "It shall come to pass in the last days that I will pour out my spirit upon all flesh and they shall prophesy" [Acts 2:16–17].

—Origen, First Principles 2.7.2

CHRISTIANS are the living temple of God, who lives in them by the Holy Spirit. In keeping with his own moral interests, as well as those of early Christianity in general, Origen stressed the need to be worthy of the indwelling Holy Spirit.

In general, all Christians endeavor to erect altars and statues that are not lifeless and without feelings, nor receptive of gluttonous demons who occupy lifeless objects, but receptive of the Spirit of God, who lives in images of virtue as in those who resemble the "image of the Creator" [Col 3:10]. So the Spirit of Christ rests on those—if I may call them such—who are conformed to him. . . .

We avoid building lifeless and dead temples to the Giver of all life. Let anyone who wishes hear how our bodies (we were taught) are a "temple of God" [1 Cor 6:19]; and "if anyone" through licentiousness or sin "destroys the temple of God" [1 Cor 3:16–17] he himself will be destroyed, because he has been truly ungodly toward the true temple.

—Origen, *Against Celsus* 8.18–19

Spiritual Beings

Angels of God

AFTER affirming that Christians confess "a God, a Son (his Word), and a Holy Spirit," Athenagoras speaks of other spiritual beings.

Even so we also understand that there are other powers that have authority over and through matter. One in particular is hostile to God. . . . God brought angels into existence to exercise providence over the things regulated by him so that he might have the all encompassing and general providence of the universe—he himself holding the supreme authority and power over all and administering the universe steadfastly, like a ship responding to the helm of wisdom—and that the angels who have been appointed over the parts might have providence over them. Just as human beings have free will with respect to virtue and evil . . . so also the angels. Some, with the free will given by God, remained in those things for which God created and ordered them; but others mocked both their rank and the constitution of their being.

—Athenagoras, *Plea for the Christians* 24

It has been passed on in the proclamation of the church that there are certain angels of God and good powers that are his ministers on behalf of the salvation of human beings. However, it was never clearly made known when these were created or what their nature is.

—Origen, *First Principles*, preface 10

Origen correctly understood Matt 18:10 (especially v. 6) as referring to believers and not to literal children.

Each believer, even the least in the church, is said to be assisted by an angel, who, the Savior testifies, always beholds the face of God the Father. And since this angel is certainly one with the person placed in his care, if the person is made unworthy through disobedience, then the angel of God is said to be taken from him. The part of the person that belongs to human nature, when it is separated from the divine part, is assigned a place among the unbelievers, because it did not faithfully observe the reminders made by the angel that God attached to it.

— Origen, *First Principles* 2.10.7

After quoting Heb 1:14, Origen continues:

We acknowledge that angels ascend, bearing the petitions of human beings to the purest heavenly regions of the universe and even to the purer regions above the heavens. Then they descend from there, bearing to each person according to his worth, something of the things ordered for them, in order to minister to those who receive kindness from God. We have learned from their work to call them angels but sometimes they are called "gods" in the divine Scriptures, because they are divine, but those who minister to us and bear the things of God to us are not appointed to receive reverence and worship instead of God. For every petition, prayer, intercession, and thanksgiving is sent up to the God who is over all through the High Priest who is over all angels, who is the living Word and God.

— Origen, *Against Celsus* 5.4

The Devil and His Angels

The devil, although created by God, was not created a devil.

Some say that the devil is not one of God's creatures. With respect to his being the devil, he is not a creature of God; but inasmuch as the devil exists, since he was made and there is no creator except our God, then he was created by God. Similarly, we say that a murderer is not a creature of God, not taking away the fact that he was made by God inasmuch as he is a human being. For we conclude that inasmuch as he happens to be a human being he

received his being from God, but we do not conclude that inasmuch as he is a
murderer he received this from God.

—Origen, *Commentary on John* 2.13 [7]

WHAT is true for the devil is true for demons.

According to us Christians, all demons were formerly not demons,
but they fell away from the good way. Demons are beings who fell away from
God. Therefore, whoever worships God must not serve demons.

—Origen, *Against Celsus* 7.69

IN THE following apocryphal account, Peter is speaking to Simon Magus.

I agree with you that there is a prince of evil, of whose origin the
Scriptures venture to say nothing either true or false. Nevertheless, let us pursue the various opinions as to how he came into existence—if indeed he came
into existence—and let us choose the one that is most reverential, since of all
the possible opinions we can be confident that the one that is most reverential can be attributed to God; and all the more so if, when all the suppositions
are removed, there still remains one view that is both adequate and less
dangerous. . . ."

—Pseudo-Clement, *Homilies* 19.8

PETER'S continued explanation in the Pseudo-Clementine *Homilies* that God
made the devil but made him good and is not to be blamed for his rebellion
and that sin as the cause of evil in the world is rather complicated, so we
quote the parallel passage from the *Recognitions*.

Why was that prince who rejoices in evil made?" . . . "God, foreseeing all things before the creation of the world and knowing that some of the
people who were to be would incline toward good but others indeed would
incline toward the opposite, associated those who would choose the good
with his own government and his own care, and named them his special inheritance. But he assigned those who indeed inclined toward evil to the rule
of those angels who—not because of their substance but because of their opposition—did not want to remain with God, since they were corrupted by

the vice of envy and pride. . . . This is the limit that was established: unless one first does the will of demons, the demons have no power over him." . . .

"Indeed God made the substance of all things; but if a rational mind that was made by God does not submit to the laws of its Creator and goes beyond the way of temperance prescribed for it, how is this a reflection on the Creator?"

—Pseudo-Clement, *Recognitions* 8.55, 56

Someone will say, "Why then was it necessary to make that prince who would turn the minds of human beings away from the true Prince?" Because—as I have said—God, who wished to prepare friends for his Son, did not wish them to be by nature unable to be anything else, but to be those who desired to be good through their own choice and will. . . . For nothing is worthy of praise if its nature will not permit you to turn away from it.

—Pseudo-Clement, *Recognitions* 9.4

JOHN of Damascus summed up orthodox thought on the origin of the devil and his angels.

The chief of the earthly order of angelic powers, who was entrusted by God with the guardianship of the earth, was not made to be evil by nature but was made good and for the good. From his Creator he did not have any trace of evil at all within him. But he did not sustain the brightness and honor that the Creator had given him, and by virtue of the choice of his own free will he was changed from what was in harmony with nature to what was against nature, and he was exalted and wished to rebel against God, who created him. He was the first to depart from the good and become evil. For evil is nothing other than the absence of good, just as darkness is the absence of light. . . . An innumerable multitude of angels who were subject to him were torn away along with him, followed him, and fell with him. Therefore, being of the same nature as the angels, they turned away through their own free choice from the good toward evil and became wicked.

Hence, they have no authority or strength against anyone except what God in his dispensation granted to them. . . . While they have the opportunity to attack humanity, they do not have the strength to compel anyone, for we have the power to receive or not to receive their attack. . . . One must know that what for human beings is death is for angels a fall. For after the fall no repentance is possible for them, just as after death there is no repentance for human beings.

—John of Damascus, *Orthodox Faith* 2.4

A brother made a request of Abba Poemen, "Give me a word." And he said to him, "When the kettle is on the fire, a fly or any other creature cannot touch it; but when it is cold, they sit on it. So it is for the [Christian]; as long as one abides in spiritual activities, the enemy cannot find a way to overthrow him."

—*Apophthegmata Patrum*, Alphabetical
Collection, Poemen # 111

Human Nature

God's Love for Human Beings

For God loved human beings, on account of whom he made the world, to whom he subordinated all things on the earth, to whom he gave reason and mind, whom alone he inclined to look above to himself, whom he made from his own image, to whom "he sent his one and only Son" [1 John 4:9], to whom he promised the kingdom in heaven and will give it to those who love him. When you have this full knowledge, consider how it will fill you with joy! How you will love the One who first loved you so much! By loving, you will become an imitator of his goodness. And do not marvel that a human being can become an imitator of God. It is possible, if God wills. To be happy does not mean that one dominates neighbors, wishes to have more than the weak, is wealthy, or has the power to compel those in need. We cannot imitate God in these ways, for these things are outside his majesty. Whoever takes up the burden of a neighbor, wishes to do good to someone who is worse off than he is, or supplies whatever things he has from God to those in need and becomes a god to those who receive—this one is an imitator of God.

— *Epistle to Diognetus* 10.1–6

The Lord, both as man and as God, helps and benefits everyone. As God, he forgives sins; as man, he instructs us not to sin. Therefore human beings are rightly beloved by God, since they are his creatures. Other things were created by his command alone, but human beings were created by the work of his own hands, and he breathed something of himself into them.

—Clement of Alexandria, *Instructor* 1.3.7

The Word shows his compassion and impartiality through all the saints, revealing and adapting himself, like a skillful physician, to whatever is advantageous for us and understanding the weakness of our humanity. He attempts to teach the ignorant; he returns those who err to his own true way. He is easily found by those who seek with faith; and to those who have pure eyes and holy hearts and who desire to knock at the door, he opens immediately. He casts away none of his servants as unworthy of the divine mysteries. He does not esteem the rich more highly than the poor, nor does he despise the poor because they are plain. He does not reproach barbarians, nor does he banish the eunuch as being one who is less than a human being. He does not hate the female on account of her disobedience at the beginning, nor does he treat the male as unworthy on account of his transgression. He wants everyone and desires to save everyone, wishing to restore everyone as children of God.

—Hippolytus, *On Christ and the Antichrist* 3

The Image of God

A human being is the image of God, that is, spirit; for God is spirit. . . . Now the image is not equal to the reality in every way. It is one thing to be like the reality but quite another to be the reality itself.

—Tertullian, *Against Marcion* 2.9.3

The soul was made in the image of God and came into being in his likeness, as divine Scripture teaches when it says (God speaking), "Let us make humanity in our image and likeness" [Gen 1:26]. Thus when the soul removes the filth of sin that covers it and guards only the pure image, and when this image is thoroughly brightened, then the soul beholds—as in a mirror—the Father's image, who is the Word, and in him considers the Father, whose image is the Savior.

—Athanasius, *Against the Pagans* 34

To the extent that we believe that whatever is good by nature is higher than our comprehension of it, so sorrow grows within us, because the good from which we are presently separated is so great and of such a kind that we lack the capacity to know it. Yet at one time we human beings were participants in that which is beyond all our powers of perception. The goodness that is above all thought was in our nature so that human beings seemed to be something else, since they were fashioned in the exact likeness according the image of the Prototype. . . . If this condition was once ours, should we not mourn at our misfortune when we view the contrast between our former blessedness and our present wretchedness? What was exalted has been brought low. What was made in the image of the heavenly was reduced to the earthly. What was appointed for royal rule was enslaved. What was created for immortality was destroyed by death. . . . What was without a master and possessed self-determination is now ruled by so many great evils that our tyrants cannot easily be counted. For whenever any of our passions can gain control, it becomes the master of the person whom it enslaves.

—Gregory of Nyssa, *On the Beatitudes* 3

THE CHURCH fathers did not know Hebrew and so did not recognize the poetic parallelism found in Gen 1:26, thus they made a distinction between "image" and "likeness." The following statement reflects a long line of earlier explanations.

On the one hand, God formed the human body from the earth; and on the other hand, he gave the rational and intellectual soul through the inbreathing of his own life—this is what we mean by the divine image. For the phrase "in his image" signifies our intellect and free will and the phrase "in his likeness" signifies our likeness in virtue, as far as that is possible.

—John of Damascus, *Orthodox Faith* 2.12

The Soul

THE GREEK definition of God included the quality of being deathless, so even Christian writers used the language of "god" when referring to human immortality.

God breathed into his face and man became a living soul" [Gen 2:6–7]. Hence many people say the soul is immortal. . . .

By nature, a human being is neither mortal nor immortal. For if God made him immortal from the beginning, then he would have made him a god; again if he had made him mortal, God would seem to be the cause of his death. Therefore God made man neither immortal nor mortal but—as we have said above—capable of both, so that if he inclined toward immortal things by keeping the commandments of God, he would receive from him the reward of immortality and become a god; but if he turned toward the things of death by disobeying God, he would be the cause of his own death. For God made human beings free and possessing freedom of choice. When human beings obey God, he gives them life now through his own love for humanity and mercy, in place of the death that human beings earn for themselves through neglect and disobedience.

—Theophilus, *To Autolycus* 2.19; 27

Ꝺence it appears that the soul is not naturally immortal but is brought to the goal of immortality by the grace of God through faith, righteousness, and knowledge.

—Clement of Alexandria, *Hypotyposeis,*
on 1 Pet 1:9

WHILE not accepting Plato's view of the natural immortality of the soul, many Christian writers accepted Plato's three-fold division of the soul.

Ꜩhe soul consists of three parts. The first part is the intellect, which is the rational part, the inner person, and the ruler of the visible person; God leads this part. The second is the high-spirited part, since it is like wild beasts and resides close to passion. The third and appetitive part takes many forms. . . .

It is not then the appearance of the outward person but the soul that is to be beautified with the adornment of nobleness and goodness.

—Clement of Alexandria, *Instructor* 3.1.1; 3.2.4

TERTULLIAN, unlike most Christian thinkers, accepted the Stoic view of the soul as being something material, of a finer grade than other matter but material nonetheless.

Ꮤe have assigned, then, to the soul both freedom of the will (as we wrote above) and its dominion over the works of nature. . . . We define the soul as born from the breath of God, immortal, corporeal, having shape, simple in substance, intelligent in itself, working in various ways, having free will, subject to contingent circumstances, in its moods changeable, rational, exercising control, possessing intuition, overflowing out of one source.

—Tertullian, *On the Soul* 22

TERTULLIAN thought that both the soul and the body derived from one's parents; hence body and soul come into existence simultaneously. Others who said that each soul was created also believed in the simultaneous origin of soul and body.

Indeed we say that both body and soul are conceived, formed, and brought to completion simultaneously, as well as born together, and not a moment intervenes in their conception that would allow them to be placed in chronological order. . . . Moreover, we recognize that life begins with conception, because we claim that the soul also begins with conception; for where there is life there is also a soul.

—Tertullian, *On the Soul* 27

ANOTHER Latin author, Lactantius, spoke for the majority when he said that each soul was created by God rather than deriving from one's parents.

One may also pose the question whether the soul is produced from the father or from the mother, or indeed from both. . . . For none of these three opinions is true, since souls are produced neither from both parents nor from either one. A body may be born from bodies, since something is contributed from both parents; but a soul cannot be produced from souls, because nothing can depart from something thin and incomprehensible. . . . Nothing can be generated from mortals except what is mortal. . . . From this it is evident that souls are not given by parents but by one and the same God and Father of all, who alone holds the regulation and explanation of their birth, since he alone brings it about.

—Lactantius, *On the Workmanship of God* 19.1, 2, 3, 4

GOD HAS planted thoughts of immortality in human beings.

Given that the body by nature is mortal, how is it that a person reasons about immortal things and often, where virtue demands it, risks death? Since the body lasts for only a time, how does a person imagine things that are eternal, so as to despise what lies before him and desire what lies beyond? The body cannot spontaneously have such thoughts about itself, nor can it think about things that are external to it. For it is mortal and lasts but for a time. It follows that something that thinks about things that are opposed to the body and against its nature must be distinct from the body in kind. What then can this be except a rational and immortal soul?

—Athanasius, *Against the Pagans* 32.1

And because the body is mortal, its senses also have mortal things as their objects; in the same way, since the soul contemplates and beholds immortal things, it follows that it is immortal and lives forever. The soul reasons about and thinks about things immortal and eternal, because it is itself immortal. For just as the body is mortal and its senses perceive mortal things, so it is necessary for the soul to be immortal and to live forever since it contemplates and reasons about immortal things. For thoughts and contemplations about immortality never cease from abiding in the soul, and they become fuel in it for the assurance of immortality. This then is why the soul has the capacity for contemplating God and is its own way to God, since it receives not from without but from within itself knowledge and apprehension of the Word of God.

—Athanasius, *Against the Pagans* 33.4

GOD MADE us for communion with him. The capacity for this communion increases with the reception of divine blessings. Gregory of Nyssa's sister, Macrina, explained this to him as follows:

The Wisdom that established the universe fashioned souls to be like receptacles with free wills, as vessels for the very purpose of being capable of receiving his blessings. They become continually larger by the addition of what he pours into them. Participation in divine goodness is such that it makes the one into whom it is poured larger and capable of receiving even more.

—Gregory of Nyssa, *On the Soul and
the Resurrection*

Reason

Human beings, who are truly endowed with reason and in this respect similar to God and who are made free in their will, having power over themselves, cause themselves to become sometimes wheat and sometimes chaff [Matt 3:11]. Therefore a human being is justly condemned for this reason: although he was made a rational being, he lost true reason and lives irrationally, opposed to the righteousness of God.

—Irenaeus, *Against Heresies* 4.4.3

It is the nature of the eyes only to see, of the ears to hear, of the mouth to taste, of the nose to detect odors, and of the hands to touch. But things a person ought to see, hear, touch, taste, and smell are no longer a matter of the senses; these are the business of the soul and its mind to discern. For instance, the hand can take hold of a sword blade and the mouth can taste poison, but neither knows that these are harmful unless the mind discerns.

—Athanasius, *Against the Pagans* 31.3

REASON has limits; faith is superior. Revelation guides the right use of reason. The greatest ignorance lies in thinking that one knows more than one does.

If in your reasoning you have passed through the air and whatever pertains to the air, reach with me now to heaven and heavenly things. Let faith rather than reason lead us, if perhaps you have learned the weakness of reason in matters nearer to you and have come to know reason by knowing the things that are beyond reason, so that you may not be altogether earthly or of the earth, being ignorant even of your own ignorance.

—Gregory of Nazianzus, *Oration* 28.28

The Desire for God

The mind burns with an inexpressible desire to know the reason for those things that we see God do. Without doubt, we believe that this desire, this longing, was placed in us by God. Just as our eyes naturally seek light and sight, and our body naturally desires food and drink, so our mind possesses a proper and natural desire to know the truth of God and the causes of things. We have received this desire from God not so that it should never be satisfied or never be capable of being satisfied; if the love of the truth were never to achieve part of its desires, then it might seem that this was placed in our minds by God in vain. Because of this, even in this life those who laboriously devote themselves to the study of piety and religion—however small may be the portion they grasp of the many and immense treasures of divine knowledge—receive much benefit by the very circumstance that their soul and mind are occupied in these pursuits and make progress in their eager desire. Moreover, because their minds are directed toward the study and love of the investigation of truth, they become better prepared to receive future instruction.

—Origen, *First Principles* 2.11.4

The sole distinction—or certainly the greatest distinction—between human beings and animals is religion.

—Lactantius, *Divine Institutes* 2.3.14

It is agreed upon, therefore, by the common consent of the whole human race that religion ought to be practiced. However, I must explain how the human race is in error on religious matters. God willed human nature to eagerly desire two things: religion and wisdom. But human beings make mistakes in this regard, because they either undertake religion without wisdom or study wisdom alone and leave out religion, when one without the other cannot be true. Therefore, because they disregard the wisdom that teaches them that there cannot be many gods, they fall into a multiplicity of religions that are false; or they study a wisdom that is false, because they neglect the religion of the Supreme God, who is able to instruct them in the knowledge of the truth. People who have undertaken either of these courses follow a life that is devious and full of many errors, because human duty and all truth are included in these two inseparably united pursuits.

—Lactantius, *Divine Institutes* 3.11

The Equality of Human Beings

I believe that one heaven is common to all persons, and that the revolution of the sun and the moon and the order and arrangement of the stars are also held in common by us all, as is the share and benefit of day and night; so also the changes of the seasons, the rains, the fruits, and the living force of the air; and likewise the flowing rivers are a plentiful wealth to all; the earth is one and the same, the mother and the tomb from which we were taken and to which we shall return, none having a greater share than another. And further—above these—we have in common our reason, the law, the prophets, the very sufferings of Christ by which we were all without exception remade; we who partake of the same Adam, were deceived by the serpent, were put to death by sin, were saved again through the heavenly Adam and brought back by the tree of shame [the cross] to the tree of life, from whence we had fallen.

—Gregory of Nazianzus, *Oration* 33.9

Women

THE EQUALITY shared by all human beings applied to males and females alike. Much has been said in recent years about the negative attitudes toward women that were expressed by some early Christian authors. We include here a few positive statements as a way of bringing a measure of balance to the discussion and of maintaining the general thrust of this collection. This positive evaluation was typified in the treatment of Mary, who was viewed as reversing the disobedience of Eve.

And just as it was through a virgin who disobeyed that man was stricken and fell and died, so too it was through the virgin who obeyed the word of God that man resuscitated by life received life. For the Lord came to seek back the lost sheep, and it was man who was lost; and therefore he did not become some other formation, but he likewise, of her that was descended from Adam, preserved the likeness of formation; for Adam had necessarily to be restored in Christ, that mortality be absorbed in immortality, and Eve in Mary, that a virgin, become the advocate of a virgin, should undo and destroy virginal disobedience by virginal obedience.[2]

—Irenaeus, *Demonstration of the Apostolic Preaching* 33

We have been born of man and woman; children owe one debt to both of their parents.

. . . If you ask about the worst, the woman sinned—and so did Adam. The serpent deceived them both; it was not the case that one was weaker and the other stronger. But consider something better: Christ saves both by his passion. Was he made flesh for the man? He was made flesh also for the woman. Did he die for the man? The woman also is saved by his death. He is called the seed of David, and so perhaps you think the man is honored? But he is born of a virgin, and this is on behalf of women. Therefore he says that the two shall be one flesh [Gen 2:24], so the one flesh is to have equal honor.

—Gregory of Nazianzus, *Oration* 37.6–7

THE BLAME placed on Eve for her part in the first transgression is amply compensated by reference to the woman's role in the story of redemption, Mary Magdalene as well as the Virgin Mary.

Since, as the apostle says, "The woman, being deceived, was in transgression" [1 Tim 2:14] and her disobedience led the revolt against God, for this cause she became the first witness of the resurrection [John 20:1–18] that she might correct the outcome of her disobedience by her faith in the resurrection. And just as at the beginning she became a minister and adviser to her husband on behalf of the words of the serpent and brought into human life the beginning of evil and its consequences, so in ministering the words of Christ—who put to death the rebellious dragon—to his disciples she became humanity's guide to faith. It was fitting that the first sentence of death be annulled through her.

—Gregory of Nyssa, *Against Eunomius*
3.10.16 [12.1]

We understand that the virtue of man and woman is the same. For if there is one God for both, there is one Instructor for both, one church, one temperance, one sense of shame, a common nourishment, a united marriage, with respiration, sight, hearing, knowledge, hope, obedience, and love all the same. The life of men and women is common; they also have in common grace, salvation, virtue, and training. . . . Therefore men and women also share in common the name "human being."

—Clement of Alexandria, *Instructor* 1.4.10–11

EQUALITY in excellence means equality in responsibility. Martyrdom was a further expression of equality. It was within the context of martyrdom that Clement of Alexandria affirmed other elements of equality.

Every church is full of those—both men and chaste women—who have trained their whole lives for the death that creates life in Christ. It is possible for one who lives our manner of life, whether a barbarian, Greek, slave, old person, child, or woman, to practice philosophy without books. For self-control is common to all human beings who choose it. We acknowledge that each race has the same nature and possesses the same virtue. With regard to humanity, a woman does not possess one nature while a man manifests another; they have the same nature and so also the same virtue. If perhaps self-control, righteousness, and whatever follows these qualities are considered a man's virtue, then are men alone considered virtuous while women are licentious and unjust? It is improper even to suggest this! Therefore both men and women, both slave and free, are to cultivate self-control, righteousness, and every other virtue, since one and the same virtue pertains to the same nature. . . . Since there is sameness with regard to the soul, women will attain the same virtue. And since her body is distinctly different, she will bear children and care for the household. . . . Just as it is good for a man to die on behalf of virtue and freedom, so also for a woman. . . .

It is possible for men and women equally to share in perfection.
—Clement of Alexandria, *Miscellanies* 4.8, 19

ɧuman nature is divided into male and female, and both possess the freedom to choose between virtue and evil. For this reason the divine voice exemplified the virtuous life for each sex—Abraham for the men and Sarah for the women—so that each person might be directed by an appropriate example.
—Gregory of Nyssa, *Life of Moses* 1.12

God did not create the woman out of material that was different from that of the man. He took the elements to create her from the man. He did this so that the woman would not take a direction opposed to the man, thinking that she had a different nature. Moreover, God lays down the same laws for men and women, because the difference between them lies only in their bodily forms, not in the soul. A woman is endowed with reason just as a man is, and she has the ability to understand, knowing as well as a man what ought to be done, what to avoid, and what to look for. There are times when women are better than men at seeing what is beneficial, and they are good advisers. Both men and women must have access to the divine temples, and the law does not allow men to share in the divine mysteries and forbid this to women, but it commands that women be initiated into and participate in the sacred rites equally with men. Since the struggle for virtue is common to both, the prizes are set before women as well as men.
—Theodoret, *Cure of Pagan Diseases* 5.56–57

INSTRUCTIONS to women about their conduct often sound very similar to general Christian instruction.

Propriety in dress, watchfulness when among men, moderation in food, simplicity in the acquisition of necessities—all of these things are small when merely mentioned, but experience has taught us that their achievement requires great struggle. We can add perfection in humility so as not even to remember ancestral distinctions, nor to be boastful of any natural advantages in body or mind, nor to make other people's opinions of us a basis for pride and exaltation—all these things characterize a life lived according to the gospel. So also constant self-control, diligence in prayer, sympathetic brotherly love, sharing with the needy, subjugation of thought, contrition of heart, wholesome faith, and equanimity in despondency, never letting our minds forget the terrible and inevitable tribunal. It is to that judgment that we are all hastening; but few remember this or exert themselves with an eye toward its outcome.

—Basil of Caesarea, *Letters* 173, to Theodora

THE DESCRIPTION of his mother Nonna by Gregory of Nazianzus constitutes a tribute to the Christian ideal of womanhood.

She is a woman who—while others were being honored and extolled for their natural or artificial beauty—acknowledged but one kind of beauty: the beauty of the soul and, as far as possible, its preservation and restoration to the divine image. She has rejected pigments and devices for adornment as being more fitting for women of the stage. She acknowledged one true, noble birth: piety, and the knowledge of where we came from and where we are going. She knew that the one safe and inviolable form of wealth consists in stripping oneself of wealth for God and the poor, and especially for those of our own kin who are unfortunate. She thought that help that went only so far as meeting necessity was a reminder and not a relief from distress; more liberal beneficence brings stable honor and perfect consolation. Some women excel in thrifty management and others in piety, but she—difficult as it is to attain both—surpassed them all in both. . . .

What time or place for prayer ever escaped her? She was drawn to these things before all other things in the day; . . . Who reduced the flesh by more constant fasting and vigil? Or stood like a pillar at the singing of psalms throughout the night and day? . . . Who was a better patron of the orphan and widow? Who assisted mourners to alleviate their misfortunes as much as she did? . . . Her voice was never heard in the holy assemblies or places, except in the necessary liturgical words of the service.

—Gregory of Nazianzus, *Oration* 18.8–9

GREGORY of Nazianzus also left a moving tribute to his sister Gorgonia, in his oration at her funeral.

Who did more to open her house graciously and bountifully to those who live according to God? And—what is greater—who extended such modest and godly greetings in welcome? Further, who showed a more resolute mind in suffering? Who had a soul more sympathetic to those in distress?

Whose hand was more liberal to those in need? . . . She was the eye of the blind, the foot of the lame, the mother of orphans. . . . And best of all, what she appeared to be was not more than the truth—she cultivated well her piety in secret before the One who sees secret things. . . . The sole wealth she left to her children was her example to be imitated and the honor for her good deeds.

. . . She was considered to be more manly than the noblest of men and all women because of her prudent intensity in chanting the Psalms, her converse with the divine oracles—either in explaining them or in their timely recollection—the bending of her knees, which had grown hard and almost been planted in the ground, her tears that cleansed her stains with a broken heart and spirit of humility, her prayer that rose heavenward, and her un-wandering mind that was elevated high above the earth. In all these things— or in any one of them—who among men or women can boast of sur-passing her? . . .

O womanly nature, overcoming the manly in the common struggle for salvation and demonstrating that male and female are distinctions of body and not of soul!

— Gregory of Nazianzus, *Oration* 8.12, 13, 14

JEROME had contact with a number of aristocratic women in Rome, and he left records of their virtues. One who was notable, whose intellectual abilities matched those of Jerome himself, was Marcella, whom he described in a let-ter he wrote to another woman, their mutual friend Principia.

Our widow had clothing that would keep out the cold and not ex-pose her figure. Of gold, she rejected even a ring for sealing, preferring to store away her money in the stomachs of the needy rather than in purses. . . .

Her eagerness for the divine Scriptures was incredible. . . . This meditation in the law [Pss 119:11; 1:2 have been cited] was not a repetition of the written words . . . but of action. . . . Marcella fasted, but in moderation. . . .

We judge virtues not by sex but by character. . . .

Since at that time my name was esteemed by some for the study of the Scriptures, she never came to see me that she did not ask me some ques-tion about the Scriptures, nor would she at once acquiesce to my explanation but—on the contrary—proposed questions, not to be contentious but to learn the answers to those objections she thought might be made to my state-ments. What virtue, what intellect, what holiness, what purity I found in her

I am afraid to say. . . . I will say only that whatever was brought together in me through long study and constant meditation, so that it became part of my nature, this she tasted, learned, and made her own. Consequently after my departure from Rome, if any dispute arose about any testimony of Scripture, they made their way to her to settle it. . . .

When the soldiers entered [at the taking of Rome by the Goths in 410], . . . she thanked God that he had preserved you untouched, in answer to her prayer. She said that she was also thankful that the capture of the city had not made her poor, but had found her so.

—Jerome, *Letters* 127.3, 4, 5, 7, 13

The Church

If the prayer of one or two has such power [Matt 18:19–20], how much more the prayer of the bishop and the whole church! The person who does not come to the assembly shows arrogance, already having separated himself.

—Ignatius, *Ephesians* 5.2–3

WHEN Ignatius wrote about withdrawing from the assembly of the church, he had in mind schismatics who withdrew on doctrinal grounds. In contrast, the *Didascalia* spoke of the indifference of church members.

Now when you teach, command and warn the people to be constant in assembling in the church and not to withdraw themselves but always to assemble, lest anyone diminish the church by not assembling and cause the body of Christ to be short of a member. . . . Seeing that you have Christ for your head . . . be not then neglectful of yourselves and deprive not our Savior of his members, and do not rend and scatter his body. And make not your worldly affairs of more account than the word of God; but on the Lord's Day leave everything and run eagerly to your church, for she is your glory. . . . Be constant therefore in coming together with the faithful who are being saved in your mother the church, the living and lifegiving.[3]

—*Didascalia* 13

If the word "sacred" is received in a twofold way—both for God himself and for what is prepared in his honor—should we not properly say that the church is sacred, since it came into being for the honor of God according to holy knowledge, is exceedingly worthy of God and not prepared by craftsman's art, and is not embellished by the hand of a vagabond but made into a temple by the will of God? For I do not call the church a place but the assembly of the elect.

—Clement of Alexandria, *Miscellanies* 7.5

All the prophets declared concerning Christ that a day would come when, having been born with a body of the race of David, he would build an eternal temple for God—which is called the church—and assemble all nations to the true religion of God. This is the faithful house, the everlasting temple; and if anyone has not sacrificed in it, he will not have the reward of immortality. Since Christ was the builder of this great and eternal temple, he must also hold an everlasting priesthood in it; and only through him who built it can we approach the temple and enter into sight of God.

—Lactantius, *Divine Institutes* 4.14.1–3

The Holy Spirit builds the church, which is indeed the temple, home, and city of God.

—Tertullian, *Against Marcion* 3.23.2

The apostles founded churches in every city. From these, the other churches subsequently derived the tradition of the faith and the seeds of doctrine, and are deriving them daily so that they may become churches. On this account they themselves are also regarded as apostolic, since they are the offspring of apostolic churches. . . . Therefore, although there are so many of them and they are so great, the churches are the one, earliest church that was founded by the apostles, from which they all come. In this way—insofar as they are all one—all are early and apostolic. The proof of their unity is their fellowship in peace, their title of brotherhood, and their common bond of hospitality. . . .

It is manifest that all doctrine that agrees with the apostolic and original mother churches of the faith must be regarded as truth, containing without doubt what the churches received from the apostles, the apostles from Christ, and Christ from God. On the other hand, all doctrine that savors of being contrary to the truth of the churches, apostles, Christ, and God must be presumed to be false. . . .

We hold communion with the apostolic churches because our doctrines are not in any way different.

—Tertullian, *Prescription against
Heretics* 20–22

HIPPOLYTUS gave an early formulation of the comparison of the church with a ship. His starting point was the likeness of a mast on a sailing vessel to a cross.

The world is the sea on which the church, like a ship, is tossed about in the deep but not destroyed, for she has her skilled Pilot, who is Christ. And in her midst she also bears the trophy over death, the cross of the Lord. Her prow is the East, her stern is the West, and her hold is the South. Her tillers are the two Testaments, and the ropes that stretch around her are the love of Christ that binds the church tightly together. The fishing net is the laver of regeneration, which renews believers. . . . Like the wind, the Spirit from heaven is present, by whom believers are sealed for God. Iron anchors accompany her, which are the holy commandments of Christ himself—strong as iron. She has sailors on the right and on the left, lieutenants like holy angels by whom the church is always supported and guarded. Her ladder that leads up high into the sail yard signifies the image of the passion of Christ that draws the faithful to ascend toward heaven. And the top sails of the sail yard, which are most highly praised, are the company of prophets, martyrs, and apostles who rest in the kingdom of Christ.

—Hippolytus, *On Christ and Antichrist* 59

ORIGEN'S comparison of the church to the tabernacle, based on the instructions for building the tabernacle in Exod 26, contains a significant passage on the holiness of the church and its teachings.

We know without a doubt that the one who builds a sanctuary to the Lord in purity of heart and body will see God. Therefore let us all together—and each individually—build a sanctuary to the Lord. In a manner of speaking we all together build the church as a holy sanctuary "not having spot or wrinkle" [Eph 5:27].

—Origen, *Homilies on Exodus* 9.3

THE PRESENCE of hypocrites in the church has always been a problem, it seems, and an excuse advanced by doubters.

Although there seem to be tares in the church, nevertheless neither our faith nor our love ought to be hindered, causing us to withdraw from the church. We ought to labor in such a way that we become wheat, so that when the wheat begins to be gathered into the Lord's barns, we may receive the fruit of our work and labor [compare Matt 13:24–30, 36–43].

—Cyprian, *Letters* 54[50].3.1

The church is one, although widely spread abroad into a multitude through the increase of its fruitfulness. It is like the sun, which has many rays but the light is one; or like a tree, which has many branches but the strength is one, coming from its tenacious root; or like many rivers that flow from one source, the multiplicity appears diffused in the liberality of its overflowing abundance but unity is preserved in its origin. . . . Thus the church, suffused with the light of the Lord, sheds her rays throughout the whole world, yet it is one light that is everywhere suffused; the unity of the body is not separated. The abundance of her productivity spreads her branches over the whole earth. She widely expands her rivers that flow so liberally, yet her head and origin are one. She is one mother, abundant in the success of her fruitfulness: from her womb we are born, by her milk we are nourished, and by her spirit we are kept alive. . . .

"Where two or three are gathered together in my name, I am with them" [Matt 18:19–20]. He does not divide people from the church, since he himself built and made the church. But in rebuking the faithless for their discord and commending peace to the faithful by his word, he shows that he is with two or three who pray in unity rather than with a great many who disagree, and that more can be obtained by the petition made in concord by a few than by the discordant prayer of many.

—Cyprian, *On the Unity of the Church* 5; 12

THE CONTEXT of the following selection is Basil's discussion of the gathering together of the waters on the third day of creation.

If the sea is beautiful and worthy of divine praise, then how much more beautiful is the gathering of the church, where the blended voices of men, women, and children are sent up in prayers to God like a wave carried to the shore. A profound calm preserves this church unmoved, while evil spirits are unable to disturb it with heretical words. Be worthy, then, of the approbation of the Lord by preserving this good order in a most seemly manner in our Lord Jesus Christ, to whom be glory and power for ever and ever. Amen.

—Basil of Caesarea, *Hexaemeron* 4.7

IT IS natural to look back to earlier days as being a time of greater faithfulness. In the fourth century Basil looked back to the times of persecution as being spiritually better for the church than his own time, when there were many lukewarm members and the bitter conflicts of theological debate.

When I read your letter again and again,] I thought that we were back in the old times, when God's churches flourished, rooted in the faith and united in love, all the different members being in harmony as if one body. Then the persecutors were manifest, and with them the persecuted. The people grew more numerous by being fought against. The blood of the martyrs watered the churches and nourished many more contestants for godliness, who followed after them, stripping themselves for the struggle with the zeal of their predecessors. At that time we Christians kept the peace with one another that the Lord left with us, but now not a single trace is left us, so harshly have we driven it away from one another.

—Basil of Caesarea, *Letters* 164.1

The church of God is like a body: through some saints she performs miracles; through others she speaks the truth, through some she preserves virginity, through others she preserves marital chastity. Each performs his or her proper task, some this and others that, but they live side by side. What the soul is to the body of a person, the Holy Spirit is to the body of Christ, which is the church. The Holy Spirit does for the whole church what the soul does for every member of an individual's body. Look then and see what you ought to beware of, what you ought to observe, what you ought to fear. If it happens that any member of the human body—a hand, a finger, or a foot—is cut off, does the soul leave with what is cut off? While it is in the body, that part is alive; when it is cut off, it loses its life. It is like that with catholic Christians: they are alive only while in the body. If they become heretics and are cut off from the body, the Holy Spirit does not go with the amputated member.

—Augustine, *Sermons* 267.4

Leadership

A brother asked Abba Poemen, "Some brothers live with me; do you want me to give them orders?" The old man said to him, "No, above all do your own work; and if they want to live, they will observe for themselves." The brother said to him, "But they themselves, Father, want me to give them orders." The old man said to him, "No, be their example, not their legislator."

— *Apophthegmata Patrum,* Alphabetical
Collection, Poemen # 174

THE FOLLOWING selection describes Basil of Caesarea, one of the ablest leaders of the fourth-century church.

Seeing that tenderness makes for slackness and weakness, but severity makes for exasperation and audacity, he helped both kinds of people by showing the other quality. He mixed his resistance with gentleness, his tenderness with firmness. With a few people he had to use argument, but by his actions he was able to bring healing to many more. He did not capture people by artifice, but he won them to himself by his good will. He did not avail himself of political power, but he brought people over to his side by the moderate, not continuous, use of what he was able to do. . . . [This policy won over most people, and Basil ignored those whose ill nature was incurable, of whom the panegyrist says:] They were consumed by wearing themselves out, as rust depletes itself along with the iron on which it feeds.

— Gregory of Nazianzus, *Oration* 43.40

Pastoral Care

SPIRITUAL direction requires different treatment of different persons.

Just as the same medicine and food are not administered to all human bodies—but some receive one kind and some another, according to whether they are healthy or sick—so also souls should be taught and guided differently. . . . A word leads some; others are trained by examples. Some require goads; others, bridles. Some are sluggish and hard to motivate for the good, requiring a verbal blow to arouse them. Others are more fervent in spirit and have impulses that are difficult to hold in check, like thoroughbred colts that run far from the turning post; the word must improve them by restraining them and holding them back.

Praise benefits some; blame benefits others. Both should be spoken at the proper time, for if spoken at the wrong time or without reason, they result in harm. Encouragement corrects some; rebukes correct others. The same applies to those who are reproved in public and those who are admonished in private. For some despise private admonitions but are brought to their senses when censured by many. Others act shamelessly when censure is given openly but are receptive to secret rebuke or instruction, rendering ready obedience to sympathy.

—Gregory of Nazianzus, *Oration* 2.30–31

ONE OF the great masters of pastoral care, whose work has continued to guide pastors through the centuries, is Gregory the Great.

The guidance of souls is the art of arts. . . .

Often, when many things that cause admiration in subordinates are available and can be done, one's mind elevates itself in thought and fully brings on itself the wrath of the judge, even though it does not break forth in outward works of iniquity. The one who judges is within and what is judged is within. When, therefore, we do wrong in heart, what we do within ourselves may be hidden to others, but we nevertheless sin before the judge who is the witness. . . .

There are some who possess exceptional gifts of virtue and are exalted with great gifts for helping others grow, and who are diligent in chastity, strong in abstinence, filled with the banquets of doctrine, humble in patient long-suffering, upright in lordly courage, merciful in the grace of piety, strict in the severity of justice. If these are called to the eminence of government and refuse to undertake it, then they deprive themselves of these very gifts and more, which they received not for themselves alone but also for others . . . [John 15:16–17]. If therefore concern for feeding the sheep is the thing that testifies to one's love for Christ, then whoever is strong in virtues and refuses to feed the flock of God is convicted of not loving the Chief Shepherd. . . .

Therefore, if someone seeks the glory of honor and not a ministry of good work, he bears witness against himself that he does not desire the episcopate [1 Tim 3:1]. . . .

The conduct of a president should so far surpass the conduct of the people as the life of a shepherd is supposed to differ from the flock. . . . It is therefore necessary that he be pure in mind, exceptional in conduct, discreet in keeping silence, profitable in speech, a compassionate neighbor to each individual, exalted—above all—in contemplation, a humble associate of those who live well, upright in his zeal for justice against the vices of those who do wrong, not lessening his care for inward things when occupied with outward things, and not neglecting to provide for outward things when concerned about inward things.

—Gregory the Great, *Pastoral Rule* 1.1,
4, 5, 8; 2.1

Teaching

A teacher] gives himself on behalf of the church, on behalf of the pupils whom he has "begotten" [1 Cor 4:15] in faith; he serves as an example for those who are able to receive the highest activity of that Teacher, who loves both God and humanity, as a demonstration of the truth of his words, as an expression of love for the Lord. This person is not enslaved with fear but is true in word, patient in labor, unwilling to lie in spoken word; thus he always accomplishes what is without sin, since a lie—inasmuch as it is spoken with a certain deceit—is not an empty word but works evil. Therefore only a gnostic [i.e., truly spiritual] teacher testifies to the truth both in deed and word, for he always acts uprightly in all things—in his word, his act, and his very thoughts.

—Clement of Alexandria, *Miscellanies* 7.9.52

Amma Theodora said, "A teacher must be a stranger to the desire to rule, an alien to vainglory, far from pride, not deceived by flattery nor blinded by gifts, not overcome by the stomach nor controlled by anger. Rather, a teacher should be long-suffering, gentle, and as humble as possible; he should be approved and patient, provident and a lover of souls.

—*Apophthegmata Patrum,* Alphabetical
Collection, Theodora # 5

Syncleitica said, "It is dangerous for one to teach who has not been trained in the practical life. It is like someone who has an unsound house and receives guests; he will cause harm by the collapse of the dwelling. In the same way, those who have not first built themselves up destroy those who come to them. For they may summon them to salvation by their words, but by their evil conduct they injure even more those who follow them."

—*Apophthegmata Patrum,* Alphabetical
Collection, Syncleitica # 12

I know an inexperienced disciple who boasted to certain persons about the accomplishments of his teacher. He thought that by doing this he could gain glory for himself from another's fruit. Instead he acquired dishonor for himself, for everyone said to him, "And how did a good tree produce an unfruitful branch?"

—John Climacus, *Ladder of Paradise* 4

The Religious Calendar

ORIGEN responded to the charge made by the pagan critic Celsus that Christians did not participate in public feasts. After quoting Gal 4:10–11, he acknowledges that Christians observe certain days, but then he explains that the true spiritual significance of these days is that they are signs of daily devotion.

On the subject of observing days, if someone replies by pointing to the things we do on certain days—the Lord's Days, Preparation Days, Passover, or Pentecost—let it be said in response that the perfect Christian, who in word, deed, and thought always belongs to the Word of God (who is the Lord by nature), is always the Lord's; he keeps the Lord's Day every day. And the perfect Christian—who is always preparing to live the true life, abstains from the pleasures of human life that deceive the majority, does not foster the "mind of the flesh" [Rom 8:6] but "mortifies the body and brings it into subjection" [1 Cor 9:27]—is always observing Preparation Days. Again, the one who considers that "Christ our Passover was sacrificed" [1 Cor 5:7] and that it is necessary to keep the feast by eating the flesh of the Word, never ceases from keeping the Passover. Since Passover means "crossing over," this person is always crossing over from the affairs of this life to God in his thinking and in every word and every action, and he is eagerly hurrying toward the city of God. Moreover, the person who is able to say truly, "We are risen with Christ" [Col 2:12], and also, "He raised us with him and made us sit together in the heavenly places in Christ" [Eph 2:6], is always living in the season of Pentecost; this is especially true when, like the apostles of Jesus who "went up to the upper room" [Acts 1:13–14], this person spends time in supplication and prayer so as to become worthy of some measure of the tongue of fire from God and of "the rushing mighty wind" [Acts 2:2] from heaven, which is powerful both in abolishing the evil in human beings and the things that result from it.

—Origen, *Against Celsus* 8.22

THERE was a dispute in the second century over the date and manner of observing Easter. Although the basis of the dispute is different today, the Eastern and Western churches still have a different date for Easter. Irenaeus sought to make peace, with counsel that may still be relevant.

The controversy is not only about the day but also about the form of the fast itself [that preceded Easter Sunday]. Some think it is necessary to fast for one day, some for two days, others for more. Some count their day of fasting as forty hours, day and night. Such variety of observances did not originate in our own time but much earlier, when those who, without strictness it seems, maintained a simple and individual practice that they established for the future. Nonetheless all of these lived in peace and we also live in peace with one another, and the disagreement over the fast confirms our agreement in the faith.

—Irenaeus, cited in Eusebius, *Church History* 5.24.12–13

THE BIRTH of Christ was probably observed on January 6 by Gregory of Nazianzus. He gives directions on how not to celebrate Christmas.

Let us not put wreaths on our porches, arrange dances, nor decorate the streets. Let us not feast the eyes nor charm the ears with pipe-playing. Let us not enfeeble the sense of smell, nor pander to the sense of taste, nor gratify touch. These are ordinary paths to evil and entrances for sin. Let us not be effeminate in clothing that is soft and flowing, whose beauty is useless, gleaming with gems and radiant with gold. But let our beauty be natural, without the artifice of false colors and not procured contrary to the image of God. Let us not be "in revelry and drunkenness," with which—I know—"sexual intercourse and licentiousness" [Rom 13:13] are closely connected. . . . Let us not attempt to excel one another in intemperance. In my thinking, every excess and whatever goes beyond need is intemperance. And we do these things while others, who are of the same clay and composition as we are, go hungry and in need!

—Gregory of Nazianzus, *Oration* 38.5

Revelation

God's Self-Revelation

KNOWLEDGE of God comes from revelation and must be received in faith. See also Knowledge of God in this chapter, and Chapter III under Grace.

No person saw or gained knowledge of God, but he made himself known. God made himself known through faith, by which alone one is permitted to see God. For God, the Master and Maker of all things, who created all things and set them in order, not only loves humanity but is also long-suffering. And so he always has been, is, and will be kind, good, without wrath, and true—and only God is Good.

— Epistle to Diognetus 8.5–8

THE SUPREME revelation is through Christ, God's Son and Word.

The Lord showed himself to his disciples as the Word who gives knowledge of the Father and . . . through whom God is known. . . . For no one is able to know the Father except by the Word of God, that is, by the Son who reveals him; nor is it possible to know the Son except by the good pleasure of the Father. . . . For this purpose the Father revealed the Son so that through him he might be manifested to all and might receive into incorruption and eternal rest those righteous ones who believe in him (indeed to believe in him is to do his will). . . . The Father therefore revealed himself to all by making his Word visible to all. And in turn the Word showed the Father and the Son to all, since he has been seen by all.

— Irenaeus, *Against Heresies* 4.6.1, 3, 5

Since by divine inspiration the truth is revealed to those of us who have received the mystery of true religion, and since we follow God, the teacher of wisdom and the guide to virtue, we call all people together to heavenly sustenance, without making any distinction with regard to sex or age.

— Lactantius, *Divine Institutes* 1.1.19

The Christian faith, which has been preached to all nations by his disciples in accordance with our Lord's command, is neither from human beings nor by them but by our Lord Jesus Christ himself, who is the Word, the Life, the Light, the Truth, God, Wisdom, and everything else that he is by nature. For this cause especially he was made in the likeness of humanity, sharing our nature. He was in our likeness in all things yet without sin. . . . So we do not subtract, change, or add anything to this faith, which was delivered to the apostles by God . . . for whatever is said that is not in exact accord with the truth is assuredly false.

— Gregory of Nyssa, *Against Eunomius* 2.1 [1, 3]

The Truth of Christianity

Could it have come to pass without the help of God that Jesus, wishing to spread his word and teaching in a few years, could have done this to such an extent that everywhere in our world not a few Greeks and barbarians, persons wise and persons without understanding, were so favorably disposed to his word that they contended on behalf of Christianity even unto death, rather than deny it (which no one is reported to have done for another doctrine)? . . . If the person who reasonably considers these things will agree that no improvement among human beings occurs without divine help, then how much more confidently—after comparing the former and later lives of many who have come over to his word, and after considering the acts of licentiousness, injustice, and greed that each was formerly engaged in—will that person declare this about Jesus. . . .

Anyone who examines the subject will see that Jesus attempted and accomplished something that surpasses human nature. For from the beginning, when everyone in the whole world opposed the spreading of his word—the kings at the time and the generals and governors under them, and almost everyone who was entrusted with authority, even the magistrates of cities, soldiers, and people—he still conquered, since it is the nature of the Word of God not to be hindered. And he became stronger than these adversaries and overcame all of Greece and most of the barbarian world, converting myriads of souls to his religion.

—Origen, *Against Celsus* 1.26; 27

Would any rational person say that a better way of life—one that daily lessens the number of evils—comes about through deceit?

I think the conduct of his disciples is clear and obvious: they devoted themselves to a teaching that endangered their very lives—which they would not have taught so strenuously if they had invented the resurrection of Jesus from the dead—and in addition, not only prepared others to despise death but also first did so themselves.

—Origen, *Against Celsus* 2.50, 56

Scripture

THERE were advantages to the revelation being recorded in Scripture.

So that we might more fully and more definitely approach God and his attitudes and will, God added a literary document, so that whoever wishes may search for God, and searching may find, and finding may believe, and believing may serve him.

—Tertullian, *Apology* 18.1

THE READING of Scripture was important in Christian assemblies, and the Scriptures that were read were the basis of the teachings given. Tertullian describes what the Scriptures meant to Christians.

We meet together in order to read the sacred texts, if the nature of the times compels us to warn about or recognize any present concern. In any case, with the holy words we feed our faith, we arouse our hope, we confirm our confidence. We strengthen the instruction of the precepts even more by inculcating them.

—Tertullian, *Apology* 39

There is, brothers and sisters, one God, whom we know in no other way than from the holy Scriptures. For just as a person who wishes to gain experience in the wisdom of this world attains this only by becoming familiar with the dogmas of philosophers, so all of us who wish to gain experience in godliness gain this from no other source than the oracles of God. Let us pay attention then to whatever the divine Scriptures proclaim; and whatever they teach, let us learn.

—Hippolytus, *Against Noetus* 9

THE FOLLOWING passage specifically speaks about the books of the prophets.

We do not attempt to make any change in the words that were spoken of old by the prophets, but we make public their words that have been written and read them to those who are able to believe rightly. This benefits both parties: it benefits the one who speaks, by holding in memory and setting forth correctly the things that were previously stated; and it benefits those who hear by their attending with the mind to the things spoken . . . and receiving in faith what has been said.

—Hippolytus, *On Christ and the Antichrist* 2

ORIGEN, in preaching about the campsites in the wilderness wanderings of Israel (Num 33), draws the following lesson.

The true food for our rational nature is the word of God. . . . If we compare this food with food for the body, the word of God contains milk—that is, knowledge of the outward and simple teachings such as moral instruction, which is given to those entering into divine studies as rudiments of rational learning. When they read a passage from the divine books that is not obscure, they receive it readily. . . . Another person, upon reading the Gospels, the Apostle, or the Psalms accepts these readily and with joy, rejoicing to find there a remedy for weaknesses. But if the book of Numbers is read, especially the passage we have before us, no remedy for weakness nor anything for the salvation of the soul is there. . . . [Just as there are different foods for different animals and human beings of different ages], so also for rational nourishment. I speak of the divine books.

One should not criticize or reject passages of Scripture that appear to be more obscure, more difficult to understand, or that contain things that a beginner, a child, or one who is weak in understanding cannot use, or because in their view the words seem to have no utility and contribute nothing to salvation. . . . All of these texts are words of God, and their diversity offers nourishment that is adapted to the capacity of our souls. . . . If we pay careful attention, for example, to the reading of the Gospel or the teaching of the Apostle in those places where we take delight and find nourishment that is suitable and pleasing, we will also find hidden secrets by studying and going deeper into the precepts of the Lord. If we reject and avoid what seems to be obscure and difficult, and keep to the principle of rejecting what is obscure, then we must abandon even those passages that inspire the most confidence in us, for they contain much of the same difficulty and obscurity. These passages do, however, contain many clear and simple words that are capable of edifying the hearer, even one of little intelligence. . . . But we must not say that the words of the Holy Spirit contain anything useless or superfluous, even if they appear to contain certain obscurities. Instead, we ought to turn, . . . [and] ask God about their meaning . . . so that we may pass from weakness to strength, from childhood to maturity.
—Origen, *Homilies on Numbers* 27.1

According to our faith in the doctrine that we hold with certainty to be divinely inspired, we assuredly believe that it is not possible to set forth and display this higher and more divine reason concerning the Son of God in any other way than by means of the Scriptures alone that were inspired by the Holy

Spirit—that is, the Gospels and Apostolic writings, and the Law and the Prophets—as Christ himself affirmed. . . . Although no one can speak in a way that is worthy of God the Father, it is nevertheless possible to grasp some knowledge of him from the visible creation and from those things that the human mind naturally feels; and in addition, this knowledge can be confirmed from the holy Scriptures. [Knowledge of the Son of God and the Holy Spirit, he proceeds to say, comes only from the Old and New Testaments.]

—Origen, *First Principles* 1.3.1

THE CONVICTION that the Scriptures manifest internal harmony and consistency flowed from belief in the divine inspiration of Scripture.

I will not dare to think or say [that the Scriptures are contradictory or in error], but if some Scripture is brought forward that has an alleged contradiction, I will for myself rather confess that I do not understand the things said; and I will strive to persuade those who assume that the Scriptures are contradictory rather to think the same as I do.

—Justin Martyr, *Dialogue* 65.2

IRENAEUS affirmed the basic clarity of Scripture, in spite of some difficulties.

The entire Scriptures, Prophets and Gospels, can be clearly, unambiguously, and harmoniously understood by everyone, even if everyone does not believe them. . . .

If, however, we cannot discover solutions to all of the things that we inquire about in the Scriptures, we should not then inquire about another God besides the One who is. For this is the greatest impiety. We ought to leave such things to the God who made us, knowing most certainly that the Scriptures are perfect, being spoken by the Word of God and his Spirit.

—Irenaeus, *Against Heresies* 2.27.2; 28.2

CLEMENT of Alexandria considered the effects of Scripture and the relationship between knowledge of them and knowledge in general. See also Chapter III, under Faith.

When the Scriptures are read, one person is strengthened in faith, another in character, and another is rescued from superstition by knowledge of matters. . . . For knowledge is necessary for the exercise of the soul and for holiness of character. It makes the faithful worthy of respect and accurate observers of affairs. For just as belief is impossible without instruction, so comprehension is impossible without knowledge.

—Clement of Alexandria, *Prophetic Eclogues* 28

FOR CHRISTIANS, Christ was the key to the interpretation of Scripture. Irenaeus expressed this with reference to the Old Testament.

If anyone, therefore, reads the Scriptures attentively, he will find in them a discussion of Christ and a foreshadowing of the new calling. . . . When the law is read by Christians, it is a treasure hidden in a field [Matt 13:44], revealed and explained in the cross of Christ, enriching the understanding of human beings and showing the wisdom of God, manifesting his dispensations for human beings.

—Irenaeus, *Against Heresies* 4.26.1

MANY of those who had a classical education found the style of Scripture unworthy. Origen defended the simplicity of Scripture.

I have said these things in defense against the charge made by Celsus and others that the wording of the Scriptures, which appears to be put in the shade by the wording of brilliant compositions, is unworthy. The prophets among us, as well as Jesus and his apostles, observed a manner of diction that not only contained the truth but was also able to win over the multitudes, until each one who had been persuaded and brought in could make progress, according to his capacity, toward the ineffable things that are expressed in words that appear to be unworthy. . . . The divine word says that what is spoken is not sufficient to reach the human soul—even if it is itself true and worthy of belief—unless divine power is given to the one who speaks and grace appears plainly in his words. Without divine help this does not occur, even in those who speak effectively.

—Origen, *Against Celsus* 6.2

SCRIPTURE is accommodated to human capabilities, so it speaks of God in human terms.

When we talk with very young children, we do not show off our ability at speaking, but we adjust ourselves to the weakness of those to whom we speak; we say and do those things that appear to be useful for changing and correcting children as children. In the same way, it seems that the word of God accommodates and moderates the things written in the Scriptures to the ability of the hearers, according to what is suitable and beneficial in the message.

— Origen, *Against Celsus* 4.71

THERE are things in Scripture for all levels of understanding.

When gathered all together, these passages convince the person who applies himself to their reading that the books of the Gospel are not only simple—as some suppose—but by divine arrangement have become simple to those who are simple; but to those who desire and are able to hear more acutely, there are hidden within them matters that are wise and worthy of the word of God.

— Origen, *Commentary on Matthew* 10.1

THERE is a danger of reading into Scripture what one wants to, or of bringing an extraneous system of thought to its interpretation.

If, on the grounds of trusting in the Scriptures, anyone dares even to hear anything against God, let that person first of all consider along with me the fact that if anyone shapes a dogma according to his wishes and plausible to himself before carefully searching the Scriptures, he will be able to produce many testimonies from them to support the dogma he has formed.

— Pseudo-Clement, *Homilies* 3.9

WE MUST live—not admire—Scripture.

An old man said, "The prophets wrote the books; then came our ancestors, who lived by them. Those who came later understood them from the heart. Then came the present generation, who copied them out and put them on their shelves unused."

— *Apophthegmata Patrum*, Anonymous
Collection, # 228 Nau

Isidore said: "Whoever wants to be always with God must pray often and read [Scripture] often. For when we pray, we speak with God; but when we read, God speaks with us. All [spiritual] progress proceeds from reading and meditation. What we do not know, we learn by reading; and what we learn, we keep by meditation.

"Reading the holy Scriptures confers a double advantage: It educates the intellectual faculty of the mind, and by taking a person's attention away from the world's vanities it leads to the love of God. . . .

"No one is able to understand the meaning of holy Scripture except by the familiarity of frequent reading."

—The Defensor of Ligugé, *Book of Sparkling Sayings* 81.17–18, 21, quoting Isidore of Seville, *Sententiae* 3.8.2, 4; 3.9.1

The Last Things

The Second Coming of Christ

The Jews, as those to whom the prophets spoke, also knew that Christ was to come. Indeed, even now they look for his advent and the greatest cause of disagreement between them and us is that they do not believe he has already come. For two advents of Christ were predicted: the first has already been fulfilled in the lowliness of the human condition; and the second, which is imminent, will be fulfilled when the world ends in all the majesty of Deity revealed. By not recognizing the first, they regard the second—which was the one more obviously predicted and the one for which they hope—as the only one.

—Tertullian, *Apology* 21.15

We announce not only one advent of Christ but also a second, which is far more glorious than the former. For the former demonstrated his patience, but the latter brings the crown of a divine kingdom. Now in most respects all things are twofold in our Lord Jesus Christ. His generation is twofold—one from God before the ages and one from a virgin at the close of the ages. His descent is twofold—one unobserved, "like rain on a fleece" [Ps 72:6], and the second is his manifest appearance, which is to come. In his former advent he was wrapped in swaddling clothes and placed in a manger; in his second he "covers himself with light as a garment" [Ps 104:2]. In his first advent "he endured the cross, despising the shame" [Heb 12:2]; in his second he will come attended by an army of angels and receive glory. We stand not only upon his first advent but also expect his second. . . . The Savior comes not to be judged again but to judge those who judged him. . . . At his first advent he came because of the divine dispensation, and he taught people with persuasion; but this time they will have him for their King by necessity—even if they do not want him.

—Cyril of Jerusalem, *Catechetical Lectures* 15.1

We should not be troubled by the brief delay of that for which we hope, but we should be diligent so that we may not be rejected from what we hope for. It is as if one were to tell some inexperienced person beforehand, "The gathering of the crops will occur in the season of summer, the granaries will be filled, and the table will be full of food at the season of plenty." Only a foolish person would seek to hasten the coming of that season. He ought to be sowing seeds and diligently preparing the fruits for himself. The season will surely come—whether he desires it or not—at the appointed time. The one who has prepared an abundance of crops for himself beforehand and the one who is left destitute of all preparation at the hour of harvest will not see that time the same way. Even so, I think that since the divine proclamation makes clear to all that the season of change will come, it is one's duty not to be curiously inquisitive about the times, for Jesus said that "it is not for us to know the times and seasons" [Acts 1:7]. Nor ought one to pursue calculations that weaken the soul with regard to the hope of the resurrection. Rather, placing confidence in the faith of things expected, one must acquire in advance the grace that is to come, through a good way of life.

—Gregory of Nyssa, *On the Making of Man* 22.8

Resurrection

To the objection that a future resurrection of the dead is impossible, Athenagoras succinctly summed up the Christian response.

The statement that is far more acceptable and the truest of all is the assertion that what is impossible for human beings is possible for God.

—Athenagoras, *On the Resurrection* 9

In the following passage Justin Martyr offers an analogy that illustrates the possibility of resurrection.

To anyone who thinks about it, what could be more incredible, supposing we were not in a body, than to say that bones, nerves, and flesh come into existence from a small drop of human seed and are shaped into the form that we see? Let this now be stated as a hypothesis: if you were not such as you are and from such parents, and someone said to you and strongly affirmed—after having shown you the human seed and a sculptured image—that they are the same and from the same thing, would you believe it before seeing it come to pass? No one would dare to contradict this! In the same way, although you have never seen a dead person raised, you are disbelieving. But just as you would not believe at the beginning that from a small drop such a person can come into being—yet you see them coming into being—so also understand that it is not impossible for human bodies that have been dissolved and dispersed in the manner of seeds in the earth to be raised at the time appointed by God and to be clothed with incorruption [1 Cor 15:53].

—Justin Martyr, *1 Apology* 19

SEVERAL authors made the point that it is "easier" for God to reconstitute a human being than to create one in the first place.

For just as I did not exist before I came into being and did not know who I was, since I existed only in the underlying substance of fleshly matter, but believe that I, who formerly did not exist, came into existence and exist now, so I, who came into existence and through death no longer exist and are no longer seen, will come into existence again, even as I formerly did not exist but then was born. Even if fire utterly destroys my flesh, the world receives the vaporized matter. Even if I am consumed by rivers or seas, or torn apart by wild animals, I am stored up in the treasuries of a rich Master. The poor, godless person does not know what is stored up, but God the King—when he wills—will restore the substance visible to him alone to its original condition.

—Tatian, *Oration to the Greeks* 6.2

But how," you say, "can the matter of a body that has been dissolved reappear again?" Consider yourself, O man, and you will come to faith in the resurrection. Reflect on what you were before you came into being—nothing at all. For if you had been anything, you would remember it. You, then, who were nothing before you came into being and likewise are made nothing when you cease to be, why can you not come into being again out of nothing, at the will of the same Creator whose will brought you into being out of nothing? . . . Give an account—if you can—of how you were created, and then you can ask how you will be re-created. Indeed, it will be easier for you to be made what you once were, since at one time, equally without difficulty, you were made what you never were before.

—Tertullian, *Apology* 48

BOTH the just and the unjust will be raised, but to a different end.

Our [Christian] system promises eternal life to those who adhere to it and observe it; on the other hand, it threatens eternal punishment in eternal fire to those who are profane and antagonistic; while to both classes alike a resurrection from the dead is preached.

—Tertullian, *To the Pagans* 1.7

ALTHOUGH they affirmed the resurrection of the same body in which one lives while on earth, several writers pointed out that the defects of our present bodies will be transformed.

If God does not raise people entire, he does not raise the dead. . . . God is quite able to remake what he once made. . . . In the great future there is no need for fear of blemished or defective bodies. . . . Our flesh shall remain even after the resurrection; . . . it is the same flesh, but at the same time incapable of suffering, because it has been liberated by the Lord for the very end and purpose of being no longer capable of enduring suffering.

—Tertullian, *On the Resurrection of the Flesh* 57

A FREQUENTLY recurring motif in support of the necessity of the resurrection was that the body was intimately connected with both the good deeds and the sins committed in this life, and so it should share in the experience of the rewards and punishments for this conduct.

We shall, then, all be raised with eternal bodies but not all bodies will be alike. If a person is righteous, he will receive a heavenly body so as to live worthily with the angels; but if a person is a sinner, he will receive an eternal body that is capable of enduring the penalties of sins, so as to burn eternally in fire but never be consumed. . . . Since then the body is our minister in all things, it shall also share in the future results of the things that have been done.

—Cyril of Jerusalem, *Catechetical Lectures* 18.19

GREGORY of Nyssa said that the resurrection will be a restoration to the original created nature before sin entered the world.

In the superabundance of his power, the divine power does not simply restore to us the body that was once dissolved, but makes great and beautiful additions to it, whereby our human nature becomes even more magnificent. . . . We say that the resurrection is nothing other than the restoration of our nature to what it originally was.

—Gregory of Nyssa, *On the Soul and the Resurrection*

OUR RESURRECTED bodies will be like Christ's.

One of the old men questioned Amma Theodora saying, "In the resurrection of the dead, how are we raised?" She said, "We have as a pledge, example, and firstfruit the one who died for us and was raised, Christ our God."[4]

—*Apophthegmata Patrum,* Alphabetical Collection, Theodora # 3

CHAPTER V

Christian Living

> We have as our lawgiver the true God, who teaches us to
> practice righteousness, to be pious, and to do good.
> —Theophilus, *To Autolycus* 3.9

*T*HE THREE QUALITIES LISTED in the quotation above—righteousness, piety, and doing good—can be viewed as constitutive of the Christian life: right conduct before others, piety toward God, and good deeds toward those in need. We have structured this chapter, however, not according to these qualities (although they occur in many of the selections) but in another way. We begin with general descriptions of Christian living that were made by a few early Christian writers. The way so many of these writers state their descriptions in terms of what Christians actually do—not simply as teachings of what Christians should do—is indeed impressive. We know from other statements that not all Christians lived up to these ideals, but there was a distinctive quality of life practiced by early Christians that caught the attention of non-Christians and that could be appealed to by those who defended the Christian faith.

From these general descriptions we turn to statements about the general principles of Christian living and its relationship to God: loving, imitating, pleasing, fearing (or reverencing), following (serving), and seeking God. The very name "Christian" was understood to indicate the special status Christians possessed in their relationship to God and Christ. Jews who believed in Christ, but who continued to keep many Jewish rituals and customs, came to be regarded as an anomaly by both Jews and Gentile Christians. Their presence, however, is a reminder not only of Christianity's ability to accommodate different racial and cultural settings, but also of the possibility of finding a middle way in the often difficult relations between Christians and Jews.

Many Christian authors described the spiritual life in terms of progress toward perfection; and some defined perfection in terms of progressive growth toward absolute perfection. For many Christians, this included the concrete reality of persecution and even martyrdom. The more ordinary and daily expression and development of spirituality included instruction and advice in the disciplines of meditation, Scripture reading, and fasting (in our treatment prayer receives separate and special attention). The ultimate goal of the spiritual life was the vision of God, glimpses of which were granted to a few in this life but which most would receive in the life to come.

Worship, often described in the language of spiritual sacrifice, was an expression of the Christian life. As such, it was not confined to the corporate assemblies of the church but was also expressed in daily attitudes and experience. The faithful sang hymns and engaged in prayer in their daily lives, in addition to their collective assemblies. The literature of the ancient church contains many discussions of prayer, which often took the form of commentaries on the Lord's Prayer. The Lord's Supper, the Eucharist, was the center of public assemblies.

Christian authors realistically assessed the trials and temptations that confronted those who sought to live a life that was pleasing to God. Pleasure was recognized as a major temptation; and sufferings that were brought about by the presence of evil in the world posed a major challenge, not only in terms of the actual experience of suffering but also as a practical intellectual question that asked why a good God allowed such things to happen to his people. The ultimate trial was death and the grief that accompanies death; Christian hope provided a response to both of these.

We conclude this chapter with selections that illustrate specific qualities that characterized Christian living: faithfulness, obedience, hope, hospitality, purity, unity, respect for human life (including opposition to abortion), nonviolent resistance to enemies, charity (including its practical expression in almsgiving), and self-control.

General Descriptions

Christians are not distinguished from the rest of people by country, language, or customs. They do not dwell in cities of their own, nor do they use a strange language, nor practice a peculiar way of life. Their teaching was not discovered through the speculation or consideration of people who are full of curiosity, nor do they busy themselves with human doctrine as some do. Although they dwell in Greek and barbarian cities, as each has received his lot, and follow the local customs in dress, food, and the rest of life, they display the marvelous and admittedly unusual constitution of their own citizenship. That is, they live in their native countries, but as sojourners.

As citizens, they share all things; and as foreigners, they endure all things. Every foreign land is their homeland, and every homeland is a foreign land to them. They marry as all people do. They bear children, but they do not abandon their offspring. They furnish a common table but not a common bed. It is their lot to live "in the flesh," but they do not live "according to the flesh" [2 Cor 10:3].

They pass their time upon the earth, but their citizenship is in heaven. They are obedient to the appointed laws, but in their own lives they surpass the laws. They love all and are persecuted by all. They are not understood, and they are condemned. They are put to death, and they are made alive. "They are poor, yet they make many rich" [2 Cor 6:10]. They lack all things, and they abound in everything. They are dishonored, and they are glorified in their dishonor. They are spoken of as evil, and they are justified. "They are reviled, and they bless" [1 Cor 4:12]. They are insulted, and they give honor. While doing good, they are punished as evil. Being punished, they rejoice as being made alive. They are fought against as foreigners by the Jews, and they are persecuted by Greeks. And those who hate them cannot state a reason for their enmity.

— *Epistle to Diognetus* 5

[T]he Christians] know and trust in God, the Creator of heaven and of earth, in whom and from whom are all things, to whom there is no other god as companion, from whom they received commandments that they engraved upon their minds and observe in the hope and expectation of the world that is to come. Wherefore they do not commit adultery nor fornication, nor bear false witness, nor embezzle what is held in pledge, nor covet what is not theirs. They honor father and mother, and show kindness to those near to them; and whenever they are judges, they judge uprightly. They do not worship idols [made] in the image of man; and whatsoever they would not that others should do to them, they do not do to others; and of the food that is consecrated to idols they do not eat, for they are pure. And their oppressors they appease and make them their friends.[1] They do good to their enemies. Their women are pure and virgins and do not offer their wombs; and their men exercise self-control from every unlawful union, and especially from impurity; their wives similarly exercise self-control, for they cling to the great hope of the world to come. If they have bondmen and bondwomen or children, they persuade them to become Christians so that they might be friends, and when they have become such, they call them brethren without distinction. They do not worship strange gods.

They are gentle, moderate, modest, and truthful. They love one another. They do not overlook the widows, and they save those who are orphaned. The person who possesses material goods ministers ungrudgingly to those who do not. When they see strangers, they take them under their own roof and rejoice over them as true brothers and sisters, for they do not call themselves brothers and sisters according to the flesh but according to the soul. And whenever they see that one of their poor has died, each one of them contributes ungrudgingly to his burial, according to their ability. And if they hear that some are condemned or imprisoned on account of the name of their Lord, they make contributions and send them what they need; and if possible, they redeem them. And if there is any that is a slave or a poor person, they fast two or three days and what they were going to set before themselves they send to them, considering themselves to give good cheer even as they are called to good cheer.

They observe carefully the precepts of God and live in a holy and just manner, as the Lord their God commanded them. They give thanks to him every morning and every hour for food, drink, and other good things. If any righteous person among them dies, they rejoice and offer thanks and pray concerning that one; and they escort the body as if he were setting out on a journey. When a child is born to one of them, they give thanks to God; and if it should die as an infant, they give thanks the more, because it has departed life sinless. But if anyone should die in sin they weep, since that person goes to punishment.

— Aristides, *Apology* 15

Christians exhibit temperance, exercise self-control, preserve monogamy, guard chastity, cast out unrighteousness, root out sin, care for righteousness, live the law, practice godliness, confess God; with Christians truth arbitrates, grace is maintained, peace shelters, the holy word guides, wisdom teaches, life arbitrates, God rules.

— Theophilus, *To Autolycus* 3.15

Among us you may find uneducated persons, workmen, and old women who cannot express the benefit that comes from our doctrine through words, but their deeds do this. For they do not call to mind the words, but they exhibit good works. When they are struck, they do not strike back; when robbed, they do not go to the law. They give to those who ask and they love their neighbors as themselves.

—Athenagoras, *Plea for the Christians* 11

Therefore also we have no need of the Law as pedagogue [Gal 3:24–25]. Behold, we speak with the Father and stand face to face with him, become infants in malice, and made strong in all justice and propriety. For no more shall the Law say: "Thou shalt not commit adultery," to him who has not even conceived the desire of another's wife [Matt 5:27–28]; or "Thou shalt not kill," to him who has put away from himself all anger and enmity [Matt 5:21–22]; "thou shalt not covet thy neighbor's field, or his ox, or his ass," to those who make no account whatever of earthly things, but heap up profit in heaven [Matt 6:19–20]. Nor "an eye for an eye and a tooth for a tooth," to him who counts no man his enemy, but all his neighbors, and therefore cannot even put forth his hand to revenge [Matt 5:38]. Nor will it demand tithes of him who has vowed to God all his possessions, and who leaves father and mother and all his kindred, and follows the Word of God [Matt 19:29]. Nor will he be commanded to leave idle one day of rest, who is constantly keeping sabbath, that is, giving homage to God in the temple of God, which is man's body [1 Cor 3:16–17], and at all times doing the works of justice.[2]

—Irenaeus, *Demonstration of the Apostolic Preaching* 96

We [Christians] do not deny a deposit that is left with us; we never defile anyone's marriage by adultery; we manage the affairs of our wards dutifully; we give aid to the needy; we render to no one evil for evil. We repudiate those who pretend falsely to belong to us. Who among us is called into account on any other charge [than being Christian]? . . . It is for such innocence, for such integrity, for righteousness, for purity, for faithfulness, for truth, for the living God that we are consigned to the flames.

—Tertullian, *To Scapula* 4.7–8

What mark do we [Christians] exhibit except the fundamental wisdom that causes us not to worship worthless works made by human hands, the self-control that restrains us from what belongs to another, the chastity that restrains us from polluting with even a look, the compassion that inclines us toward the needy, the truth itself by which we give offense, and the very liberty for which we have learned to die? Whoever wishes to understand who the Christians are must refer to these characteristics for their identification.

—Tertullian, *To the Pagans* 1.4

It is natural that we love those who love us. But righteous persons attempt also to love their enemies, to bless those who slander them, even to pray for their enemies and be merciful to those who do them wrong. Thus they also refrain from doing wrong, and similarly they bless those who curse them, forgive those who strike them, yield to those who persecute them, greet those who give them no salutation, share what they have with those who do not have, persuade anyone who is angry with them, conciliate the enemy, exhort the disobedient, instruct the unbeliever, comfort the mourner. When distressed they endure, and when treated ungratefully they do not become angry.

Having devoted themselves to loving their neighbor as themselves, they do not fear poverty, but by distributing their possessions to those in need they too become poor. Nor do they punish sinners. For since they do not want to be punished when they sin, those who love their neighbor as themselves do not punish others who sin. And just as they desire to be praised, blessed, honored, and forgiven of all their sins, they do the same to their neighbor, loving each one as themselves. In a word, what they wish for themselves they wish also for their neighbor.

—Pseudo-Clement, *Homilies* 12.32

THE FOLLOWING selection provides a specific example of Christian conduct during a time of epidemic in third-century Alexandria.

Indeed, through their exceeding love and merciful kindness, many of our brothers and sisters did not spare themselves but kept close to one another and cared for the sick without taking thought for themselves. They ministered to them earnestly, treating them in Christ and gladly departing from this life along with them. Filled up with the suffering of others and drawing upon themselves the disease of their neighbors, they willingly accepted their pains. And many who tended the sick and restored them to health themselves died, having transferred to themselves the death that lay upon others.

—Dionysius of Alexandria, quoted by
Eusebius, *Church History* 7.22.7

God requires from human beings only purity of mind and a spotless spirit; and by this standard he calculates deeds of virtue and godliness. He is pleased with works of goodness and gentleness. He loves the meek and hates agitators. Loving faith, he punishes unbelief. He tears down all presumptuous power, and he takes vengeance on the insolence of the proud. He completely overthrows the arrogant and haughty; he rewards the humble and forgiving as they deserve. Even so he highly honors and strengthens with his special help a righteous kingdom and maintains the royal conscience in the tranquility of peace.

—Emperor Constantine to the King of Persia, quoted in Eusebius, *Life of Constantine* 4.10

Abba Poemen said, "These three things are the most useful of all: to fear the Lord, to pray, and to do good to one's neighbor."

—*Apophthegmata Patrum*, Alphabetical Collection, Poemen # 160

THE THEME of the two ways and the choice that must be made was common among pagan and Jewish moralists. The following is a Christian adaptation of this theme.

There are two different roads: one is broad and easy, the other narrow and difficult. And there are two guides, who each attempt to lure the traveler. Now that our mental development has matured, life seems to be divided into virtue and vice. The soul looks at each one in turn and judges the consequences of each. The life of sinners offers all the pleasures of the present age; the life of the righteous points only to the good things of the future. The way of those who are being saved promises great goods in the future but pain in the present. The pleasant and undisciplined way of life does not look to the future but proposes only present enjoyment. Every soul, therefore, becomes confused and wavers in its deliberations. When it considers eternity, it chooses virtue; when it considers the present, it prefers pleasure.

—Basil of Caesarea, *Homilies on the Psalms* 1.5, on Ps 1:1

Some Principles for Christian Living

Loving God

It is necessary, therefore, for good people to love God's way above all things. That is, they must love God's way more than riches, glory, rest, parents, relatives, friends, and everything in the world. The person who perfectly loves possession of the kingdom of heaven will without doubt reject every practice of evil habit, negligence, idleness, malice, anger, and all similar things. For if you prefer any of these things to the kingdom of heaven—so that you love the vices of your own lust more than God—you will not possess the kingdom of heaven, for it is truly foolish to love anything more than God. For parents will die, relatives do not abide, and friends change. God alone is eternal and abides unchangeable.

—Pseudo-Clement, *Recognitions* 3.54

Imitating God

In loving, we imitate God's kindness. Do not marvel that a person can be an imitator of God. One can, if willing. For happiness is not found in ruling over one's neighbor, nor in wishing to have more than the weak, nor in being rich and powerful over those who occupy a lower station. Neither does one imitate God by doing these things; these things are outside his majesty. But whoever takes his neighbor's burden upon himself—whoever is willing to benefit another who is worse off, whoever takes the things received from God and distributes them to those who are in need—this person becomes a god to those who receive. This person is an imitator of God.

—*Epistle to Diognetus* 10.4–5

If someone puts on the name of Christ but does not demonstrate through his life what is meant by this name, he betrays the model that was given to us, putting on a lifeless mask that gives human character to a monkey. For it is not the nature of Christ to be something other than righteousness, purity, truth, and alien to every evil. Nor is it the nature of one who is truly a Christian to fail to manifest his participation in these virtues. Therefore, if one wishes to define the meaning of Christianity, we shall say it this way: Christianity is the imitation of the divine nature. Let no one dispute this definition as being excessive and going beyond the lowliness of our nature; the definition does not go beyond our nature. For if one considers the first constitution of humanity, he will find that the definition does not exceed the measure of our nature that is found in Scripture. For the first creation of man was according to the imitation of the likeness of God [Gen 1:27]. . . . The name of Christianity pertains to bringing humanity back to its original good condition. But if human beings were originally created in the likeness of God, perhaps we have not defined Christianity beyond the intention of its name when we declare that it is the imitation of the divine nature. . . .

Therefore, he who commands us to imitate the heavenly Father commands us to be pure from earthly passions. Separation from these passions is not effected by a change of place, but is accomplished only by choice.

—Gregory of Nyssa, *On the Christian Profession*

The greatest honor to God is to know him and become like him. Nothing is like God, but what is most pleasing to him is that we become like him as much as possible.

—*Sentences of Sextus* 44–45

Pleasing God

The person who chooses to "please people" [Gal 1:10] "cannot please God" [Rom 8:8], since the multitude chooses what is pleasurable, not what is profitable. But one who pleases God becomes, as a consequence, well pleasing to good people.

—Clement of Alexandria, *Miscellanies* 7.12

The will of God is what Christ both did and taught: humility in conduct, steadfastness in faith, respect in words, righteousness in deeds, mercifulness in works, disciplined in morals; unable to do harm and able to bear harm when it is done to oneself; to keep peace with brothers; to love God with one's whole heart, loving in him what is Father and reverencing in him what is God; to prefer nothing at all to Christ, because he preferred nothing to us; to adhere inseparably to his love; to stand by his cross bravely and faithfully when there is any contention concerning his name and honor; to exhibit constancy in word when we make confession, confidence when we contend in a judicial inquiry, and patience in death when we are crowned [with martyrdom]. This is what it means to be a fellow heir with Christ; this is what it means to do the commandments of God; this is what it means to carry out the will of the Father.

—Cyprian, *On the Lord's Prayer* 15

Fearing God

THE FEAR of God is often better expressed by the word "reverence." Clement of Alexandria distinguished two kinds of fear.

There are two kinds of fear. One is associated with reverence, such as citizens have for good rulers and we have for God, even as wise children have for their fathers. . . . The other kind of fear is associated with hatred, such as slaves have for harsh masters. . . . With regard to godly piety, what is voluntary and according to free choice is altogether separate from what is done out of necessity.

—Clement of Alexandria, *Instructor* 1.9.87

Anthony the Great said, "Keep the fear of God always before your eyes. Remember the 'One who puts to death and makes alive' [1 Sam 2:6]. Hate the world and all that is in it. Hate all fleshly ease. Renounce this life so that you may live with God. Remember what you promised God, for he will require it from you on the day of judgment."

—*Apophthegmata Patrum,* Alphabetical Collection, Anthony # 33

A brother asked Abba Euprepios, "How does the fear of God come into the soul?" The old man said, "If a person has humility and poverty and does not judge, the fear of God comes to him."

—*Apophthegmata Patrum,* Alphabetical Collection, Euprepios # 5

THE FEAR of God knows no other fear, not even of demons. Athanasius quotes Anthony as saying:

We must fear only God, but we must despise the demons and have no dread of them at all."

—Athanasius, *Life of Anthony* 30

SEE ALSO John Climacus, *Ladder of Paradise* 21, quoted in Chapter II, under Negative Attitudes and Actions—Fears.

Following God

IN COMMENTING on Exod 33:17–23, Gregory of Nyssa draws a comparison between Moses and a person who waits on the divine voice and prays that he might follow behind God.

When the Lord [Christ] who spoke to Moses came to fulfill his own law, he likewise gave a clear explanation to his disciples, laying bare the meaning of what had previously been said in a figure when he said, "If anyone wants to be a follower of mine" [Luke 9:23], and not, "If anyone will go before me." And to the one asking about eternal life he proposes the same thing, for he says, "Come, follow me" [Luke 18:22]. Now, the one who follows sees the back [Exod 33:23].

So Moses, who eagerly seeks to behold God, is now taught how he can behold him: to follow God wherever he might lead is to behold God. His passing by signifies his guiding the one who follows, for someone who does not know the way cannot complete the journey safely in any other way than by following behind the guide. He who leads, then, by his guidance shows the way to the one following. The one who follows will not turn aside from the right way if he always keeps the back of his leader in view.[3]

—Gregory of Nyssa, *Life of Moses* 2.251–52

Seeking God

Seek the Lord and call on him when you find him" [Isa 55:6], and "Let the heart of those who seek the Lord rejoice" [Ps 105:3]. I know from these words that something must be sought, the finding of which is always to seek. For it is not one thing to seek and another to find, but the reward of seeking is the seeking itself.

—Gregory of Nyssa, *Homilies on Ecclesiastes* 7, on Eccl 3:6

The Name Christian

THE NAME "Christian" is derived from Christ.

The word of God speaks to those who believe in him, to the church that has come into being from his name and shares his name—for we are all called Christians—as being one soul, one synagogue, one church, as to a daughter. His words likewise clearly proclaim and teach us to forget our old ancestral customs [a quotation of Ps 45:10–11 follows].

—Justin Martyr, *Dialogue* 63.5

THE TITLE "Christ" meant "anointed," and Theophilus described Christians also as "anointed." It is not clear, however, whether he was referring to the literal anointing that took place in the baptismal service, or speaking meta-phorically of anointing with the Holy Spirit.

When you ridicule me by calling me a "Christian," you do not know what you are saying. In the first place, what is anointed is sweet and useful, and not ridiculous. . . . What person upon being born or competing in an athletic contest is not anointed with oil? . . . Do you not want to be anointed with the oil of God? Therefore, we are called Christians because we are anointed with the oil of God.

—Theophilus, *To Autolycus* 1.12

THE NAME *"Christos"* was close to the word *chrestos,* which meant "useful" or "good," and was probably pronounced the same, as in modern Greek. Latin speakers especially confused the two words.

Indeed the name "Christian"—so far as its meaning goes—signifies an anointing. Even when by a faulty pronunciation you call us "Chrestians" . . . , the idea of pleasantness or goodness is intoned. You are therefore hold-ing captive in innocent people also our innocent name. . . . Surely names are not worthy of being punished by the sword, the cross, or the beasts.

—Tertullian, *To the Pagans* 1.3

As THE preceding passage indicates, the accusation brought against Chris-tians was "the name," that is, the fact of their being a member of the group that followed Christ. It was customary in Roman law to judge people as members of a group and not as individuals, but Justin complained that this was unjust.

By the mere ascription of a name nothing good or bad is deter-mined apart from the practices suggested by the name. . . . For we are accused of being Christians, but to hate what is good [*chrestos*] is not just. And again, if any one of those accused verbally denies and says that he is not a Christian, you acquit that person on the grounds of not being able to convict him as a wrongdoer; but if anyone confesses to being a Christian, you punish on the basis of the confession. But you ought to examine the conduct of the one who confesses and of the one who denies, in order that it may become evi-dent through their deeds what sort of person each is.

—Justin Martyr, *1 Apology* 4.1, 5–6

Only pray that I may be strong both inwardly and outwardly so that I not only speak but also will, so that I am not only called a Christian but may also be found to be one. For if indeed I am found a Christian, I can be called one and then be faithful, when I no longer appear in the world.

—Ignatius, *Romans* 3.2

It is proper then not only to be called Christians but also to be Christians.

—Ignatius, *Magnesians* 4.1

DIVISION that denominated Christians by different names is an old problem. Compare this selection with those in Chapter II, under Division.

Since by the instigation of demons the people of God are divided and many heresies exist, we must briefly mark out the truth. . . . For when they are called Phrygians [Montanists], Novatianists, Valentinians, Marcionites, Anthropians [those who believed that Christ was only a human being], or any other name, they cease to be Christians. By sending away the name of Christ, they adopt a human and foreign vocabulary. Therefore, it is the universal [*catholica*] church alone that retains true worship. . . . Every individual assembly of heretics considers its members especially to be Christians and believes itself to be a catholic church.

—Lactantius, *Divine Institutes*
4.30.1, 10–11, 13

I honor Peter, but I am never called a Petrian; also Paul, but I am not called a Paulian. I do not allow myself to be named for human beings, since I have come into being from God. Even so, if you are called a Christian because you accept that he is God, may you be so called and may you remain in the name and in the reality. . . . The name "Christian" is a very small thing, even if you pride yourself on it. Since you accept that he is God, show your acceptance by your works.

—Gregory of Nazianzus, *Oration* 37.17–18

Jewish Christians

JUSTIN Martyr described the different attitudes held by Gentile Christians and non-Christian Jews toward Jewish believers who wanted to continue to live as Jews. His dialogue partner, the Jew Trypho, raised a question about this.

If some now desire to live in observance of the ordinances laid down by Moses and also to believe in this Jesus who was crucified, acknowledging that he is God's Messiah who will absolutely judge all and to whom belongs the eternal kingdom, can these also be saved?" . . .

"It seems to me, O Trypho, that such a one will be saved if he does not strive to persuade other people—I mean those of the Gentiles who have been 'circumcised' from their error through Christ—to observe these practices with him by saying they will not be saved unless they observe these practices in every respect, just as you said at the beginning of our discussion that I will not be saved unless I observe these things."

He said, "Why then did you say, 'It seems to me that such a one will be saved,' unless there are some who say that such persons will not be saved?"

I answered, "There are [those who say this], Trypho, and they do not seek fellowship with such [Jewish believers] by keeping company with them or welcoming them to their houses. I do not agree with them. But if those [Jews] who through weakness of judgment wish to continue observing the ordinances from Moses that they can still keep—which we understand were appointed because of the hardness of their [the Jewish people's] hearts—after placing their hope in Christ and observing the eternal natural laws of righteousness and godliness, and choose to live together with faithful Christians without persuading them—as I said before—to be circumcised like they are, to keep Sabbath, or to keep any other such ceremonies, then I declare that we ought to welcome and have fellowship with them as kinsmen and brethren.

"But Trypho," I said, "if some of your race who believe in Christ compel the Gentiles who believe in Christ to live according to the law laid down by Moses in every respect, or choose not to fellowship with them, then I do not approve of these. I understand equally that Gentiles who are persuaded by Jewish believers to live according to the law, along with observing their confession of faith in the Messiah of God, will be saved. Those who at one time confessed and recognized Jesus as the Christ and then for some reason began to live according to the law, denied that Jesus is the Christ, and did not repent before their death, I declare will in no way be saved. Those from the seed of Abraham who live according to the law and do not come to faith in Jesus as the Christ before the end of life I likewise declare will not be saved, especially those who cursed and do curse those who believe that Jesus is the Christ."

—Justin Martyr, *Dialogue* 46; 47

THE FOLLOWING statement from a Jewish Christian source expresses a viewpoint that has become more acceptable in modern times than it was in the early centuries.

The Hebrews are not condemned because they are ignorant about Jesus, on account of the One who hid him from them, provided that they practice the things given by Moses and not hate him whom they do not know. Nor are Gentiles condemned who are ignorant of Moses, on account of the One who hid him, provided that these also practice the things spoken by Jesus and not hate him whom they do not know. They do not benefit by calling their teachers "Lord" and not doing what servants should do [Luke 6:46]. . . . If one is worthy of recognizing that both preach one doctrine, then this person is rich in God, understanding old things as new in time and new things as old.

—Pseudo-Clement, *Homilies* 8.7

Spirituality and Spiritual Disciplines

Spiritual Progress

Now can there be instruction without exercise, or progress without practice?

—Ambrose, *Duties* 1.10.31

Offer to God your heart in a soft and pliable condition, and preserve the form in which the Creator formed you. . . . If you are exceedingly hardened, reject God's workmanship, and remain ungrateful toward him because you were made a human being, becoming ungrateful to God, you lose both his workmanship and life. For creation is characteristic of the goodness of God, and to be created is the characteristic of human nature. If then you hand over to him what is yours—that is, faith and subjection to him—you will receive his workmanship and will become a perfect work of God.

—Irenaeus, *Against Heresies* 4.39.2

We obtain a certain portion of his Spirit now in order to perfect us and prepare us for incorruption, as we little by little become accustomed to receive and bear God. The apostle calls this a "pledge" [Eph 1:14], that is, a portion of the honor promised us by God. . . . This pledge makes us like God and accomplishes the will of the Father, for it makes human beings according to the image and likeness of God.

—Irenaeus, *Against Heresies* 5.8.1

Progress toward perfection occurs whenever one clings to the Lord through faith, knowledge, and love, and ascends with him to where the Guard and God of our faith and love is. From there, knowledge is finally delivered to those who are adapted and admitted to it, since it requires much preparation and prior training in order to hear the words spoken and to advance with fervor toward dignity of life and righteousness that is greater than that of the law. This knowledge leads us to the immortal and perfect goal.

—Clement of Alexandria, *Miscellanies* 7.10

Rational creatures . . . were given the faculty of free choice. This freedom of their will either called forth progress by their imitation of God or drew them to failure by their negligence.

—Origen, *First Principles* 2.9.6

One should not know any limit to the good and to progress, nor more reward than what has been attained, nor loss than what is left behind. One should make each step a means of approaching the next. We should not think it is a great thing to excel most people but rather a loss if we are lacking in worth. One should measure himself according to the commandments and not according to his neighbors.

—Gregory of Nazianzus, *Oration* 2.14

Once the soul is released from its earthly attachment, it becomes light and swift for its movement upward, soaring from below up to the heights.

If nothing comes from above to hinder its upward thrust (for the nature of the Good attracts to itself those who look to it), the soul rises ever higher and will always make its flight yet higher—by its desire of the heavenly things "straining ahead for what is still to come" [Phil 3:13], as the apostle says.

Activity directed toward virtue causes the soul's capacity to grow through exertion; this kind of activity alone does not slacken its intensity by the effort, but increases it.

The great Moses continually climbed to the step above and never ceased to rise higher, because he always found a step higher than the one he had attained. . . .

Although lifted up through such lofty experiences, he is still unsatisfied in his desire for more. He still thirsts for that with which he constantly filled himself to capacity, and he asks to attain as if he had never partaken, beseeching God to appear to him, not according to his capacity to partake, but according to God's true being. . . .

In another Scriptural passage the progress is a standing still, for it says, "You must stand on the rock" [Exod 33:21]. This is the most marvelous thing of all: how the same thing is both a standing still and a moving. For he who ascends certainly does not stand still, and he who stands still does not move upwards. But here the ascent takes place by means of the standing. I mean by this that the firmer and more immovable one remains in the Good, the more he progresses in the course of virtue.[4]

— Gregory of Nyssa, *Life of Moses*
2.224–27, 230, 243

Spiritual substances are brought into being by creation. They always look to the First Cause of all beings, and they are kept in the Good by continual participation in the Transcendent One. In a certain sense they are always being created, since they are changed for the better through their growth in good things. In this regard no limit is perceived, and their growth to the better is not circumscribed by any boundary. Rather, the good that is always present—no matter how great and complete it might seem—is in every way the beginning of a greater and superior condition. Thus the apostolic word is verified by stretching forward toward the things ahead, forgetting the things previously accomplished [Phil 3:13]. For what is found is always a greater and superior good and holds the attention of those who participate in it, and the enjoyment of what is more esteemed does not leave room for looking back to the past and erases the memory of inferior things.

— Gregory of Nyssa, *Commentary on Canticles* 6, on Song 3:1

The soul that looks to God and adopts a desire for his incorruptible beauty possesses a longing that is ever new for what lies ahead; her desire is never made dull by being fully satisfied. Hence, she does not cease from always "stretching forward to what is before" [Phil 3:13], and she goes forward from her present condition, entering into the inner sanctuary where she has never been, and considering everything great and marvelous that has appeared to her to be inferior to what will follow, since what has been found is always more beautiful than what was previously received.

— Gregory of Nyssa, *Commentary on Canticles* 12, on Song 5:7

Perfection

The perfection of everything which can be measured by the senses is marked off by certain definite boundaries. . . . But in the case of virtue we have learned from the apostle that its one limit of perfection is the fact that it has no limit. For that divine Apostle, great and lofty in understanding, ever running the course of virtue, never ceased "straining toward those" things "that are still to come" [Phil 3:13]. Coming to a stop in the race was not safe for him. Why? Because no Good has a limit in its own nature but is limited by its opposite, as life is limited by death and light by darkness. And every good thing generally ends with all those things which are perceived to be contrary to the good.

Just as the end of life is the beginning of death, so also stopping in the race of virtue marks the beginning of the race of evil. . . .

We should show great diligence not to fall away from the perfection which is attainable but to acquire as much as is possible: To that extent let us make progress within the realm of what we seek. For the perfection of human nature consists perhaps in its very growth in goodness.[5]
—Gregory of Nyssa, *Life of Moses* 1.5–6, 10

PROGRESS toward perfection involves overcoming ever-stronger enemies of the spiritual life.

Athletes who compete in physical contests do not contend against the same opponents over whom they prevailed when they were young in wrestling school. But as they grow stronger, they prepare for bigger and stronger antagonists. If they prevail over these, they prepare for those who are superior, always competing with more powerful opponents who correspond to their increased strength. In the same way, the one who has been trained through victories over enemies in such contests brings more notable victories to himself, since he struggles with more notable and greater antagonists.
—Gregory of Nyssa, *On the Titles of the Psalms* 2.13.197

Martyrdom

WE QUOTE from perhaps the first literary work devoted to an account of martyrdom, certainly the most important such account from the early church.

Blessed and noble then are all the martyrdoms that took place according to the will of God. For we who are most reverent must assign authority over all things to God. For who would not marvel at their nobility, patient endurance, and love for the Lord? Some were torn in pieces by scourging, so that the construction of their flesh even to the inner veins and arteries was visible, yet they endured and the bystanders were moved to pity and mourning for them. Some of them attained such nobility that they neither murmured nor groaned. They demonstrated to all of us that at the hour when the most noble martyrs of Christ were being tortured, they were absent from the flesh, or rather that the Lord was present and spoke with them. Paying attention to the grace of Christ, they despised worldly tortures and in a single hour purchased eternal life. To them, the fire of their inhuman torturers was cool, for they held before their eyes the escape from eternal and unquenchable fire. They looked with the eyes of their heart to the good things reserved for those who endure, "things which neither ear has heard, nor eye seen, nor has entered into the human heart" [1 Cor 2:9], which the Lord showed to them, since they were no longer humans but were already angels. Similarly those who were condemned to the wild beasts endured terrible punishments. They were stretched on instruments of torture and were punished with many other tortures with the intention that constant punishment might bring them to denial.

The devil used many devices against them. But thanks be to God: the devil had no power against any of them.

— Martyrdom of Polycarp 2–3

The jealous and envious evil one who opposes the race of the righteous, when he saw the greatness of Polycarp's martyrdom and his blameless manner of life from the beginning—his being crowned with immortality and his carrying off the indescribable prize—took care that his bodily remains not be taken away by us, although many desired to do this and to have fellowship with his holy flesh. Therefore, he put forward Nicetes . . . to ask the proconsul that his body not be given to us, "Lest they leave the crucified one and begin to worship this one." . . . They do not know that we cannot leave the Christ, who suffered for the salvation of the whole world—the innocent for sinners—nor can we worship any other. For we worship this one who is the Son of God, but we rightly love the martyrs as disciples and imitators of the Lord because of their unsurpassable good will for their King and Teacher. May we be their partners and fellow disciples!

— Martyrdom of Polycarp 17

CLEMENT extended the idea of martyrdom to the daily martyrdom of a life lived in faith, picking up the primary meaning of *martus* as "witness" as well as the technical Christian meaning of "martyr."

Because of the commandment, the true gnostic reverently avoids denying Christ in order that he may become a martyr in reverence. He does not sell his faith, not because he hopes for the gifts promised but because his love for the Lord gladly leads him to depart from this life. . . . We call martyrdom "perfection," not because a person comes to the end of life as the rest of human beings do, but because it demonstrates the perfect work of love. . . .

If the confession before God is martyrdom, every soul that has lived purely in the knowledge of God and has obeyed his commandments is a martyr in life and in word. Whenever that person is released from the body, he or she pours out the faith like blood in all aspects of life, day by day, until its departure [Matt 19:29; Mark 10:29–30]. . . . This does not signify simple martyrdom but "gnostic" martyrdom, which is to live according to the rule of the Gospel through love for the Lord . . . to leave worldly family, to leave all possessions and wealth in order to lead a life without passion.

—Clement of Alexandria, *Miscellanies* 4.4.14–15

What a beautiful spectacle to God when a Christian struggles with pain; is matched against threats, punishments, and torture; with a laugh tramples on the clamor for death and the horror of the executioner; holds up his liberty against kings and princes; yields to God alone, whose he is; like a triumphant victor he mocks the judge who passed sentence against him. For the person who obtains what he contends for is the victor.

—Minucius Felix, *Octavius* 37.1

TERTULLIAN stated the principle that martyrdoms actually caused the church to grow and affirmed that the confession of faith in martyrdom brought forgiveness of sins.

We Christians increase in number as often as we are cut down by you. The blood of Christians is seed. . . . That very "obstinacy" that you reproach us for is your teacher. For who, upon contemplating it, is not aroused to inquire about this obstinacy? Who, upon investigation, does not join us? When he joins, he longs to suffer so that he may procure the full grace of God. For all sins are forgiven by this act. . . . There is a rivalry between the affairs of God and those of human beings: we are condemned by you; we are acquitted by God.

—Tertullian, *Apology* 50.13, 15–16

AFTER citing examples of pagans who chose death for some higher cause, and of Jesus and Paul, Origen states:

Many among us, knowing that if they confessed Christianity they would be put to death but if they denied it they would be set free and their possessions returned, willingly despised life and chose death for the sake of their religion.

—Origen, *Against Celsus* 2.17

God says through the prophet, "In an acceptable time I heard you, and in the day of salvation, I came to your aid" [Isa 49:8]. What is a more acceptable time than when, on account of piety toward God in Christ, we in this world are led away under guard in procession, going in triumph rather than being triumphed over? The martyrs in Christ take off along with him "the rulers and authorities" [Col 2:15], and they share in his triumph, becoming partakers in his sufferings even as they partake of the benefits obtained by his sufferings. These benefits include triumph over the "rulers and authorities," whom in a little while we shall see conquered and put to shame. What day more fully qualifies as the day of salvation than the day of our release from this life?

—Origen, *Exhortation to Martyrdom* 42

LACTANTIUS put the best interpretation possible on the situation that many denied their faith in times of persecution, but he is correct that most of them returned to the church when persecution ended and that the endurance of the faithful won many to the faith.

The number of Christians is always being increased by those converted from the worship of the gods but is never lessened even in persecution itself—although human beings may sin and be defiled by sacrificing [to the gods], they still are not turned away from God, for truth prevails by its own power. Who, then, is so lacking in intelligence or so blind that they cannot see which side is wise? . . . Thus it happens that when peace is given by divine agency, all those who were frightened off return and, moreover, new people join us on account of the marvelous display of virtue. For when the people see persons torn to pieces by various kinds of torments, yet keep their patience unconquered while their executioners are fatigued, they suppose (as is really the case) that neither the consent of so many nor the constancy of those dying is without meaning, and that patience itself could not overcome such torture without God's help.

—Lactantius, *Divine Institutes* 5.13.1, 10–11

Meditation

Abba Theonas said, "When we turn our mind from the contemplation of God, we become enslaved by fleshly passions."

—*Apophthegmata Patrum*, Alphabetical
Collection, Theonas # 1

For prayer, see below.

Reading Scripture

Let no day pass by without reading—at a suitable time—some portion of the sacred lessons, allowing time for meditation. And never cast off the practice of reading the sacred Scriptures; for nothing feeds the soul and enriches the mind as much as those sacred lessons do.

—Theonas, *To Lucianus* 9

You then, my true son, give primary attention to reading the divine Scriptures. Be attentive: for we must be attentive when reading the things of God, so that we not say or think anything too reckless about them. . . . Being attentive to divine reading, seek correctly and with unwavering faith in God the meaning of the divine Scriptures that is hidden to the many. Never cease knocking and seeking [Matt 7:7], for prayer is indispensable in understanding divine things.

—Origen, *Letter to Gregory* [the
Wonderworker] 3

The best way to discover our duty is to study the divinely inspired Scriptures, for in them we find both instructions about conduct and the lives of blessed men, delivered in writing. They are laid before us like living images

of the godly life for the imitation of their good works. When we devote ourselves to the imitation of what is offered there, we find the appropriate medicine for whatever deficiency or illness we feel we have, as from a pharmacy.
— Basil of Caesarea, *Letters* 2.4

Holy Scripture is presented to the mind's eye as a kind of mirror so
that our inner appearance can be seen in it. In this mirror we recognize both
the ugliness and the beauty of our soul. We can tell what progress we are making, or see our utter lack of progress. . . . The virtues of people in the Bible may
support our hope, and their faults may clothe us with the protection of humility. The former, through the joy they cause, give our spirits wings; the latter, by
causing fear, put a check on our actions. By listening to Scripture the soul
learns both the confidence of hope and the humility of fear.
— Gregory the Great, *Moralia in Job* 2.1.1

The nature of water is soft, that of a rock is hard. But if a narrow-
necked bottle is hung above a stone, drop by drop the water wears away the
rock. So it is with the word of God: it is soft and our heart is hard. But when a
person hears the word of God, often then his heart is opened to the fear of God.
— *Apophthegmata Patrum*, Alphabetical
Collection, Poemen # 183

SEE ALSO Chapter IV, on the doctrine of Scripture.

Fasting

THE SHEPHERD of Hermas encouraged the use of fasting for benevolent
purposes.

On the day when you fast, taste nothing except bread and water.
Reckon how much the food of that fast day was going to cost and give this
amount to a widow or orphan, or anyone in need. Thus you shall be humble-
minded, that by your humble-mindedness the person who has received may
fill his [or her] soul and pray to the Lord on your behalf."
— Hermas, *Similitudes* 5.3.7 [56.7]

MANY texts speak of the true fast as not a literal abstaining from food. In this
passage the heavenly Shepherd instructs Hermas.

I say that what you think is a fast is not a fast. Listen," he says, "and I will teach you about a full and acceptable fast to the Lord. God does not want a vain fast [a literal fast at set times], for you accomplish nothing for righteousness by fasting in this way. But do this kind of fast for God: do nothing evil in your life but serve the Lord with a pure heart, keeping his commandments and walking in his ordinances, and let no evil desire arise in your heart. Trust in God that if you do these things, fear him, and maintain self-control over every evil thing, then you will live in God. If you do these things, you will perform a great and acceptable fast to the Lord."

—Hermas, *Similitudes* 5.1.3–5 [54.3–5]

Fastings indicate avoidance of all evils of every kind—those in deed, in word, and in thought itself.

—Clement of Alexandria, *Miscellanies* 6.12

FASTING was associated with prayer and with mourning.

Fasting accompanies prayer. . . . Abstinence from food is always a corollary of grief, just as an abundance of food is associated with gladness.

—Tertullian, *On Fasting* 7

AS A MONTANIST, Tertullian argued for fixed fasts of longer duration and greater severity than his catholic opponents. He states their position in this way.

They [Catholics] think that the days of fasting are those determined in the gospel, "when the Bridegroom is taken away" [Matt 9:14–15]; and they assume that these are the only legitimate days of fasting for Christians, since the old legal and prophetic customs are abolished. . . . Beyond that, fasting according to the new discipline is to be done without distinction of days, by choice and not by requirement, at the times and for the needs chosen by each individual. And this was observed by the apostles, who imposed no other yoke of fixed days of fasting to be observed by all in common, nor similarly of station days [half fasts] that even they themselves keep on the fourth and sixth days [Wednesday and Friday], which they continue at random, not subject to a legal precept nor extended beyond the end of the day.

—Tertullian, *On Fasting* 2

OVER against heretics who avoided meat and wine at all times as being part of an evil creation, Cyril of Jerusalem stated the catholic position that abstention from these things was a discipline of foregoing something good, not the avoidance of something evil.

For we fast by abstaining from wine and meats, not as hating something abominable, but looking for our reward in order that, by disregarding things that are apprehended by the senses, we might enjoy a feast that is spiritual and intellectual. . . . Do not despise those who eat but who partake of food on account of the weakness of the body. . . . When you abstain from these things, do not abstain as if they were abominable, since then you would have no reward, but disregard them, good as they are, for the sake of the better spiritual things set before us.

— Cyril of Jerusalem, *Catechetical Lectures* 4.27

ONE OF the desert fathers speaks of the spiritual benefits of fasting.

Abba Doulas said, "If the enemy forces us to give up our quietness, we must not listen to him. For nothing is like quietness and abstinence from food. They combine to fight together against him. For they give keen insight to the inner eyes."

— *Apophthegmata Patrum*, Alphabetical Collection, Doulas # 1

THERE was also a warning against spiritual pride by those who engage in more rigorous spiritual disciplines.

Isidore said, "If you fast regularly, do not be filled with pride. If you think highly of yourself because of fasting, then it would be better for you to eat meat. It is better for a person to eat meat than to be filled with pride and boast about it."

— *Apophthegmata Patrum*, Alphabetical Collection, Isidore of Pelusium # 4

The Vision of God

THE GOAL of Christian spirituality was often expressed in terms of seeing God.

The true gnostic prays in thought at every hour, becoming akin to God through love. First of all, this person asks for forgiveness of sins. And after sinning no more, he still asks to do well and to understand the creation and administration of the world by the Lord, so that, becoming "pure in heart" [Matt 5:8], he may by the knowledge of God through the Son be initiated into the beatific vision "face-to-face" [1 Cor 13:12].
— Clement of Alexandria, *Miscellanies* 6.12

Gregory of Nyssa integrated the goal of the vision of God into his view of spirituality as perpetual progress in perfection.

This truly is the vision of God: never to be satisfied in the desire to see him. But one must always, by looking at what he can see, rekindle his desire to see more. Thus, no limit would interrupt growth in the ascent to God, since no limit to the Good can be found nor is the increasing of desire for the Good brought to an end because it is satisfied.[6]
— Gregory of Nyssa, *Life of Moses* 2.239

What food and drink are to the body—that is, the things by which our nature is preserved—looking toward the Good is to the soul. This also is truly a gift of God: to fix one's gaze on God. . . . For as a fleshly person gains strength by eating and drinking, so a person who looks to the Good—the true Good would be the One who alone is Good—has the gift of God in all his labor, that is, always to look toward the Good in Christ Jesus our Lord.
— Gregory of Nyssa, *Homilies on Ecclesiastes* 8, on Eccl 3:12–13

Worship

All human wisdom consists in this alone, the knowledge and worship of God.
— Lactantius, *Divine Institutes* 3.30

The following general statement contrasts pagan and Christian worship.

We [Christians] praise [the Maker of the Universe] as much as we are able by the word of prayer and thanksgiving for all the things with which we are supplied, since we have learned that the only honor worthy of him is not to consume with fire the things made by him for our sustenance but to use them for ourselves and those in need; and, being thankful in word, to send up to him honors and hymns for our creation, for all the means of health, the various qualities of the different classes of things, the changes of the seasons, while making petitions for our coming into incorruption by faith in him.

—Justin Martyr, *1 Apology* 13

CHRISTIANS had to defend their practice of worshiping the one God alone against demands that they worship the civil gods of paganism and the Roman emperor.

A human being is to be honored in a manner appropriate to a human being, but only God is to be reverenced. He is not visible to human eyes, nor is he comprehensible by any means. Only if commanded to deny him will I disobey—I will rather die than to be shown an ungrateful liar. . . . I refuse to worship what has been made by him for our sakes. The sun and the moon came into being for the sake of human beings. How then can I worship my servants? How can I declare wood and stones to be gods? The spirit that pervades matter is less than the more divine Spirit; what is similar to matter is not to be honored equally with the perfect God. Neither is the unnameable God able to be bought off with gifts, for he who is without need of anything is necessarily misrepresented by us if we say he is in need.

—Tatian, *Oration to the Greeks* 4

SOME authors affirmed that worship is not confined to special days and places but that the whole of life rightly lived is worship.

We are commanded to worship and honor the Word, since we are persuaded that he is Savior and Leader, and through him to worship the Father, not on special days as others do, but to do this continually throughout the whole of this life and in every place. . . . A true gnostic honors God. That is, he acknowledges God's grace of knowledge and manner of life, not in a special place, at certain festivals, and on appointed days but his whole life in every place, even if he happens to be alone or where there are some who are believers. The presence of a good man always improves the one with whom he associates on account of reverence and respect for him. If so, then is it not reasonable that the person who through knowledge, life, and thanksgiving is always present unceasingly with God would grow better than he now is in all things—in deeds, words, and disposition? . . . Keeping festival in all of life, persuaded that God is present in everything everywhere, we practice farming, giving praise; we sail in ships, singing hymns; we live our lives according to another system of government.

—Clement of Alexandria, *Miscellanies* 7.7

In the following selection Clement of Alexandria speaks about activities that encompass the whole of life in a way that draws on the language of Christian worship assemblies (he probably has these in mind also).

A good conscience preserves sanctity toward God and justice toward human beings. It keeps the soul pure with holy thoughts, pure words, and just deeds. By thus receiving the Lord's power, the soul practices to be god, considering nothing to be bad except ignorance and action that does not accord with right reason. It always gives thanks in all things to God through righteous hearing and divine reading, true inquiry, holy oblation, blessed prayer, praising, hymning, blessing, singing Psalms. Such a soul is never separated from God at any time.

—Clement of Alexandria, *Miscellanies*
6.14.113.3

Even in times of persecution Christians continued to hold their assemblies. Some wanted to suspend these meetings or flee at the threat of persecution; Tertullian argued otherwise.

Some with a weak and cold faith will tremble and seize upon those who assemble in church and say, "When we meet in disorder, at the same time, and quite a number come together in church, we will be sought out by the pagans—and we are fearful lest the pagans are disturbed." Do you not know that God is Lord of all? If God wills, then you will experience persecution; but if it is not his will, the pagans will be quiet. . . .

You say, "How shall we gather together; how shall we celebrate the Lord's services?" In the same way as the apostles, who were protected by faith, not by money. If this faith can move a mountain [1 Cor 13:2], how much more a soldier? May your safeguard be wisdom, not a bribe. . . . If you are not able to assemble by day, you have the night, illuminated by the light of Christ against the night.

— Tertullian, *On Flight* 3.2; 14.1

TERTULLIAN also spoke about private devotions.

He tastes with his spirit: if he makes a prayer to the Lord, he is near to heaven; if he is pouring over the Scriptures, he is altogether in them; if he sings a psalm, it pleases him; if he adjures a demon, he is confident in himself.

— Tertullian, *Exhortation to Chastity* 10

PRIVATE devotion served as preparation for public worship.

They said concerning Abba Poemen that when he was preparing to attend the assembly for worship, he used to sit by himself, examining his thoughts for about an hour, and then he would set out.

— *Apophthegmata Patrum*, Alphabetical Collection, Poemen # 32

THE WORSHIPER becomes like the object of worship, hence Lactantius said that the conduct of pagan deities did not inspire righteous living.

It is not difficult to explain why the worshipers of the gods are unable to be good and just. For how can those who worship gods who shed blood—Mars and Bellona—abstain from shedding blood themselves? Or how shall those who worship Jupiter, who drove away his father, spare their parents? Or those who worship Saturn spare the infants who are born to them? How can those who worship a naked and adulterous goddess [Venus], who was—so to speak—prostituted among the gods, respect chastity? How will those who know the thefts of Mercury, who taught that deceit is not fraud but cleverness, abstain from robbery? How shall those who worship Jupiter, Hercules, Liber, Apollo, and others—whose debaucheries with males and females are well known—control their lusts? . . . For in order to placate a deity whom you worship one must do those things that please and delight the deity. So it comes about that a god shapes the life of the worshiper according to the quality of its own divine nature, because the most religious form of worship is imitation.

—Lactantius, *Divine Institutes* 5.10.15–18

LACTANTIUS devoted book 6 of *Divine Institutes* to the consideration of true worship. As a transition to the subpoint on spiritual sacrifices, we include some selections from this book.

I now come to the highest and greatest part of this work, which is to teach the religious observances and sacrifice by which God is to be worshiped. For this is the duty of human beings, and this alone constitutes the highest activity and the basis of a happy life for everyone, since we were created and received the breath of life from him . . . for the purpose of worshiping God the Creator of the sun and the sky with a pure and unblemished mind. . . . For the holy and unique Majesty desires only innocence from human beings. If a person offers this to God, he makes a sufficiently pious and religious sacrifice. . . .

Therefore would someone who offers the light of tapers and candles to the one who is the author and giver of light be considered of sound mind? Truly he requires of us another kind of light, which does not produce smoke, . . . the serene and clear light of the mind. . . . This is the religion of heaven, which consists not in corruptible things, but in the virtues of the soul that is derived from heaven. This is true worship: the mind of the worshiper presenting itself as an unblemished sacrificial victim to God. . . .

Whoever, therefore, observes these heavenly precepts is the true worshiper of God. That one's sacrifices are gentleness of spirit, an innocent life, and the doing of good deeds. The person who exhibits these qualities makes a sacrifice with every good and pious deed that is done. For God does not desire as a sacrificial victim a dumb animal's life and blood but the person's own life. . . .

What then is pure? What is worthy of God except what he requires in his divine law? . . . The incorporeal, which is pleasing to him, is to be offered to God. The gift to him is integrity of the soul, the sacrifice is praise and hymn; for since God is unseen, he ought to be worshiped with those things that are not seen. Therefore, no other religion is true except the one that consists in virtue and justice. . . . For God ought to be worshiped in word, since God is Word, as he himself confessed. Therefore, the highest religious ceremony in the worship of God is praise directed to God from the mouth of a just person. For this to be acceptable to God, it must be a work of humility, fear, and the greatest degree of devotion; for those who trust in their integrity and innocence incur the charge of conceit and arrogance, and consequently forfeit the reward of virtue. . . . In summary, one should have God within oneself, consecrated in the heart, because one is a temple of God.

—Lactantius, *Divine Institutes* 6.1.2, 4;
6.2.5–6, 13; 6.24.26–27;
6.25.5, 7, 12, 15

Spiritual Sacrifice

AGREEING with the thought of some Greek philosophers and poets, Christians substituted spiritual sacrifice for the material sacrifices of paganism.

The Creator and Father of the universe does not need blood, the odor of a burnt offering, nor the fragrance of flowers and incense, for he himself is the perfect fragrance, self-sufficient, and in need of nothing. The greatest sacrifice to him is for us to know who stretched out and made round the heavens, who established the earth at the center, who gathered together the water into the seas and distinguished the light from the darkness, who adorned the sky with stars and made every seed to sprout on the earth, who made animals and created humans. . . . Why ought I to offer whole burnt offerings, since God has no need of them? It is necessary to offer the bloodless sacrifice, to bring the "rational worship" [Rom 12:1].

—Athenagoras, *Plea for the Christians* 13

COMPARE the above with Tatian, *Oration to the Greeks* 4, cited above.

Sacrifices do not make a person holy, for God does not need sacrifice. It is the conscience of the person who presents the offering that makes the sacrifice holy. When this is pure, it moves God to accept the gift as from a friend. . . . Therefore when the church makes its offering with singleness of mind, God rightly considers her gift a pure sacrifice.

—Irenaeus, *Against Heresies* 4.18.3–4

We rightly do not sacrifice to God, who needs nothing, but supplies all things to every person. We glorify the One who was sacrificed for us by sacrificing ourselves for him. . . . For God delights in our salvation alone. Rightly then we do not bring a sacrifice to the One who is not won over by pleasures. . . . The Divine is not charmed or influenced by sacrifices,

dedications, glory, honor, or any such things, but likewise he appears to excellent and good people.

—Clement of Alexandria, *Miscellanies* 7.3

Every place where we entertain the thought of God is truly sacred.
. . . [The true gnostic's] whole life is a holy festival. His sacrifices are prayers,
praises, reading the Scriptures before meals, psalms and hymns at mealtime
and before going to bed, and prayers again during the night. These activities
unite him with the divine chorus, and by continual remembrance he arranges
himself for everlasting contemplation. What then? Does he not know the
other kinds of sacrifice, the giving of both money and teachings to those who
are in need? Surely he does.

—Clement of Alexandria, *Miscellanies* 7.7

What image can I make of God, since—when we think correctly—
a human being is himself the image of God? What temple can I erect for him,
when this whole universe made by his work is unable to hold him? And how
can I, a human being lodged in such an expanse, confine a power of such
majesty in one building? Is it not better to dedicate our minds, to consecrate
our inmost hearts? Shall I offer to God sacrifices and victims that he provided
for my use, thereby rejecting his gift? That is ingratitude, since the acceptable
sacrifice is a good spirit, a pure mind, and a sincere conscience. Therefore,
the one who cultivates innocence makes supplication to God; the one who is
attentive to justice offers libations to God; the one who avoids fraud propiti-
ates God; and the one who rescues a person from danger sacrifices the best
animal. These are our sacrifices; these are our sacred rites. Among us, the
most just person is the most religious.

—Minucius Felix, *Octavius* 32.1–3

The mind of a pious person is a holy temple of God.
A pure and sinless heart is the best altar for God.
The only suitable sacrifice to God is the doing of good deeds
for people because of God.

— *Sentences of Sextus* 46–47

Let us offer our very selves, the possession most precious to God
and most appropriate. Let us give back to the Image [Christ, Col 1:15] what is
according to the Image [Gen 1:26].

—Gregory of Nazianzus, *Oration* 1.4

For all together we are God's temple and individually we are each a temple [1 Cor 3:16–17]. . . . When our heart rises to him, it is his altar. We find acceptance in him by the Priest, his Only Begotten. We sacrifice bleeding victims when we contend for his truth unto the shedding of our blood. We burn the sweetest incense when we are aflame with pious and holy love in his sight. We vow and return to him what he has given us—and our very selves. By solemn feasts and on appointed days we consecrate the memory of his blessings, lest by the passing of time ungrateful forgetfulness steal upon us. We sacrifice to him the sacrifice of humility and praise on the altar of the heart with the fire of fervent love.

—Augustine, *City of God* 10.3.19

Hymns and Praise

THE ODES of Solomon is the oldest surviving Christian hymnbook—just how early is not certain, but many place it at the beginning of the second century.

I am putting on [the love of the Lord].
And His members are with Him,
And I am dependent on them; and He loves me.
For I should not have known how to love the Lord,
If He had not continuously loved me.
Who is able to distinguish love,
Except Him who is loved?
I love the Beloved and I myself love Him,
And where His rest is, there also am I.[7]

— *Odes of Solomon* 3.1–5

I praise Thee, O Lord,
Because I love Thee.
O Most High, forsake me not,
For Thou art my hope.
Freely did I receive Thy grace,
May I live by it.

. . . .

Indeed my hope is upon the Lord,
And I will not fear.
And because the Lord is my salvation,
I will not fear.
And He is as a Crown upon my head,
And I shall not be shaken.
Even if everything should be shaken,
I shall stand firm.
And though all things visible should perish,
I shall not die;
Because the Lord is with me,
And I with Him.
Hallelujah.[8]

— Odes of Solomon 5.1–3, 10–15

As the occupation of the ploughman is the ploughshare,
And the occupation of the helmsman is the steering of the ship,
So also my occupation is the psalm of the Lord by His hymns.
My art and my service are in His hymns,
Because His love has nourished my heart,
And His fruits He poured unto my lips.
For my love is the Lord;
Hence I will sing unto Him,
For I am strengthened by His praises,
And I have faith in Him.
I will open my mouth,
And His spirit will speak through me
The glory of the Lord and His beauty,
The work of His hands,
And the labour of His fingers;
For the multitude of His mercies,
And the strength of His Word.
For the Word of the Lord investigates that which is invisible,
And perceives His thought.
For the eye sees His works,
And the ear hears His thought.
It is He who made the earth broad,
And placed the waters in the sea.
He expanded the heaven,
And fixed the stars.

And He fixed the creation and set it up,
Then He rested from His works.
. . . .
And the worlds were made by His Word,
And by the thought of His heart.
Praise and honour to His name.
Hallelujah.[9]

— *Odes of Solomon* 16.1–12, 19–20

Fill for yourselves water from the living fountain of the Lord,
Because it has been opened for you.
And come all you thirsty and take a drink,
And rest beside the fountain of the Lord.
Because it is pleasing and sparkling,
And perpetually refreshes the self.
For much sweeter is its water than honey,
And the honeycomb of bees is not to be compared with it;
Because it flowed from the lips of the Lord,
And it named from the heart of the Lord.
And it came boundless and invisible,
And until it was set in the middle they knew it not.
Blessed are they who have drunk from it,
And have refreshed themselves by it.
Hallelujah.[10]

— *Odes of Solomon* 30.1–7

Sing psalms to the Lord, his saints." It is not the one who brings forth the words of the psalm with his mouth who sings to the Lord, but those who send up psalmody with a pure heart, are holy, and preserve righteousness before God. These are able to sing psalms to God, harmoniously following the spiritual rhythms.

— Basil of Caesarea, *Homilies on the Psalms* 29.3, on Ps 30:4

THE PSALMS formed the basic hymnbook of the early church.

All of the Psalms have been spoken and arranged by the Spirit so that the emotions of our soul may be understood in them according to what was written beforetime, and so that all of them may have been written as about us and become our very own words, for a reminder of our emotions and a corrective of our conduct. Those things the psalmists have said are types and characterizations of us. . . .

Now it is necessary to include the reason why such words are sung with melody and song. For some of the unlearned among us, although believing that the words are inspired by God, nevertheless think that the Psalms are sung on account of the euphony and for pleasure to the ear. But this is not so, for the Scripture does not seek the sweet and beguiling, although even these qualities were intended to benefit the soul in all things. Melody has two purposes. First, it was fitting that divine Scripture sing hymns to God vocally, not only in the single tone of prose but also in the full range of the voice. . . . Second, just as harmony unites musical instruments and accomplishes one symphony, so the Word desires that human beings not be inharmonious and divided within. . . . The harmonious recitation of the Psalms is an image and type of the tranquil and calm constitution of the mind. For as we make known and signify the thoughts of the soul through the words that we utter, so the Lord wishes the melody of the words to be a symbol of the spiritual harmony in the soul; thus he decreed that the odes be sung harmoniously and the Psalms be recited as an ode.

—Athanasius, *Letter to Marcellinus* 12; 27–28

THREE different methods of singing were employed in the early church: antiphonal, responsorial, and unison.

The customs we observe are in agreement and harmony with all the churches of God. At night our people are awake and go to the house of prayer. In labor, affliction, and continuous tears they make confession to God. At last, arising from their prayers, they enter into psalmody. At one time, divided into two groups, they sing antiphonally to one another. This practice strengthens their recitation of the words, and at the same time controls their attention and keeps their hearts from distraction. Next, entrusting to one person the task of leading the melody, the others sing the response. Thus they pass the night in a variety of psalmody interspersed with prayers. When day begins to dawn, all in common—as if of one mouth and one heart—lift up the psalm of confession to the Lord, each one making the words of repentance his or her own.

—Basil of Caesarea, *Letters* 207.3 [4]

At that time David sang the Psalms, and we today with David. He had a kithara [harp] of lifeless strings; the church has a kithara made of living strings. Our tongues are the strings of our kithara, putting forth a different sound yet a godly harmony. For indeed women and men, young and old, have different voices, but they do not differ in the words of hymnody, for the Spirit blends the voice of each and effects one melody in all. . . .

The soul is an excellent musician, an artist; the body is an instrument, holding the place of the kithara, aulos [flute], and lyre. . . . Since it is necessary to pray unceasingly, the instrument is always with the artist.

—John Chrysostom, *Homily on Psalms*
145.2, 3, on Ps 146:2, 3

The intention of our present life ought to be the praise of God. The everlasting exultation of our future life will be the praise of God, and no one can qualify for this future life unless he has practiced for it in the present.

—Augustine, *Expositions on the Psalms* 148.1

The Lord's Supper

WHETHER the following prayer belongs to a love feast, the Eucharist, or— what is more likely—an occasion where both were combined, is not clear.

We give thanks to you, Holy Father, for your holy name that you caused to dwell in our hearts, and for the knowledge, faith, and immortality that you made known to us through Jesus your Servant. To you be the glory forever! You, Lord Almighty, created all things on account of your name, and you gave food and drink to human beings for their refreshment so that they might give thanks to you, but you graciously bestowed on us spiritual food and drink and life eternal through your Servant. Above all, we give you thanks because you are mighty. To you be the glory forever! Remember, Lord, your church and deliver her from every evil, perfect her in your love, and gather her that you have sanctified from the four winds into your kingdom that you prepared for her. For the power and the glory are yours forever. Let grace come and this world pass away. Hosanna to the God of David! If anyone is holy, let him come. If anyone is not, let him repent. Maranatha! [Our Lord, come!] Amen.

—*Didache* 10

We [Christians] are the true high priestly race of God, as God himself testifies when he said that "in every place among the Gentiles they offer pure and acceptable sacrifices to him" [Mal 1:11]. God does not receive

sacrifices from anyone except through his priests. Therefore, God in antici-
pation testifies that all the sacrifices that Jesus Christ arranged to be done
through his name are well pleasing to him, namely, the Eucharist of the bread
and the cup, the sacrifices that Christians in all the earth make. . . . I also
agree that prayers and thanksgivings performed by worthy persons are the
only sacrifices that are perfect and well pleasing to God. For these alone
Christians undertake to make, even at the memorial of their solid and liquid
food that brings to mind the suffering that the Son of God endured because
of them.

—Justin Martyr, *Dialogue* 116–17

Jesus received flesh from the flesh of Mary. He walked here in that
flesh, and he gave that flesh to us to be eaten for salvation [John 6:54–63]. No
one eats that flesh without first worshiping. . . . [Jesus said] "Understand
spiritually what I say. You are not to eat this body that you see nor drink the
blood that those who crucify me will shed. I have presented a mystery to you.
Spiritually understood, it will bring life. Although this must be celebrated
visibly, it must be understood spiritually."

—Augustine, *Expositions on the Psalms*
98.9 [Engl. 99.8], on Ps 99:5

To believe in Christ is to eat the living bread. The person who believes eats. This person is invisibly filled because he is invisibly born again. . . .

Now we also receive visible food. The sacrament is one thing; the
power of the sacrament is another. Many receive at the altar and die, and indeed die by receiving [1 Cor 11:29]. . . . See then, my brothers and sisters: eat
heavenly bread in a spiritual sense; bring innocence to the altar. Even though
your sins are committed daily, let them not be deadly. Before you approach
the altar, be attentive to the words "Forgive us our debts, as we forgive our
debtors" [Matt 6:12]. You forgive, and it is forgiven you. Approach in peace,
and it is bread, not poison. . . . You can lie to God, but you cannot deceive
God. . . .

[Commenting on John 6:50:] Manna signified this bread; the altar
of God signified this bread—those things were sacraments. As signs they
were diverse; but in what they signified they are equivalent. . . . Spiritually
they are the same, but bodily they are different; because they ate manna we
eat something else. But spiritually it was the very thing that we eat [Christ].
. . . [1 Cor 10:1–4]. As was the bread, so the drink. The rock was Christ in a
symbol; the true Christ is in word and flesh. . . . What pertains to the power
of the sacrament is not what pertains to the appearance of the sacrament: it

pertains to the person who eats within, not outwardly, the person who eats in his heart rather than biting with his teeth.

[On John 6:56—the Latin text brackets the words that I have enclosed in brackets.] This is what it means to eat that food and drink that drink: to abide in Christ and to have him abide in you. Consequently, those who do not abide in Christ and in whom Christ does not abide without doubt neither eat [spiritually] his flesh nor drink his blood [although in a fleshly and visible way biting with their teeth the sacrament of the body and blood of Christ]. Rather, they eat and drink the sacrament of something so great to their judgment when they presume to come to the sacraments morally unclean.

—Augustine, *Homilies on the Gospel of John* 26.1, 11, 12, 18, on John 6:41–59

As a deer desires the springs of waters, so my soul desires you, my God" [Ps 42:1]. . . . It is the same with the monks who sit in the desert and burn from the poison of evil demons. They desire the Sabbath and Lord's Day so that they may come to the springs of waters, that is, to the body and blood of the Lord, so that they may be purified from the bitterness of the Evil One.

—*Apophthegmata Patrum*, Alphabetical Collection, Poemen # 30

Prayer

Definition and Description

CLEMENT of Alexandria has a small treatise on prayer in his *Miscellanies*. We include some selected quotations.

We must offer God not expensive sacrifices, but those he loves. The compounded incense that was commanded in the Law [Exod 30:34] is the blending of many tongues and voices in prayer. . . .

We pray for those things that we ask for, and we ask for those things that we desire. Our prayers and our desires correspond; they aim at the good things and the benefits available in creation. The true gnostic, therefore, makes prayers and requests for the truly good things that pertain to the soul . . . so as no longer to possess good things (like lessons that are presented) but to be good. . . .

Thus prayer is—to speak more boldly—talking with God. Even if whispering or not opening the lips we speak through our silence, we cry out from within. God unceasingly gives ear to all inner speech. . . .

While some set aside appointed hours for prayer, as for example the third, sixth, and ninth hours, the true gnostic prays throughout his whole life, endeavoring to be with God through prayer. . . .

Since God knows those who are worthy of good things and those who are not, he gives what is appropriate to each person. Therefore he would not give to those who are unworthy, even if they asked often, but he would give to those who are clearly worthy. Nevertheless petition is not redundant, even if he gives good things without being asked. . . .

It is possible to send up prayer without the voice, by concentrating all the inner spiritual being on the voice of the mind in an undistracted turning to God. . . .

He does not use many words in voiced prayer, since he has learned what things one must ask for from the Lord. He will pray in every place, but not openly and obviously to the crowd. He prays while engaged in walking, in conversation, in quiet times, in reading, and in doing works that accord with reason in every situation.

—Clement of Alexandria, *Miscellanies* 7.6–7

For us [Christians] altars are the spirit of each righteous person, from which incense is sent up that is truly and rationally fragrant, that is, prayers [Rev 5:8] from a pure conscience.

—Origen, *Against Celsus* 8.17

The rest of the Christians do not use in their prayers the names applied to God that are found in the [Hebrew] divine Scriptures. The Greeks use Greek names and the Romans use Roman names, and in the same way all pray in their own language to God, praising him as they are able. For the Lord of every language hears those who pray in every language, hearing—if I may say it this way—as if from one voice what is expressed in many languages.

—Origen, *Against Celsus* 8.37

THE FOLLOWING passage defines the different words for prayer in 1 Tim 2:1.

I consider then that "supplication" is the petition sent up with entreaty to obtain something that a person lacks; "prayer" is sent up by someone with words of praise in a dignified manner concerning important matters; "intercession" is a request concerning others by someone who has a greater measure of confidence; "thanksgiving" is the acknowledgment with prayer of the good things caused by God, when the one making the acknowledgment comprehends the greatness—or what seems to be great to the one who has benefited—of the blessing that came to him.

—Origen, *On Prayer* 14.2

ORIGEN outlined the elements of prayer.

These are the four topics of prayer. At the beginning and introduction of the prayer, let each one offer—as far as one can—words of praise to God through Christ, who is acknowledged and praised together with him, in the Holy Spirit. After this, let each person set in order common thanksgiving for the benefits received by many people that lead to thanksgiving and for those things God has done for each individual. After the thanksgiving, it seems to me that everyone should make bitter accusation before God for their own sins, and ask first for healing so that they may be delivered from the habit that brings about sin and second for forgiveness of past sins. Fourth, after the confession, it seems to me that one must offer petition for the great and heavenly matters, both in general and for oneself, and for one's family and those who are dearest. And finally, let the prayer be concluded with words of praise to God through Christ in the Holy Spirit.

—Origen, *On Prayer* 33.1

When we stand for prayer, beloved brothers and sisters, we ought to be watchful and apply ourselves vigorously to prayer with the whole heart. Let every carnal and worldly thought disappear, and do not let the mind at that time think on anything except only what is being prayed. . . . Let the heart be closed against the adversary and open only to God, and do not allow the enemy of God to approach at the time of prayer. For he frequently steals upon us, penetrates our hearts, and by subtle deception calls our prayers away from God. The result is that we have one thing in our heart and another in our voice, when we ought to pray with a sincere intention to God not with voice alone but also in mind and thought. What a weakness it is to wander in mind and to be carried away by inappropriate and profane thoughts when you entreat the Lord, as if there might be something greater you ought to think about than what you are saying to God. How can you petition to be heard by God when you do not hear yourself?

—Cyprian, *On the Lord's Prayer* 31

We must devote ourselves more to prayer. For prayer is like the leader of the chorus of virtues. Through it we ask for the other virtues from God. The person devoted to prayer has fellowship with God and comes in contact with him through a mystical holiness, a spiritual energy, and an inexpressible disposition. Taking the Spirit as our guide and fellow contestant, our love for the Lord is kindled, and we seethe with longing. Since no satiety in prayer is found, we are always burning with passion for the Good and stirring up desire in the soul. . . .

According to Scripture it is not our falling to the knee and placing ourselves in the position of those who pray that is excellent and pleasing to God, while our thoughts wander away from him. Rather, what pleases God is the rejecting of all idleness of thought and every improper attention to the body in order to deliver the soul over to prayer.

—Gregory of Nyssa, *On the Christian Mode of Life*

The brethren also asked him [Agathon] 'Amongst all good works, which is the virtue which requires the greatest effort?' He answered, 'Forgive me, but I think there is no labor greater than that of prayer to God. For every time a man wants to pray, his enemies, the demons, want to prevent him, for they know that it is only by turning him from prayer that they can hinder his journey. Whatever good work a man undertakes, if he perseveres in it, he will attain rest. But prayer is warfare to the last breath.'[11]

—*Apophthegmata Patrum*, Alphabetical Collection, Agathon # 9

Abba Zenon said, "Whoever wants God to hear his prayer quickly, when he rises and stretches out his hands to God, he will pray from his soul for his enemies before anything else, even his own soul's welfare. Through this virtuous deed, whatever is asked of God, he will answer."

—*Apophthegmata Patrum*, Alphabetical Collection, Zeno # 7

Some asked Abba Macarius, "How ought we to pray?" The old man said to them, "There is no need to make long prayers, but extend your hands and say, 'Lord, as you will and as you know, have mercy.' If the conflict is urgent within you, say, 'Lord, help.' He knows what is good for us, and he acts with mercy toward us."

—*Apophthegmata Patrum*, Alphabetical Collection, Macarius # 19

Abba Nilus said, "Whatever you do in vengeance to a brother who has harmed you, it will all come back to your heart in your time of prayer."

Again he said, "Prayer is the outgrowth of gentleness and absence of anger."

Again he said, "Prayer is a remedy against grief and despondency." . . .

Again he said, "Whatever you have endured in living a disciplined life, you will find its fruit in the time of prayer." . . .

Again he said, "Do not wish that things in regard to yourself happen as seems good to you, but as pleases God; then you will be untroubled and thankful in your prayers."

— *Apophthegmata Patrum*, Alphabetical Collection, Nilus # 1–3, # 5, # 7

The Necessity and Frequency of Prayer

A Christian—even an unlearned one—is persuaded that every place in the world is part of the universe and that the whole world is the temple of God. He prays "in every place" [1 Tim 2:8], shutting his eyes of sense and raising the eyes of his soul, he rises above the whole world. He does not stop at the vault of heaven, but being led by the divine Spirit, he comes in thought to the place above the heavens, and arriving as it were outside of the world, he sends up prayer to God. He does not pray for the ordinary circumstances of life, for he has learned from Jesus to seek nothing small, that is, nothing having to do with the senses, but only the great and truly divine things. These things are contributed and given by God to lead us to blessedness with him through his Son, the Word, who is God.

— Origen, *Against Celsus* 7.44

A person who "prays without ceasing" [1 Thess 5:17]—deeds of virtue and fulfillment of the commandments being included as a part of prayer—combines prayer with the necessary deeds and proper actions with the prayer. For only in this way can we accept that "pray without ceasing" is a saying that can be put into practice, that is, if we can say that the whole life of a holy person is one great combined prayer, of which what we commonly call prayer is a part. This latter ought to be observed at least three times every day. [Dan 6:10; Acts 10:9–11; Ps 5:3; 141:2; 119:62; and Acts 16:25 are quoted.]

— Origen, *On Prayer* 12.2

If I have righteousness," someone will perhaps ask, "what need is there for prayer, since my actions suffice to accomplish everything? Moreover, the One who gives knows what we need." We need prayer because it is no small bond of love for God, producing in us the habit of conversation with him and leading us in the love of wisdom. If someone who associates with a remarkable person profits much from the association, how much more does the one who talks constantly with God. We do not know the benefit of prayer as we should, since we do not apply ourselves to it with diligence and do not make use of it according to God's laws. If we are going to converse with persons who are above us, we are careful that our appearance, our walk, and our clothing are as they should be for conversing with them. Yet in approaching God we yawn, scratch ourselves, turn this way and that, pay little attention. . . . If we approach him with proper reverence, as those who are about to hold conversation with God, then we would know how much benefit we enjoy, even before receiving what we ask for.

— John Chrysostom, *Commentary on the Psalms* 4.2, on Ps 4:1

The Power of Prayer

GREGORY of Nyssa proceeds from expressing the necessity of frequent prayer to a description of the power of prayer, and so offers a transition to this new topic.

Most people bypass and neglect prayer, this holy and divine work. Concerning this subject, therefore, it seems to me of first importance to insist as much as possible in this discourse that it is absolutely necessary to devote oneself to prayer. . . .

If prayer precedes one's occupation, sin finds no entrance into the soul. When the remembrance of God is firmly established in the heart, the devices of the enemy remain ineffective, and righteousness will always mediate in disputes. . . .

In prayer, a person is present with God, for the person who prays is separated from the enemy. Prayer safeguards self-control, controls the temper, restrains pride, cleanses us of malice, overthrows envy, destroys injustice, and corrects impiety. Prayer is the strength of bodies, the prosperity of the home, the good will of the city, the strength of the kingdom, the victory in war, the security of peace, the bringing together of enemies, the preserver of allies. Prayer is the seal of virginity, the pledge of marriage, the shield of the traveler, the guard of those who sleep, the courage of those who keep watch, the productivity of farmers, the deliverance of sailors. . . . Prayer is conversation with God, the contemplation of unseen things, the fulfillment of things desired, equal in honor with the angels, the progress of good things, the overthrow of evils, the correction of sinners, the enjoyment of the present, and the substance of things hoped for.

—Gregory of Nyssa, *On the Lord's Prayer* 1

It was the will of Christ that prayer would not be effective for any evil. He conferred all its power for good. Thus prayer knows nothing except to call souls of the fallen back from the very path of death, to restore the weak, to cure the sick, to purify those possessed by demons, to open the doors of a prison, to loose the bonds of the innocent. Prayer washes away sins, repels temptations, extinguishes persecutions, consoles the discouraged, delights the generous, accompanies travelers, calms waves, paralyzes robbers, supports the poor, rules the rich, lifts up the fallen, upholds those who are falling, maintains those who are standing. Prayer is a wall of faith, our arms and weapons that protect us on every side against our enemy. Thus we never go forward unarmed.

—Tertullian, *On Prayer* 29

We must propitiate the one God who is over all and pray that he will be gracious, making him favorably disposed by godliness and virtue. . . . We boldly say that when people with free choice set before themselves the better things, many myriads of sacred powers [angels] unbidden pray together with them.

—Origen, *Against Celsus* 8.64

THE FOLLOWING statement was made with reference to the prayer of Hezekiah in 2 Kgs 20:1–7.

Thickness of walls is no hindrance to prayers sent up with devotion.

—Cyril of Jerusalem, *Catechetical Lectures* 2.15

People who pray like Elijah [1 Kgs 17:19–24; 18:36–44] and Hannah [1 Sam 1:10–11], even before they receive what they ask for, enjoy many good benefits from their prayer—restraining all their passions, assuaging their anger, casting out envy, melting their desire, weakening their longing for the things of this life, establishing their soul in great calm, and finally lifting it to heaven itself. . . . Prayer especially softens hardness of heart. Therefore when you practice prayer, seek not only to receive what you ask for but also to make your soul better by prayer. This is the function of prayer. The person who prays in this way rises above the concerns of this life, gives wings to the mind, makes thoughts lighter, and is conquered by none of the passions.

—John Chrysostom, *Commentary on the Psalms* 130.1–2

The Lord's Prayer

TERTULLIAN comments on the character of the Lord's Prayer as a summary of Bible teaching.

In fact, a summary of the whole gospel is included in the Lord's Prayer. . . .

In these summaries of a few words how many sayings of the prophets, evangelists, and apostles are touched on—sermons of the Lord, parables, examples, precepts! How many duties at the same time are captured! The honor of God in "Father"; the testimony of faith in "name"; the offering of obedience in "will"; the remembrance of hope in "kingdom"; the petition for life in "bread"; the confession of "sins" in the prayer for forgiveness; the concern for "temptation" in the request for protection. What about this is to be wondered at? God alone is able to teach how he wants to be approached in prayer.

—Tertullian, *On Prayer* 1.6; 9

CYPRIAN expands on the corporate intention of the Lord's Prayer.

Above all, the Teacher of peace and Master of unity did not want prayer to be individual and private, so as to pray only for oneself. We do not say, "My Father who is in heaven," nor "Give me my bread today," nor does each ask that the debt be forgiven for himself alone, nor request that he alone not be led into temptation and that he alone be delivered from evil. Our prayer is public and in community, and when we pray we ask not for one person but for the whole people, because we the whole people are one. The God of peace and Master of concord who teaches unity desires that we each pray for all, even as he carried all in one.

—Cyprian, *On the Lord's Prayer* 8

"OUR FATHER in heaven"

We shall use the name "Father" for God reluctantly if we are not genuine children, lest in addition to our other sins we also become guilty of the charge of impiety. . . .

Therefore the saints, being an image of the Image—the true Image being the Son—imitate his Sonship, becoming conformed not only "to the body of the glory" [Phil 3:21] of Christ but also to the One who is "in the body." They become conformed "to the body of his glory" by being transformed through "the renewing of the mind" [Rom 12:2]. . . .

When the Father of the saints is said to be "in heaven" we should not take this to mean that he is circumscribed in bodily form and lives "in heaven," for if God is contained by heaven, then he is less than heaven. But we must believe that by the ineffable power of his Godhead all things are contained and held together by him.

—Origen, *On Prayer* 22.3–4; 23.1

ᗞow great is the kindness of the Lord! How abundant his goodness and regard for us when he willed that we make our prayer in his sight and call him "Father," and that just as Christ is Son of God we also are named children of God! None of us would dare to utter that name in our prayer unless he permitted us to pray in this way. Therefore, dearest brothers and sisters, we ought to remember and know that when we call God Father we ought to act as children of God, so that just as we take pleasure from God as Father so he might take pleasure from us.

—Cyprian, *On the Lord's Prayer* 11

"HALLOWED be your name."

We pray that his name be hallowed, not that it is the place of human beings to wish God well—as if there could be another who could wish God well or as if he might be adversely affected if we did not wish him well. But clearly, it is fitting for God to be blessed in every place and time because of the remembrance always owed by every person for his benefactions. . . . Moreover, when is the name of God not holy and hallowed through himself, since he himself sanctifies others? . . . So we speak this for the glory of God. In addition, when we say, "Hallowed be your name," we make that petition for ourselves, so that his name may be hallowed in us who are in him and that at the same time his name may be hallowed in others for whom the grace of God is waiting.

—Tertullian, *On Prayer* 3

A name is an appellation that manifests in a summary fashion the general character of the particular quality of the object being named. . . . In the case of human beings, since their particular qualities change, it is suitable that, according to Scripture, their names are changed. For when the quality of Abram changed, he was called Abraham; and when the quality of Simon changed, he was named Peter; and when the quality of Saul the persecutor of Jesus changed, the name Paul was given. In the case of God, who is himself un-changeable and exists always unalterable, there is always one name, like the name "I am," which he gave himself when he spoke in Exodus [Exod 3:14], or some other such name. Since, therefore, we all have some conception con-cerning God and some ideas about him, but we do not all know what he is—indeed these are few and, if I may say so, there are even fewer who comprehend his holiness in all its aspects—then we are rightly taught to make our thought concerning God holy. Then we may see the holiness of him who creates, exer-cises providence, judges, elects, rejects, receives, turns away from, and counts worthy of reward and punishes each according to worth. In these and similar things, if I may say so, the particular quality of God is characterized.

— Origen, *On Prayer* 24.2–3

Therefore, when I pray, "May your name be hallowed in me," by the meaning of these words I pray the following: By working together with your help may I become blameless, righteous, godly, keeping away from all evil, speaking the truth, working righteousness, walking in the straight path, shining in self-control, adorned with incorruption, beautified in wisdom and prudence, meditating on things above, despising what is earthly, distin-guished by an angelic way of life.

— Gregory of Nyssa, *On the Lord's Prayer* 3

"YOUR kingdom come."

It is evident that one who prays for the kingdom of God to come prays rightly for the kingdom of God to spring up, bear fruit, and be per-fected in himself. Every saint who is ruled by God as king and who obeys the spiritual laws of God dwells in himself as in a well-governed city. The Father is present with him, and Christ rules together with the Father in the soul that has been perfected. . . . I think that the kingdom of God is to be understood as the blessed constitution of the spirit and the ordered state of wise thoughts. And the kingdom of Christ is the saving words that go forth to those who hear and the works of righteousness and the other virtues that are accomplished, for the Son of God is Word [John 1:1] and Righteousness [1 Cor 1:30]. . . .

Moreover, concerning the kingdom of God we must also make this distinction that just as there is no "partnership between righteousness and iniquity," no "fellowship between light and darkness," and no "agreement of Christ with Beliar" [2 Cor 6:14–15], so there is no coexistence of the kingdom of God with the kingdom of sin. If we want to be ruled by God as king, then "let not sin ever rule in your mortal body" [Rom 6:12], and let us not obey its commandments when it summons our soul "to do the works of the flesh" [Gal 5:19] and other things alien to God. . . . Even now, may our corruptible nature be clothed with sanctification in holiness and all purity, and may "our mortal nature be clothed with incorruption" [1 Cor 15:53–54], that is, the Father's immortality; for death is abolished so that we may be ruled by God as king and exist already in the good things of regeneration and resurrection.

— Origen, *On Prayer* 25.1, 3

We pray that the kingdom of God may be represented in us, just as we ask that his name may be hallowed in us. When does God not reign, or when does that kingdom begin with him, which always was and does not cease to be? We pray for the coming of our kingdom promised to us by God and obtained by the blood and passion of Christ, so that we who were formerly servants in the world might afterward reign when Christ reigns.

— Cyprian, *On the Lord's Prayer* 13

If we pray for the kingdom to come upon us, we ask by the power of God for these things: may I be delivered from corruption; may I be set free from death; may I be released from the bonds of sin; may death no longer rule over me. May the tyranny of evil no longer be effective against us; may war not have power over us nor lead us into captivity by sin. But let your kingdom come upon me so that the passions that now overpower and rule me may depart from me, or rather may they be annihilated.

— Gregory of Nyssa, *On the Lord's Prayer* 3

"Your will be done."

We add "Your will be done in heaven and on earth," not because there stands in the way any power by which the will of God may be done any less, prompting us to pray for him that his will may be successful. Rather, we ask that his will may be done in everyone. . . . The sense of the petition is that the will of God may be done in us on earth so that—one may be sure—it is done in heaven. What indeed does God will but that we walk according to his discipline?

—Tertullian, *On Prayer* 4

The will of God is the salvation of human beings. If now we stand to say, "Your will be done in me," we must renounce everything from our former life that was outside the divine will. . . . The doing of the divine will casts out a double idolatry: both the folly of idols and the desire for gold and silver.

—Gregory of Nyssa, *On the Lord's Prayer* 4

"ON EARTH as it is in heaven"

One can take the words "as in heaven, so on earth," which are found only in Matthew, in common with the three petitions, so that what is set down for us in the prayer may be spoken as "May your name be hallowed, as in heaven so on earth," "your kingdom come, as in heaven, so on earth," and "your will be done, as in heaven so on earth." For the name of God is hallowed by those in heaven, and the kingdom of God is present among them, and the will of God has been done by them. All these things are lacking to us upon the earth, but they can exist among us if we prepare ourselves to be worthy to attain God's hearing concerning all of these things.

—Origen, *On Prayer* 26.2

"GIVE us this day our daily bread."

This petition may be understood both spiritually and literally, because each understanding provides divine usefulness for salvation. For the bread of life is Christ, and this bread is not everyone's but is ours. Even as we say "Our Father" because he is the Father of those who have understanding and believe, so also we speak of "our bread" because Christ is the bread of us who are in union with his body. We ask that this bread be given to us daily. . . .

This petition may also be understood that we who have renounced the world and rejected its riches and displays should ask for food and sustenance for ourselves . . . [Luke 14:33]. The person who undertakes to be a disciple of Christ, renouncing all things according to the word of the Master, ought to pray for food day by day and not extend the desires of his petition for a long period of time . . . [Matt 6:34]. With good cause, therefore, the disciple of Christ—who is prohibited from thinking about tomorrow—asks for sustenance for the day.

—Cyprian, *On the Lord's Prayer* 18–19

We were commanded to seek only what suffices to sustain physical existence. We say to God, "Give us bread"—not delicacies, wealth, showy purple clothing, gold ornaments, precious stones, silver vessels. . . . When he says "bread," he includes all bodily requirements. If then we ask for these things, let it be clear in the mind of the one praying that the concern is for transitory things; but if we ask for good things for the soul, the petition looks to what is enduring and immortal. He especially commands the one who prays to look concerning this.

—Gregory of Nyssa, *On the Lord's Prayer* 4

"Forgive us our debts, as we also have forgiven our debtors."

A petition for pardon is a confession by which the person who asks for pardon acknowledges sin. Thereby repentance acceptable to God is also demonstrated, because he desires it more than the death of the sinner [Ezek 33:11]. "Debt" in Scripture is a figure of sin, because sin in the same way is a debtor to judgment, and the justice of retribution is unavoidable unless payment is made.

—Tertullian, *On Prayer* 7

We should ask for our debts to be forgiven according to our forgiveness of our debtors, since we know that it is not possible to obtain what we ask in regard to our sins unless we ourselves acted the same way toward those who sinned against us. . . . There remains no excuse for you on the day of judgment when you will be judged according to your own sentence, and what you did, this also you will experience. For God commands that we be at peace, in harmony, and in agreement in his house. What he made us according to the new birth he wants us to persevere in as reborn persons, so that we who have begun to be children of God may abide in the peace of God and may be one soul and one mind with those with whom we are one spirit. . . . Our peace and brotherly agreement is the great sacrifice to God.

—Cyprian, *On the Lord's Prayer* 23

"Do not bring us into the time of trial, but rescue us from the evil one."

All the life of man upon the earth is temptation" [Job 7:1, Greek]. Therefore, let us pray to be delivered from temptation, not that we be without temptation, for this is impossible, especially for those on the earth—

but that we not yield when we are tempted. For I think that the person who yields when tempted "enters into temptation," being entangled in its nets.

Therefore it is necessary to pray, not that we may not be tempted (for this is not possible), but that we may not be brought under the power of the temptation, which those who are entangled in it and conquered by it experience.

—Origen, *On Prayer* 29.9, 11

These words show that the adversary can do nothing against us unless God previously permits it, so that all our fear, devotion, and obedience may be turned to God, since in temptations nothing evil is allowed unless power is given from him. . . .

When we ask that we not come into temptation we are warned of our infirmity and weakness and, accordingly, we make this request lest anyone insolently praise himself; lest anyone proudly and arrogantly claim anything for himself; lest anyone take possession of glory as his own—either from confession or suffering—when the Lord himself taught humility.

—Cyprian, *On the Lord's Prayer* 25–26

Prayer at Meals

CLEMENT of Alexandria refers to the two parts of a banquet, the eating followed by the drinking. During the latter part, singing was often a component of the entertainment.

As it is fitting to bless the Creator of all before we partake of food, so also when drinking it is proper to sing praise to him as we partake of the things he has made.

—Clement of Alexandria, *Instructor* 2.4.44.1

THE FOLLOWING is a sample prayer to be used at mealtime.

Blessed be you, O Lord, who has nourished me from my youth and who gives food to all flesh. Fill our hearts with joy and gladness that, always having all we need, we may abound in every good work, in Christ Jesus our Lord, through whom may glory, honor, and power be yours forever. Amen.

—*Apostolic Constitutions* 7.49.68

Challenges to Christian Living

Trials and Temptations

IN THE following selection Origen is speaking of flight from persecution, but his principle has a broader application.

It is necessary to endure very nobly and courageously any unavoidable testing that comes upon us, but when it is possible to avoid it, it is reckless not to do so.

—Origen, *Commentary on Matthew* 10.23

The devil presents enticing forms and easy pleasures to the eyes so that he might destroy chastity by the sight. He tempts the ears with sonorous music so that by the hearing of sweet sounds he might sap the strength and weaken the vigor of Christians. He provokes the tongue by abuse; he incites the hand to the aggressiveness of murder by harassing injuries. He provides the opportunity for dishonest gain so that he may make a swindler. He piles up pernicious profits so that he may capture a soul by money. He promises earthly honors so that he may take away the heavenly; he shows the false so that he may steal the true. When he cannot deceive secretly, he threatens plainly and openly, threatening the terror of violent persecution so as to subdue the servants of God.

—Cyprian, *On Jealousy and Envy* 2

ATHANASIUS quoted Anthony as saying:

The demons deceive the pagans with fantasies, and out of envy for us Christians they make every effort to hinder our entry into heaven so that we will not ascend to the place from which they fell. Because of this, there is need for much prayer and discipline in order that a person may receive through the Spirit the gift of discernment of spirits and be able to know their characteristics. . . .

"When the demons see all Christians—and especially the monks—working cheerfully and making progress, they attack them first through temptations and by placing stumbling blocks that wear them down; these stumbling blocks are evil thoughts. But there is no need to be afraid of their suggestions, for by prayers, fastings, and faith in the Lord the demons imme-diately fail in their efforts."

—Athanasius, *Life of Anthony* 22–23

THE FOLLOWING selection is a letter of consolation that was written on the death of a loved one.

Afflictions do not come in vain to the servants of God from the Lord who oversees us, but they come as a testing of genuine love for the God who created us. For as the toils of their contests bring crowns to athletes, so also testing by trials leads Christians to perfection, if we accept with proper patience in all thanksgiving the things the Lord administers.

By the goodness of the Master all things are dispensed. Nothing that happens to us should be received as grievous, even if at the present time it touches our weakness. For even if we are ignorant about how the things that come to us from the Master can be considered good, we still ought to be persuaded that this is so. For what happens is assuredly beneficial, either to us on account of the reward of endurance, or to the soul that is taken away so that it might not by tarrying longer in this life be filled with the evil that is natural to life. For if the hope of Christians were limited to this life, we would rightly consider early separation from the body hard to bear; but if the true life for those who live for God begins when the soul is released from these bodily bonds, then why do we grieve as those who have no hope [1 Thess 4:12]?

—Basil of Caesarea, *Letters* 101

THE NEXT selection follows a quotation of 2 Cor 6:14.

Since a fellowship of light with darkness is impossible and incon-sistent, a person who possesses both of these opposites becomes his own enemy. Being divided between virtue and vice, a battle line of opposing ar-mies is drawn up within him. Just as it is impossible for two enemies both to be victors over the other—for the victory of one certainly causes the death of the adversary—so also in this civil war brought about by a mixed life it is impossible for the better army to conquer, except through the total and absolute destruction of the other. . . . As long as we have the two and hold on to these opposites, one with each hand, it is impossible for the same person to participate in both. For when one grasps hold of evil, virtue is totally destroyed.

—Gregory of Nyssa, *On Perfection*

A brother asked one of the fathers, saying, "What shall I do? I am always thinking about fornication; it does not leave me one hour of rest, and my soul is distressed." The old man said to him, "Whenever the demons suggest these thoughts, do not enter into conversation with them. For it is the nature of demons always to throw out suggestions, and they are not negligent in doing so; nevertheless they do not compel. You have the power to welcome or not to welcome them. . . ." The brother answered and said to the old man, "What then shall I do, since I am weak and passion conquers me?" He said to him, "Consider carefully your thoughts, and whenever they begin to speak to you, do not answer them, but rise, pray, and put forth repentance, saying, 'Son of God, have mercy on me.'"

—*Apophthegmata Patrum,* Anonymous
Collection, # 184 Nau

A brother asked one of the fathers whether or not someone is defiled by thinking a foul thought. There was a discussion of this subject. Some said, "Yes, he is defiled"; others said, "No, or else we who are ordinary people could not be saved; the important thing is not to carry out the thoughts with the body." The brother went to a very experienced old man and asked him about this matter. The old man said to him, "It is required of each person according to the measure of virtue attained by each person." The brother urged the old man, "For the Lord's sake, explain your meaning." The old man said, "Look, a desirable object lies here and two brothers come in. One has a great measure of virtue; the other has less. If the perfect one says, 'I want to have this object,' and he does not entertain the thought but quickly cuts it off, then he is not defiled. If the one who has not reached such a great measure of virtue desires the object and meditates on the thought but does not take it, he is not defiled."

—*Apophthegmata Patrum,* Anonymous
Collection, # 216 Nau

THE ABSENCE of temptation may be a warning to us, not of our strength but our weakness.

The same abba [Bessarion] said, "When you are at peace, without having to struggle, humiliate yourself for fear of being led astray by joy which is inappropriate; we magnify ourselves and we are delivered to warfare. For often, because of our weakness, God does not allow us to be tempted, for fear we should be overcome."[12]

— Apophthegmata Patrum, Alphabetical
Collection, Bessarion # 9

Abba Poemen said of Abba John the Dwarf that he besought God, and the passions were taken from him, and he became free of care. He went and told a certain old man, "I see myself at rest and without any inner conflicts." The old man said to him, "Go, beseech God that inner warfare come to you so that you may have the affliction and humility you formerly possessed, for the soul makes progress through conflicts." Therefore, he besought God, and when conflict came, he no longer prayed for it to be taken from him, but he said, "Give me, Lord, endurance in these conflicts."

— Apophthegmata Patrum, Alphabetical
Collection, John the Dwarf # 13

It is said that there are five reasons why God allows the demons to wage war against us. The first is so that, through fighting and resisting, we might come to the discernment of virtue and vice. The second is so that, through warfare and labor, we might obtain virtue and possess it firmly and unchangeably. The third is so that we not become proud as we progress toward virtue, but learn humility. The fourth is so that when we are tempted by evil we may hate it with a hatred made perfect. The fifth and principal cause is so that as we become free of passions we will forget neither the weakness that is common to humanity nor the power of the One who helps us.

— Maximus the Confessor, *Charity* 2.67

Pleasure

The history of Moses [Num 25] teaches us that of the many passions which afflict human thinking there is none so strong as the disease of pleasure. That those Israelites, who were manifestly stronger than the Egyptian cavalry, had prevailed over the Amalekites, had shown themselves awesome to the next nation, and then had prevailed over the troops of the Midianites, were enslaved by this sickness at the very moment they saw the foreign women only shows, as I have said, that pleasure is an enemy of ours that is hard to fight and difficult to overcome.

By vanquishing by her very appearance those who had not been conquered by weapons, pleasure raised a trophy of dishonor against them and held up their shame to public scorn. Pleasure showed that she makes men beasts. The irrational animal impulse to licentiousness made them forget their human nature. . . .

What, then, are we taught by this account? This: That now having learned what great power for evil the disease of pleasure possesses, we should conduct our lives as far removed from it as possible; otherwise the disease may find some opening against us, like fire whose very proximity causes an evil flame. . . .

In order that we might be kept far from such evil, the Lord in the Gospel with his own voice cuts out the very root of evil—namely, the desire which arises through sight—when he teaches that the person who welcomes passion by taking a look gives an opening to the disease harmful to the self [Matt 5:28–29].[13]

— Gregory of Nyssa, *Life of Moses* 2.301–304

Things pursued by the flesh—even if they are especially enticing to the senses at the present time—bring enjoyment only for a moment. For no bodily activity can bring lasting pleasure. The pleasure of drinking ceases with the satisfaction. Likewise with eating, fullness quenches the appetite. And in the same way, any other desire dies away in the participation of what is desired; even if the desire returns, it dies again. No sensual pleasure endures forever nor does it stay the same: even among the pleasures one thing is good in childhood, another in the prime of life, another in middle age, another at the next age, and yet another in old age when we are bent to the earth. But Solomon says, "I sought that good which is equally good in every age and every time of life, which does not expect satiety and finds no fullness."

— Gregory of Nyssa, *Homilies on Ecclesiastes* 2, on Eccl 2:3

Enemies

Do not consider if David had enemies, but whether or not he himself made them enemies. For Christ did not command us not to have enemies—for this is not within our control—but he commanded us not to hate; we are in control of this, but not of whether we have enemies. It does not lie within our power to avoid being hated without cause, but this lies within those who hate. The wicked are accustomed to hate the good falsely and without cause. . . . For there is no necessity to consider how we might not have enemies, but how we might not have them justly and for good reason, and how, if we are hated many times, we might not hate and turn away from them. For this is enmity: to hate and turn away from someone. So when I am hated and do not hate, that person considers me an enemy, but I do not consider that one as my enemy. When I pray, when I wish good to them, how can I consider such persons enemies?

—John Chrysostom, *Commentary on the Psalms* 7.5

Sufferings

THIS passage was written at the time of a plague.

It disturbs some that the power of this disease attacks Christians and pagans alike. They think that if a Christian is immune from contact with evils, then he should happily have full enjoyment in this world and age and be preserved for future joy without experiencing all of the contrary things here. It disturbs some that mortality is common to us as well as to others. For what in the world is not common to us and others, as long as we have this body in common, according to the law of our first birth? As long as we are in this world, we are joined equally with the human race in the flesh, but we are separated in spirit. Therefore, until this corruptible is clothed with incorruption and this mortal receives immortality [1 Cor 15:53], and the Spirit leads us to God the Father, whatever disadvantages of the flesh there may be are common to us and the human race. When there is a lack of food owing to the earth being barren, famine distinguishes no one. When any city is captured by the invasion of an enemy, captivity devastates all alike. When the calm clouds withhold rain, there is one drought for all. When craggy rocks break up a ship, the shipwreck is common to all who sail on the ship without exception. A weakness of the eyes, an attack of fever, or health of the members is common to us and others, as long as this common body is borne in the world.

Moreover, if the Christian knows and maintains the condition and law in which he believes, he knows that he must have more difficulties than others in this world, since he must struggle more with the attacks of the devil.

—Cyprian, *On Mortality* 8–9

In our bodily weakness and infirmity we must always fight and struggle. This fight and struggle cannot be sustained except through the power of patience. When we are examined and investigated, sufferings are introduced and multiple kinds of temptations are imposed—by the loss of capacities, by the heat of fevers, by the torments of wounds, by the loss of loved ones. Nothing distinguishes between the unjust and the just more than adversity: the unjust person complains and blasphemes while the righteous person demonstrates patience.

—Cyprian, *On Patience* 17

For it is not a blessed thing to be in suffering, but it is blessed to be victorious over suffering and not to be broken by the disturbance of temporal pain. . . .

It may be that there is some bitterness in these sufferings and that strength of soul cannot hide the pain. Neither do I deny that the sea is deep because it is shallow beside the shore; nor that the sky is clear because at times it is hidden by clouds; nor that the earth is fruitful because in some places there is barren gravel; or that fields are abundant because they customarily have fruitless weeds mixed in them. Similarly I consider that the harvest of a blessed conscience may be interrupted by some bitterness of pain.

—Ambrose, *Duties* 2.5.19, 21

God's patience invites the wicked to repentance even as God's punishment educates the good in patience. So too God's mercy embraces the good to comfort them, just as God's severity seizes the wicked to punish them. It pleased divine providence to prepare good things in the future for those who are righteous that the unrighteous will not enjoy, and bad things for the impious that those who are good will not suffer. He willed that temporal goods and evils be common to both alike, so that we might not too eagerly strive after the goods that wicked persons are thought to possess, nor shamefully avoid the evils that even good people often experience.

There is a great difference in the purpose of those things that are called favorable and those that are called adverse. For a good person is neither lifted up by temporal goods nor broken by evils. A bad person, on the other hand, because of being corrupted by good fortune, feels punished by misfortune. . . . If every sin were struck with obvious punishment now, nothing would be reserved for the last judgment; on the other hand, if Divinity did not openly punish any sin now, no one would believe that there is divine providence. And so it is with other things as well; if God did not through his most evident generosity give to those who ask, we would say that these things do not belong to him; or if he gave them to everyone who asks, we would decide that people serve God only for rewards, and our service would make us not pious but greedy and covetous instead. Although both good and bad people suffer, we must not suppose that there is no difference between them, since there is no difference in what they suffer. . . . In the same affliction, the wicked hate God and blaspheme, while the good pray and praise.

—Augustine, *City of God* 1.8.1–2

Evil in the World

WHY IS there evil in a world created by a good God? This is an old problem, often raised. Compare Chapter III, on Free Will. Tertullian begins by quoting the argument against the goodness and power of God and then proceeds with his response.

   If God is good, knows the future, and is able to prevent evil, then why did he allow human beings, his very image and likeness and indeed (with regard to the soul) his own substance, to be deceived by the devil and fall away from obedience of the law into death? For if he who did not wish such a thing to occur is good, possesses foreknowledge (he was not ignorant of what would occur), and is powerful in that he could prevent it, then what occurred under these three conditions of divine majesty [that is, the fall of humanity into sin] would not have occurred. But since it occurred, the contrary is certainly proved, that is, we should not believe that God is good, prescient, or powerful, since no such thing would have occurred if he is such a God (good, prescient, and powerful). But such has actually occurred because he is not such a God." In reply, we must first defend in the Creator these qualities that are called into doubt. . . .

   Therefore, if God possessed those qualities according to which nothing evil could or ought to have occurred to human beings—yet it nonetheless did occur—we ought to look at the human condition and ask whether what could not have occurred through God is more likely to have occurred through this human condition. I find, then, that God created human beings free in will and power. Nothing is a clearer indication of God's image and likeness in them than this expression of God's own condition [of freedom]. . . .

   Therefore, the necessary consequence was that God, once having granted liberty to human beings, must withdraw from his own liberty, that is, he must restrain within himself both his own foreknowledge and his superior power by which he could have intervened and prevented human beings from falling into danger through the wrong use of their liberty. Now, if he had intervened, he would have withdrawn the freedom of will that his reason and goodness had permitted.

—Tertullian, *Against Marcion* 2.5.1–3,
5; 2.7.2–3

GOD'S providence overrules evil for good.

Nothing opposes God or withstands him who is Lord and Almighty. But the counsels and activities of those who rebelled against him,
being limited, come from an evil inclination. In the same way, bodily ill-
nesses come from a bad disposition; but they are overruled by his general
providence for a healthful outcome, even though the cause produces illness.
Therefore, the greatness of divine providence does not allow the evil that results naturally from voluntary apostasy to remain uselessly unprofitable, nor
for it to be altogether injurious. For it is the work of divine wisdom, excellence, and power not only to do good—for this is the nature of God, so to
speak, just as the nature of fire is to warm, and the nature of light to give
light—but also especially to bring to some good and useful end what proceeds from the evils planned by some beings and to use profitably those
things that seem to be bad, as the testimony that comes from a time of trial.
— Clement of Alexandria, *Miscellanies*
1.17.85.6–86.3

THE PRESENCE of evil is necessary for the development of virtue.

Virtue cannot be discerned unless it has vices opposed to it, nor can
it be perfected unless it is exercised against what is contrary to it. For God
wanted there to be this difference between good and bad things, so that we
might know good from bad and bad from good. The nature of the one cannot be known if the other is removed. Therefore, God did not exclude the
bad, so that the nature of virtue could be manifest.
— Lactantius, *Divine Institutes* 5.7

EVIL has no real subsistence but is the absence of good.

All wickedness is characterized by the absence of the good. It does
not exist by itself and is not contemplated as a substance. For evil is not present in itself apart from free choice, but it is the nonexistence of the good that
is designated as evil. That which is not has no substantial existence, and
the Creator of the things that have substantial existence is not the Creator
of what does not have substantial existence. God, therefore, is external to
the cause of evils, since he is the Maker of things that are, not of things
that are not. He created sight, not blindness, and he manifested virtue, not its

absence. . . . If, when the light shines clearly in a bright sky, someone closes their eyelids so as not to see, the sun is not the cause of that person's not seeing.

—Gregory of Nyssa, *Catechetical Oration* 7

IN ANOTHER passage Gregory of Nyssa made the same point using other words: evil has no real existence in and of itself.

Since evil is considered in contrast to good and God is absolute virtue, then evil is outside of God. Its nature is not comprehended as being anything in and of itself, but in not being good. We call "evil" whatever is outside the good. Thus evil is considered in contrast to the good, even as non-being is distinguished from being. Just as those who close their eyes to the light are said to see darkness—for not seeing is seeing darkness—even so, when we through free impulse departed from the good, then the unreal nature of evil gained existence in those who departed from the good, and it exists as long as we are outside the good.

—Gregory of Nyssa, *Homilies on Ecclesiastes* 7, on Eccl 3:7

To receive what we desire, to find what we seek [Matt 7:8], and to enter where we want depends on our choice and is within our power, whenever we will. Consequently, the opposite notion is established along with this: the inclination toward the worse is compelled by no external necessity. Evil exists by being chosen; it comes into existence when we choose it. Evil does not exist anywhere in and of itself apart from deliberate choice.

—Gregory of Nyssa, *On the Beatitudes* 5

Death

We Christians are persuaded that when we depart from the present life, we shall live another life that is better than the present life, heavenly and not earthly. Then we shall abide near God and with God and be unchanging and passionless in soul, not as flesh—although we shall have flesh—but as heavenly spirit. Or if we fall with the rest of the people, our life will be worse and in fire.

—Athenagoras, *Plea for the Christians* 31

Not even impatience at the loss of our loved ones is excused, even though asserting our right to feel pain might serve as an excuse. For we remember the admonition of the apostle, who said, "Do not grieve at the falling asleep of anyone, as the pagans who have no hope do" [1 Thess 4:13]. And he speaks rightly. For since we believe in the resurrection of Christ, we believe in the resurrection of ourselves, for whom he both died and arose. Therefore when the resurrection of the dead is established, the pain of death and the impatience that accompanies pain disappear. For why do you feel pain, if you do not believe that someone perishes? Why do you bear impatiently the temporary taking away of the one whom you believe will return? What you consider as death is a departure on a journey. The person who goes before you is not to be lamented, although obviously he will be missed. But the sense of loss is to be tempered by patience. . . . If we impatiently feel pain over those who have attained what Christians pray for ["to be with Christ," Phil 1:23], we show ourselves unwilling to attain it.

—Tertullian, *On Patience* 9

Beloved brothers and sisters, let us be prepared for the whole will of God with a sound mind, firm faith, and strong virtue. Leaving aside the fear of mortality, let us think on the immortality that follows. By this let us show ourselves to be what we believe, so that we do not grieve over loved ones who have departed. And when the day of our own summons comes, let us go to the Lord willingly and without hesitation. . . .

We regard paradise as our homeland; we begin already to have the patriarchs as our parents. Who would not hasten to prepare and run to see our homeland and greet our parents? A great number of our loved ones await us there—parents, brothers and sisters, children—a very large crowd longs for us, already assured of their own safety but concerned for our salvation. What a great joy it is both to them and to us to come into their presence and embrace! How great the pleasure of the heavenly kingdom, the highest and perpetual happiness, without fear of death and with eternity of life! There, we find a glorious chorus of apostles, a number of rejoicing prophets, innumerable martyrs crowned for the victory in their contest and suffering, triumphant virgins who by their strength of continence subjugated the passion of the flesh and body. There, the merciful receive a reward for doing works of righteousness, for feeding and giving gifts to the poor—by following the Lord's commandments they exchanged their earthly possessions for heavenly treasures. To these, beloved brothers and sisters, let us hasten with eager desire. Let us desire to be with these quickly, and quickly come to Christ.

—Cyprian, *On Mortality* 24; 26

If someone asks us whether death is good or bad, we answer that its quality depends on the nature of a person's life. For just as a life itself is good if it is lived with virtue but bad if lived in wickedness, so also death is appraised according to the past actions committed in a person's life. So, if one's life was passed in God's religion, then death is not evil, because it is a translation to immortality. But if one's life was otherwise, then death is necessarily evil, because it transfers to eternal punishment.

—Lactantius, *Divine Institutes* 3.19

THE FOLLOWING passage is from a letter of consolation written to a person who was grieving the death of his son.

It is God's command that those who put their trust in Christ not grieve for those who fall asleep, because of the hope of the resurrection and because great crowns of glory from the Judge are reserved as a reward for great endurance. If we incline our thinking to these soothing thoughts, perhaps we shall find some measure of relief from our trouble. Wherefore, I exhort you as a noble contestant to stand against this great blow and not to fall under the weight of grief. . . . We are not deprived of the boy, but we have returned him to the lender. His life was not destroyed but exchanged for a better one. The earth did not hide our beloved, but heaven welcomed him. Let us remain here for a short time, and then we shall be with the one whom we miss so much.

—Basil of Caesarea, *Letters* 5.2

Those who love wisdom and are rightly guided by hope for the things to come will not consider death to be death. When they look at the dead person lying before their eyes, they will not feel the same as most persons but will remember the crowns, prizes, indescribable goods that the eye does not see and ear does not hear, and life with the angelic chorus. Just as a farmer who sees the seed break up does not fall down and become despondent, but at that very time rejoices with great joy because he knows that the break up of the seed is the beginning of a better birth and the basis of a bigger crop, so also when the righteous, who take care to live uprightly and look daily for the kingdom, see death lying before their eyes, they are not distraught—like the many—nor disturbed and troubled. For they know that death to those who have lived uprightly is a change for the better, a journey to a better place, a race to the crown.

—John Chrysostom, *Commentary on the Psalms* 49.10

IN THE following passage Augustine responds to the pagan challenges to Christian faith that arose when those who were killed in the barbarian invasions of Italy died before their normal time and could not be buried. He speaks of the certainty of death and the purpose of funerals.

Of this I am certain: death has come to no one who was not going to die sometime. The end of life makes a long life the same as a short one. For one is not better and another worse because one is longer and the other shorter, since now equally they exist no more. What difference does the kind of death that puts an end to life make? . . . A death that cuts off a good life should not be considered evil, for nothing makes death evil except the punishment that follows death. Since we are all necessarily going to die, we should not be concerned about what the cause of death will be. But we should give thought to where we are going when we die. . . .

Many bodies of Christians indeed were not buried in the earth, but no one separates them from heaven or from the earth, which is all filled with the presence of the One who knows where he will one day raise what he created. . . . Thus all of these things—the taking care of the funeral, the condition of the sepulcher, the ceremonies of the funeral procession—are solace for the living rather than support for the deceased. If an expensive sepulcher does any good for an ungodly person, then a cheap one, or none at all, would harm the godly. . . .

Nevertheless, the bodies of the deceased are not to be despised and left unattended, especially not the bodies of the righteous and faithful that the Spirit used as organs and instruments for all good works. . . . Consequently, when in the sack of that great city [Rome] or other towns the dead bodies of Christians were deprived of proper burial, it was neither the fault of the living, who could not provide these services, nor a punishment to the dead, who could not feel the loss.

—Augustine, *City of God* 1.11, 12, 13

The remembrance of death is a daily death. The remembrance of our passing away is to groan hourly. The fear of death is a characteristic of our nature that is produced by disobedience; but the terror of death is a proof of unrepented transgressions. Christ feared death—but was not terrified—in order to reveal clearly the characteristics of his two natures.

—John Climacus, *Ladder of Paradise* 6

Characteristics of the Christian Life

Faithfulness

ONE OF the most famous declarations of faithfulness from the early church was pronounced by Polycarp at his trial before the Roman governor.

When he was brought forward, the proconsul asked him if he was Polycarp. When he acknowledged that he was, the proconsul tried to persuade him, saying, "Have respect for your age," and other such things that they are accustomed to say. "Swear by the guardian spirit of Caesar, repent, say, 'Away with the atheists.'" Polycarp, with a dignified appearance, looked at all the crowd of lawless pagans in the stadium and waved his hand at them. Groaning and looking up to heaven he said, "Away with the atheists!" When the proconsul proposed that he "swear, and I will release you, revile Christ," Polycarp replied, "For eighty-six years I have served him, and he has done me no wrong. How can I blaspheme my King who saved me?"

— *Martyrdom of Polycarp* 9.2–3

THE FOLLOWING passage speaks of the change brought about by Christian teaching, followed by a statement of how persecution only causes the Christian message to spread, as pruning increases plant productivity.

Christians learned true worship of God from the law and word that went out from Jerusalem through the apostles of Jesus and have fled for refuge to the God of Jacob and of Israel. Although we were full of war, of killing one another, and of every evil, each one of us over all the earth has refashioned his instruments of warfare—swords into ploughshares and spears into agricultural implements [Isa 2:3–4]. We cultivate godliness, righteousness, kindness, faith, and hope, which come from the Father himself through the Crucified One. . . . It is evident that there is no one who can terrify or enslave those of us who have believed in Jesus over all the world. Although beheaded, crucified, thrown to wild beasts, placed in chains, fire, and all other tortures, it is plain that we do not abandon our confession. As much as these things happen, by so much more do many others become believers and worshipers of God through the name of Jesus. It is like pruning the fruit-bearing branches of a vine in order to make other branches sprout, which become flourishing and fruitful. The same thing happens with us. For the vine, planted by God and Christ the Savior, is his people.

—Justin Martyr, *Dialogue* 110.2–4

THE FAITHFUL are few in number.

Faith that has no roof but the sky is better than impiety with great wealth. Three who are gathered together in the name of the Lord [Matt 18:20] are more with God than tens of thousands of those who deny the Godhead. . . .

You count the tens of thousands, but God counts those who are saved. You count the unnumbered grains of sand, but I count the chosen vessels. For nothing is so magnificent to God as pure teaching and a soul that has been perfected in the doctrines of truth.

—Gregory of Nazianzus, *Oration* 42.7–8

ONE SHOULD be faithful in whatever circumstances of life one finds oneself. The following passage comments on the phrase "Walk in God's ways" (Ps 128:1b).

He did not say "way" but "ways," indicating that the ways are many and varied. He appointed many ways in order to make the entrance easy for us. Some are illustrious in their virginity. Some are prominent in married life. Others are honored in widowhood. Some give everything away; some, a half. Some enter by an upright life; some enter by repentance. . . . Were you not strong enough to keep your body pure after the baptismal bath? You can make yourself pure by repentance; you can through money, through almsgiving. But you have no money? You can care for the sick, visit the imprisoned, give a cup of cold water, bring the stranger into your home, give two obols (like the widow) and groan with those in pain, for this also is almsgiving. But are you completely deserted and in poverty, weak in body, and unable to go about? Bear all this with thanksgiving, and you will reap a great reward.

—John Chrysostom, *Commentary on the Psalms* 128.2

Obedience

Offer to God your heart soft and manageable, and preserve the form in which the Creator formed you, having moisture in yourself, lest by being hardened you lose the impression of his fingers. . . . If you are stubbornly hardened, reject his craftsmanship, and present yourself ungrateful to him because you were made a human being, by being ungrateful to God you lose both his craftsmanship and his life. For to create is the property of God's goodness, and to be created is the property of human nature. If, therefore, you deliver to him what is yours—that is, faith in him and obedience—you will receive his craftsmanship and you will be a perfect work of God. But if you do not believe in him and flee from his hand, the cause of imperfection will be in you who did not obey, and not in him who called you.

—Irenaeus, *Against Heresies* 4.39.2–3

According to nature—that is, according to creation—I might say that we are all children of God, because we were all made by God. But according to obedience and doctrine, not all are children of God, but those who believe in him and do his will. On the other hand, those who do not believe and do not do his will are children and messengers of the devil, since they do the works of the devil.

—Irenaeus, *Against Heresies* 4.41.2

We ought, therefore, to take our stand on Christ's words and to learn and do what he taught and did. Moreover, how can a person say he believes in Christ and not do what Christ commanded us to do? How can one who does not wish to keep faith with the commandment arrive at the reward of faith?

—Cyprian, *On the Unity of the Church* 2

Hope

BIBLICAL and Christian hope is stronger than we generally think of hope today, for it involves not only desire but also expectation. This expectation stems from faith in the words of a trustworthy God.

Hope derives its existence from faith. . . . Hope is the expectation of the possession of good, and faith is necessary for expectation. . . . When it is said, "God is faithful" [1 Cor 1:9], this indicates that it is worth believing in him when he makes a declaration. Now his word makes declaration, and God himself is faithful.

—Clement of Alexandria, *Miscellanies* 2.6.27.1–3

Desire is a powerful thing, hoping for things unattainable and undertaking things impossible. But hope in the Lord is the strongest of all. For not by irrational desire but in the strength of faith I expect that a way will appear in extraordinary circumstances and that you will easily overcome all hindrances.

— Basil of Caesarea, *Letters* 145

WITH reference to the desire of Moses to see the glory of God [Exod 33:18–23], Gregory of Nyssa describes hope as the desire for what is not seen. He describes God as Beauty.

Hope always draws the soul from the beauty that is seen to what is beyond, always kindles the desire for the hidden through what is constantly perceived. Therefore, the ardent lover of beauty, although receiving what is always visible as an image of what is desired, yet longs to be filled with the very stamp of the archetype.[14]

— Gregory of Nyssa, *Life of Moses* 2.231

THE GROUND of hope is found in the incarnation of Christ, his resurrection, and the Christian's salvation.

When our defects grow numerous, despair of a remedy takes control of us, since these defects mock the soul, as the devil and his angels work through poisonous suggestions to make us despair. . . . But there is hope in that God considered it worthy to take on human nature in Christ. . . . In the resurrection of the flesh "death is swallowed up in victory" [1 Cor 15:54]. With my inner and most intense voice, "with my voice I cried to the Lord"— through whom he helps and by whose meditation he hears us—"and he heard me from his holy mountain" [Ps 3:4], and "I slept, and I took rest; and I rose up because the Lord took me up" [Ps 3:5]. Who of the faithful is unable to say, "I will not fear the thousands that surround me" [Ps 6:6], recalling the death of their sins and the gift of regeneration?

— Augustine, *Expositions on the Psalms*
3.10, on Ps 3:1–8

Hospitality

Abba Apollo said with regard to hospitality for the brothers, "We must bow before the brothers who come, because it is not before them that we bow but before God. When you see your brother," he said, "you see the Lord your God. We have learned this," he said, "from Abraham [Gen 18]. When you welcome the brothers, insist that they rest awhile, for this we have learned from Lot, who insisted that the angels do so" [Gen 19:3].

—*Apophthegmata Patrum*, Alphabetical
Collection, Apollo # 3

IN MONASTICISM hospitality took precedence over religious duties.

Abba Cassian told the following story: "The holy Germanus and I went to Egypt to visit an old man. Because he offered us hospitality, we asked him, 'Why do you not keep the rule of fasting when you receive visiting brothers, as we have received it in Palestine?' He replied, 'Fasting is always with us, but I cannot have you with me always. Furthermore, fasting is indeed a useful and necessary practice, but it is a matter of our free choice, while the law of God requires us of necessity to fulfill the works of love. Thus by receiving Christ in you, it is necessary to serve you with all diligence. When I send you on your way, I can resume the rule of fasting again.'"

—*Apophthegmata Patrum*, Alphabetical
Collection, Cassian # 1

Purity

It is said that persons must go to sacred services and prayers after having been washed, and so they are pure and radiant when they attend. This being adorned and cleansed outwardly serves as a sign. Purity is thinking holy thoughts. . . . For perfect purity—it seems to me—is purity of the mind, deeds, thoughts, even of words, and ultimately sinlessness in dreams. . . . Sufficient purification for a person—it seems to me—is strict and lasting repentance. We condemn ourselves for former practices, we let go of the past, and after these things we take thought, and in the mind we escape from the pleasures of the senses and from our former trespasses.

—Clement of Alexandria, *Miscellanies* 4.22

Unity

Do not attempt to make something appear plausible to yourself alone, but in church let there be one prayer, one petition, one mind, one hope in love, in blameless joy, which is Jesus Christ, than whom nothing is better. All of you hasten as to one temple of God, as to one altar, to one Jesus Christ, who proceeded from the one Father and withdrew to the One who is.

—Ignatius, *Magnesians* 7.1–2

So also the church of God, after it is purified and those who are wicked, hypocrites, blasphemers, double-minded, and who do various kinds of wickedness are cast out . . . will be one body, one purpose, one mind, one faith, one love. Then, when he has received his people in purity, the Son of God will be glad and rejoice in them.

—Hermas, *Similitudes* 9.18.3–4 [95.3–4]

The church, although dispersed throughout the world to the ends of the earth, received from the apostles and their disciples this faith: in one God the Father Almighty, the Maker of heaven, the earth, the seas, and all things in them; and in one Christ Jesus, the Son of God, who became flesh for our salvation; and in the Holy Spirit, who preaches through the prophets the dispensations of God and the comings of Christ, his birth from a virgin, his passion, his resurrection from the dead, the bodily ascension into heaven of our beloved Christ Jesus the Lord, and his appearing from heaven in glory for the summing up of all things [Eph 1:10] and to raise the flesh of all humanity. . . .

The church, having received this preaching and this faith—as we said—although dispersed throughout the world, carefully preserves it as living in one house. Similarly, it believes these things as if having one soul and the same heart, and it preaches, teaches, and delivers these things harmoniously, as if possessing one mouth. For indeed the languages throughout the world are different, but the power of the tradition is one and the same. Those churches founded in Germany do not believe differently or transmit it any differently; nor do those in Spain, among the Celts, in the East, in Egypt, in Libya, and those founded at the center of the earth [Palestine? Rome?]. But just as the sun, the creature of God, is one and the same throughout the world, so also the preaching of the truth shines everywhere and enlightens every person who wishes to come to the knowledge of the truth. The one who is exceedingly powerful in speech among the leaders in the churches will not speak things other than these, for no one is above the Teacher. Nor will the one who is weak in speech diminish what is handed down. Since the faith is one and the same, the person who is able to speak at length does not expand it and the one who speaks little does not diminish it.

—Irenaeus, *Against Heresies* 1.10.1–2

The faith is one and the same, since all [those who belong to the church] receive one and the same God the Father, believe in the same dispensation of the incarnation of the Son of God, know the same gift of the Spirit, are attentive to the same commandments, preserve the same form of constitution, which is the works of the church, expect the same coming of the Lord, and await the same salvation of the whole person, that is, of the soul and body. The preaching of the church is true and firm, in which one and the same way of salvation is displayed throughout the whole world.

—Irenaeus, *Against Heresies* 5.20.1

THE MEMBERS of the church are brothers and sisters.

There is no other cause for sharing the name of brothers and sisters among ourselves except that we believe that we are all equal. Since we appraise every human being according to the spirit and not the body—although the condition of bodies is different—slaves are not slaves to us but we consider them and call them brothers and sisters in the spirit, as well as fellow slaves in religion. Riches also do not make people outstanding, unless the riches are able to make them more illustrious by good works. For the rich are not those who have wealth but those who use their money for works of justice; those who seem to be poor become rich in this way, because they are not in want and are desirous of nothing. Since therefore we are equals in humility of mind—the free persons with the slaves and the rich with the poor—nevertheless in the sight of God we are distinguished by virtue, so that the person who is more just is the more elevated.

—Lactantius, *Divine Institutes* 5.15 [16]

WITHDRAWAL of fellowship from sinful and divisive members is necessary to maintain spiritual unity.

I certainly hope, dearest brothers and sisters—and I equally advise and urge—that if possible none of the brothers or sisters perish, but that the mother [the church] should have the joy of embracing in her bosom the one body of a like-minded people. Nevertheless, if some of the leaders of the schism and authors of dissension remain in their blind and obstinate folly and cannot be brought back to the way of salvation by wholesome advice, then the rest of you—whether enticed in your simplicity, misled by falsehood, or in some way ensnared by the cunning of deceitful skill—break the snares of deception, set yourselves free from the errors into which you have wandered, and recognize the correct path of the heavenly way . . . [2 Thess 3:6; Eph 5:6–7]. One must withdraw from those who do wrong, or rather flee from them, lest by joining in their evil course and walking in the path of error and wrongdoing you depart from the true way and become a participant in wrongdoing. For God is one, Christ is one, his church is one, the faith is one, and the people are bound together by the glue of concord into an undivided unity of the body. That unity cannot be separated, nor can that body be divided. . . . Something cut off from its mother's [church's] womb cannot live or breathe; the reality of salvation is lost.

—Cyprian, *On the Unity of the Church* 23

BASIL extended the concept of unity to include agreement in decisions.

A work done by one or two pious persons, we are persuaded, is done by the counsel of the Spirit. For whenever holy persons undertake their work with no human consideration present before their eyes and no purpose of their own pleasure, but proposing what is well pleasing to God, it is evident that it is the Lord who is directing their hearts [2 Thess 3:5]. Where spiritual men initiate plans, and the people of the Lord follow these in agreement of mind, who will doubt that the plan came about by communion with our Lord Jesus Christ, who poured out his blood for the churches?

—Basil of Caesarea, *Letters* 229.1

UNITY is displayed especially in the church assembled for worship.

The holy church of God [is composed] of many, an almost limitless number. Men, women, and children are coming into the church, reborn and re-created by her in the Spirit. They are distinguished from one another and are very different from one another in race and appearance, in nationality and languages, in manner of life and ages; in opinions, abilities, manners, customs, and interests; in knowledge, social station, fortunes, characters, and habits. But the church gives to all and grants equally the same divine character and title—that they all are from Christ and are named after Christ. The church gives one simple, indivisible, and inseparable relationship in faith, and she does not allow the many untold differences that are in each one to be recognized, because all the people are referred to and come together into the same general assembly. Accordingly, no one in any respect is separated from the community; all grow together with one another, united by the one simple and indivisible grace and power of the faith. . . . Christ keeps hold of all things for himself by one simple and infinitely wise force of goodness, like the hub with some sort of spokes fastened to it by one simple and unitary cause and force.

—Maximus the Confessor, *Mystagogy* 1

Respect for Human Beings and Human Life

The greatest impiety toward God is the ill-treatment of a human being.

—*Sentences of Sextus* 96

RESPECT for human life included respect for unborn life. Several statements mention abortion as being conduct that is forbidden to Christians. The following selection is an expansion and application of the Ten Commandments.

The way of life is this: first, you shall love God who created you; second, your neighbor as yourself. . . . The second commandment of the teaching is this: you shall not kill; you shall not commit adultery; you shall not sodomize young boys; you shall not steal; you shall not engage in the magical arts; you shall not practice sorcery; you shall not cause an abortion, nor commit infanticide after the child is born. You shall not covet the things of your neighbor; you shall not commit perjury; you shall not give false testimony; you shall not speak abusively; you shall not bear malice; you shall not be double-minded or double-tongued.

—*Didache* 1.2; 2.1–4

ONE SLANDER brought against Christians by some pagans was that they killed babies and ate their flesh. Athenagoras stated one of the responses to this charge that was offered by Christian apologists.

Who can accuse us of murder and cannibalism, since they know that we cannot endure to see a person put to death even if justly. . . . We who consider that watching someone put to death is next to killing that person have renounced the spectacles of contests between gladiators and wild beasts. How, then, can we put someone to death when we do not even watch such spectacles, so as not to inflict on ourselves guilt and pollution? By what reason can we be murderers who say that women who use drugs to cause abortion commit murder and are accountable to God for the abortion? For the same person does not think that what is in the womb is a living being, and on account of this is in God's care, and then put it to death after it has entered into life. Nor does the same person refuse to expose a child that is born on the grounds that those who expose children are their murderers, and then destroy a child they have reared.

— Athenagoras, *Plea for the Christians* 35

LACTANTIUS discussed attendance at the public spectacles, but said much more in his strictures against cruelty, including warfare and the ancient practice of exposing (abandoning on trash heaps) unwanted children.

Persons who consider it pleasurable for a human being, even if justly condemned, to be slaughtered in their sight pollute their conscience— without a doubt—just as much as they would if they were spectators and participants at a homicide committed in secret. They call sports those spectacles at which human blood is shed. Human feeling has departed so far from human beings that when they destroy human life they think they are taking part in public entertainment, themselves becoming more guilty than all those whose bloodshed gives them pleasure. I ask now if those who not only allow the killing of those who are placed under the stroke of death and are begging for mercy but even clamor for death and inflict it by their cruel and inhuman decisions, not being satisfied with wounds or content with the shedding of blood, can be pious and just persons. . . .

When God forbids us to kill, he prohibits not only murder, which is not even permitted by the public laws, but he also warns against doing what human beings consider lawful. Thus it is not permitted for just persons to engage in warfare—since justice itself is their warfare—nor indeed to condemn anyone for a capital crime, because it makes no difference whether you kill a person by the sword or by a word, when the act of killing itself is prohibited. Thus there ought to be absolutely no exception at all made to this divine precept, since it is always an offense to kill a human being, a living creature that God desires to be sacrosanct.

Therefore, let no one think that it is allowed for anyone to snuff out the life of newborn children, which is the greatest impiety. God breathes a soul into them for life and not for death. . . . What kind of persons are they who are led by a false piety to expose a child [rather than strangle it]? . . . It is as horrible to expose a child as to put it to death. . . . If anyone is unable to raise children because of poverty, it is better to abstain from intercourse with his wife than to damage the work of God with defiled hands.

—Lactantius, *Divine Institutes* 6.20.10–12,
15–17, 18, 20, 23, 25

FOR SOUL-LIFE beginning at conception, compare the following passage to Tertullian, *On the Soul* 27, quoted in Chapter IV, under Human Nature—The Soul.

Among us Christians murder is once for all forbidden. It is unlawful for us even to destroy what is conceived in the womb while blood is being taken from the mother's womb to form a human being. To prohibit birth is murder with undue haste. It makes no difference whether someone takes the life of a child who has been born or destroys a child who is going to be born. The one who is going to be a person is a person, for the fruit is always in the seed.

—Tertullian, *Apology* 9.8

CELSUS charged that the Jews originated in rebellion against the Egyptians and that Christians originated in rebellion against the Jews. Origen's reply was that Christian teaching is against all forms of violence.

Neither Celsus nor those who think like him will be able to point out any act of rebellion by Christians. If a rebellion was the cause of the bringing together of Christians, . . . the Lawgiver of the Christians would not have altogether forbidden the taking of human life. He nowhere teaches that it is just for his disciples to be violent against a human being, even if that person is very wicked—for he did not consider it proper in his divinely inspired law to allow the taking of human life in any manner whatever. If Christians took their beginning from a rebellion, they would not have adopted such mild laws, by which they were killed as sheep and did not resist those who persecuted them.

—Origen, *Against Celsus* 3.7

THERE is always a temptation to think one's own life is more valuable than another's. Ambrose addressed this situation and appeals to the Christian's principle of putting others ahead of self.

Some ask whether in the case of a shipwreck a wise person ought—if able to do so—to take a plank away from a foolish sailor? Although it might appear that the escape of a wise person from a shipwreck is of greater worth to the common good than that of a foolish sailor, nevertheless it does not seem to me that a Christian—both just and wise—ought to seek his own life by the death of another. For it is the same case as someone who encounters an armed robber; he may not hit back at the person striking him, lest while defending his safety he defile his piety.

—Ambrose, *Duties* 3.4.27

Nonviolent Resistance

We request that the deeds of all those who are charged before you be judged so that the one convicted may be punished as an evildoer but not as a Christian. But if anyone is proven innocent, may that person be released as a Christian who has done no wrong. We do not request that those who bring charges against us be punished, for their present evil and ignorance of good things are sufficient punishment.

—Justin Martyr, *1 Apology* 7.4–5

We who are called Christians . . . although we have done nothing wrong, you [imperial authorities] allow to be driven out, carried away, and persecuted, when the multitude makes war on us on account of our name alone. . . . When we are beaten, we have learned not to strike back or go to court against those who ravage and plunder us but—even if they strike us on the face—to offer also the other side, and to give to those who take away our garment our cloak also.

—Athenagoras, *Plea for the Christians* 1

The Lord commanded us not only not to hate human beings but also to love our enemies; he commanded us not only not to commit perjury but also not to swear; . . . not only not to strike another but also to turn the other cheek when struck; not only not to refuse to return the goods of another but also, if our own things are carried away, not to ask for them back; and not only not to harm our neighbors nor do anything bad to them but also to be magnanimous to those who treat us badly, to show kindness to them, and to pray for them so that by repentance they may be saved; and in nothing should we imitate the arrogance, lust, and pride of others.

—Irenaeus, *Against Heresies* 2.32.1

A true gnostic never remembers past injuries and is not violent toward anyone, even if that one deserves to be hated for his conduct. For a true gnostic worships the Creator and loves others who share life in common, showing mercy toward other persons and praying for them on account of their ignorance.

—Clement of Alexandria, *Miscellanies* 7.11

If anyone attempts to provoke you by violence, the Lord's admonition is at hand: "To the one who strikes you on the face, turn the other cheek" [Matt 5:39]. Let outrageous conduct be worn out by your patience—whatever their blow may be, joining together pain and rough treatment. The more outrageous the beating sustained, the more severe will be the affliction from the Lord, for they will be afflicted by the One for whose sake you endure. If bitterness of tongue breaks out in either cursing or insults, take note of the saying "When they curse you, rejoice" [Matt 5:11]. For the Lord himself was cursed according to the Law, and yet he alone is the Blessed One. Therefore let us as servants follow the Lord and endure cursing with patience so that we may be blessed. . . . No doubt some harm you so that you may feel pain, because the pleasure of inflicting harm is in the pain of the one being harmed. Therefore, when you prevent his pleasure by not being pained, he must necessarily be pained at the loss of his pleasure. . . .

For what is the difference between the one who provokes and the one who is provoked, except that the former is detected in wrongdoing earlier and the latter at a later time? Nevertheless the Lord, who prohibits and condemns everything wicked, accuses both of hurting a human being. It makes no difference in what order wrong is done, nor does place distinguish what is joined together by likeness of deed. An equivalent deed has equivalent deserts. It is absolutely commanded that we not repay evil with evil [Rom 12:17].

—Tertullian, *On Patience* 8; 10

No one applies the name "sheep" to those who fall in armed combat and are contending with the same fierceness, but rather to those who are killed in their own condition and patience, yielding rather than resisting.

—Tertullian, *Against Marcion* 4.39

Charity or Almsgiving

CHRISTIANS were not only not to do harm, but also to do good to others.

Do not be one who extends your hands to receive but closes them to giving. If you have possessions through the labor of your hands, give them for the ransom of your sins. Do not hesitate to give, nor grumble when you give, for you know the good Paymaster of the reward. Do not turn away from a person in need but share all things with your brother and sister, and do not say that these things are your own. For if you are partners in what is immortal, how much more in the things that are mortal!

— *Didache* 4.5–8

In a discussion of the Christian assembly for worship on Sunday, Justin Martyr described Christian benevolence.

Those who have, provide for all those who are in want. . . . Those who have means and are willing, each according to his own choice, gives what he wills, and what is collected is deposited with the president [of the assembly]. He provides for the orphans and widows, those who are in want due to sickness or some other cause, those who are in bonds, and strangers who are sojourning among us—in a word, he becomes the protector of all who are in need.

—Justin Martyr, *1 Apology* 67.1, 6

A rich person has much wealth but is poor in the affairs of the Lord, being drawn away by concern for riches. A rich person's intercession and confession to the Lord are exceedingly small, and what he has is weak, small, and lacking in power. When a rich person finds comfort in a poor person and ministers to his needs, the rich person believes that what is done for the poor will yield a reward with God. This is because the poor person is rich in intercessions and confessions that have great power with God. Therefore, the rich person ministers to the poor without hesitation. A poor person, therefore, when ministered to by a rich person, intercedes and gives thanks to God for the rich person who gave to the poor. That rich person is diligent again and again concerning the poor person, so that the latter may be unfailing in life. For the rich know that the intercession of the poor is acceptable and rich toward God. Both, therefore, complete the work. The poor person works by intercession, in which he is rich from the Lord; the poor person gives this to the Lord who ministers to him. The rich person in the same way unhesitatingly offers to the poor the riches he has received from the Lord.

—Hermas, *Similitudes* 2.5–7 [51.5–7]

Do not judge who is worthy and who unworthy, for it is possible for you to be mistaken in your opinion. In the uncertainty of ignorance it is better to do good to the unworthy for the sake of the worthy than to fail to encounter the good by guarding against those who are less good. For by being sparing and trying to test those who are well-deserving or not, it is possible for you to neglect some who are loved by God, the penalty for which is the eternal punishment of fire. But by helping all those in need you in turn must assuredly find some who are able to save you before God. . . .

Contrary to the rest of people, enlist for yourself an army without weapons, without war, without bloodshed, without wrath, without stain—pious old people, orphans dear to God, widows armed with gentleness, men adorned with love. Obtain with your wealth as guards of body and soul such as these whose commander is God.

—Clement of Alexandria, *Who Is the Rich Man Who Is Saved?* 33–34

A true gnostic impoverishes himself on account of the perfection that resides in love in order never to overlook a brother or sister who happens to be in affliction, especially if he knows that he himself can bear the condition of need easier than the other. . . . And if he suffers any hardship by supplying from his own indigence in order to do good, he does not fret at this but increases his beneficence still more.

—Clement of Alexandria, *Miscellanies* 7.12.77.6–78.1

It is disgraceful for one person to live in luxury while many are poor. How much more praiseworthy it is to do good to the many than to live extravagantly! How much wiser it is to spend money on human beings than on jewels and gold! How much more useful it is to acquire well-behaved friends than lifeless adornments! Who has ever benefited as much from lands as from gracious giving?

—Clement of Alexandria, *Instructor* 2.12.120

TERTULLIAN contrasted the use of funds by the church and the use of funds by Greco-Roman associations.

These contributions [put into the church's treasury] are the trust funds of piety. For they are not spent on banquets, drinking parties, or dining clubs; but for feeding and burying the poor, for boys and girls who are destitute of property and parents; and further for old people confined to the house, and victims of shipwreck; and any who are in the mines, who are exiled to an island, or who are in prison merely on account of God's church—these become the wards of their confession. So great a work of love burns a brand upon us with regard to some. "See," they say, "how they love one another." . . . But possibly we are thought less than real brothers and sisters because no tragedy cries aloud about our brotherhood, or because we are brothers in regard to family possessions which, among you, are the very things that dissolve brotherhood. So we who are united in mind and soul have no hesitation about sharing property. All things are common among us except our women.

—Tertullian, *Apology* 39.5–11

For if we are lending to God by giving alms to the poor, and what we give to the least we give to Christ [Matt 25:40], there is no basis for someone to prefer earthly to heavenly things nor to give priority to human over divine things.

—Cyprian, *On Works and Alms* 16

If therefore we do alms to be seen by people [Matt 6:1] and in our thoughts our aim is to appear to people to be philanthropic and to be praised for our philanthropy, our only reward is from people. And, in general, everything that is done with the doer's intention of being praised by people has no reward from the One who sees in secret [Matt 6:4] and gives his reward to those who are pure in secret. . . . Evil thoughts are the source of all sins and are able to pollute even those actions that, if they were done without evil thoughts, would justify the person doing them.

—Origen, *Commentary on Matthew* 11.15

GREGORY of Nazianzus describes his father and his mother.

It is much better to extend a hand to the undeserving for the sake of the deserving than to deprive the deserving out of fear of the undeserving. . . .

What is best and greatest of all was that all love of honor was absent from his generosity. I now make plain the extent and character of this generosity. Their possessions and their desire to share them were common to him and his wife, as they competed for excellence. The greater part of their benevolence he placed in her hand, as a most excellent and faithful steward in such

matters. . . . She considered that all their substance, whatever came to them as well as whatever had been theirs, was too little for her personal benevolence; but she would have readily sold herself and her children into slavery in order to spend the proceeds on the poor, if it had been possible, something I often heard her say. So lightly did she touch the reins of her benevolence! . . . It would not be hard to find among others magnanimity in regard to possessions . . . , but it is not so easy to find those who surrender the glory that goes with it. The love of glory supplies to most people the desire to expend their resources; where the benevolence is not seen, there also the generosity is faint.
— Gregory of Nazianzus, *Oration* 18.20–21

HAVING given various examples of types of liberality, Ambrose turns to another type of assistance that does not require the outlay of money.

Liberality [in giving money], therefore, is useful, but it is not available to everyone. For there are many good people whose resources are slim. They are content with little for their own use, but they do not have much to give to ease the poverty of others. However, there is another kind of charity available by which they are able to assist those who are less well off. For there are two forms of liberality: one form helps by actual support, that is, in the use of money; the other donates by expending good works. The latter is frequently much more illustrious and celebrated. . . .
Money is easily consumed; deliberate actions cannot be exhausted.
— Ambrose, *Duties* 2.15.73

AMBROSE narrates an incident that involved a deacon named Lawrence in the church of Rome, during the time of the persecution under Valerian in 258.

Such gold [of the Redeemer] the holy martyr Lawrence preserved for the Lord. When the treasures of the church were requested, he promised to show them. On the following day he led out the poor. When asked where the treasures that he promised were, he pointed to the poor and said, "These are the treasures of the church." And indeed they are treasures in whom Christ lives, in whom faith exists. . . . What better treasure does Christ have than those in whom he loves to be seen?
— Ambrose, *Duties* 2.28.140

SEE ALSO Chapter II, under Mercy.

Self-Control

CLEMENT of Alexandria states the quality of self-control paradoxically.

Perfect persons do not have "courage," for those who consider nothing in this life fearful are never in fearful circumstances, and without anything fearful nothing is able to remove them from their love for God. Nor do these persons have need of cheerfulness, for those who are persuaded that all things turn out well do not fall into sorrow. Nor are these angry, for there is nothing that drives them to anger, since they always love God and are altogether turned toward God alone and for this reason have hated none of God's creatures. And they are not envious, for they lack nothing to help them become like the excellent and the good. Nor do they love anything with a common affection, but they love the Creator through the things created. Neither do they encounter desire and longing for anything, nor are they in need of any other things that pertain to the soul, since they already live together with the Beloved. Since they have become friends with him by free choice and have drawn ever more closely together with him by habitual discipline, they have been blessed by an abundance of good things.

—Clement of Alexandria, *Miscellanies* 6.9

It was said of an old man that for fifty years he had neither eaten bread nor drunk wine readily. He even said, 'I have destroyed fornication, avarice and vainglory in myself.' Learning that he had said this, Abba Abraham came and said to him, 'Did you really say that?' He answered 'Yes.' Then Abba Abraham said to him, 'If you were to find a woman lying on your mat when you entered your cell would you think that it is not a woman?' 'No,' he replied, 'But I should struggle against my thoughts so as not to touch her.' Then Abba Abraham said, 'Then you have not destroyed the passion, but it still lives in you although it is controlled. Again, if you are walking along and you see some gold amongst the stones and shells, can your spirit regard them all as of equal value?' 'No,' he replied, "But I would struggle against my thoughts, so as not to take the gold." The old man said to him, "See, avarice still lives in you, though it is controlled." Abba Abraham continued, "Suppose you learn that of two brothers one loves you while the other hates you, and speaks evil of you; if they come to see you, will you receive them both with the same love?" "No," he replied, 'But I should struggle against my thoughts so as to be as kind toward the one who hates me as towards the one who loves me.' Abba Abraham said to him, 'So then, the passions continue to live; it is simply that they are controlled by the saints.'[15]

—*Apophthegmata Patrum*, Alphabetical
Collection, Abraham # 1

THE FOLLOWING passages were written about monks, but a wider application can be made, so I have substituted the word "Christian."

A Christian imitates Christ—insofar as is humanly possible—in words, deeds, and thought, and believes correctly and blamelessly in the holy Trinity. A friend of God is one who participates in all things that are natural and sinless. Insofar as he can, a Christian does not neglect good things. Self-control is to strive in the midst of temptations, trials, and tumults to imitate with all one's strength the behavior of a person who has been delivered from these things. . . . Renunciation of the world is voluntary hatred of the material nature that is praised and a denial of nature for the undertaking of what is above nature. All who readily abandon the things of life do this either for the coming kingdom, or on account of the multitude of their sins, or because of love for God. . . .

No one will enter into the heavenly bridal chamber wearing a crown without making three renunciations: first, all worldly matters, persons, and family; second, the cutting off of one's own will; and third, the renunciation of pride that follows from obedience.

—John Climacus, *Ladder of Paradise* 1; 2

ENDNOTES

Introduction

[1] An excellent English translation by Boniface Ramsey, OP, is available in *John Cassian: The Conferences* (Ancient Christian Writers 57; New York: Paulist, 1997).

[2] *The Sayings of the Desert Fathers: The Alphabetical Collection* (trans. Benedicta Ward, SLG; Kalamazoo: Cistercian Publications, 1975).

[3] *The Wisdom of the Desert Fathers: Apophthegmata Patrum (The Anonymous Series)* (trans. Benedicta Ward, SLG; Oxford: SLG Press, 1975).

[4] *Defensor de Ligugé: Livre d'étincelles* (Sources chrétiennes 77 and 86; Paris: Cerf, 1961, 1962).

I. Social Existence

[1] *The Sayings of the Desert Fathers: The Alphabetical Collection* (trans. Benedicta Ward, SLG; Kalamazoo: Cistercian Publications, 1975), 20. Used by permission of Cistercian Publications.

[2] *The Ante-Nicene Fathers* 8 (trans. B. P. Pratten; repr., Peabody: Hendrickson, 1994), 754–55. Used by permission. Melito was not the author of the original work, which was most likely composed in Syriac at a later date.

II. Good and Bad; Right and Wrong

[1] *The Nicene and Post-Nicene Fathers*, Second Series 10 (trans. H. De Romestin; repr., Peabody: Hendrickson, 1994), 22–29; translation slightly modified. Used by permission.

[2] "An Early Church Sermon Against Gambling (CPL 60)," trans. Scott T. Carroll, *Second Century* 8 (1991): 90–94. Reprinted with permission of The Johns Hopkins University Press.

[3] *The Sayings of the Desert Fathers: The Alphabetical Collection* (trans. Benedicta Ward, SLG; Kalamazoo: Cistercian Publications, 1975), 168. Used by permission of Cistercian Publications.

[4] Ibid., 119–20. Used by permission of Cistercian Publications.

III. Conversion and Salvation

[1] *St. Irenaeus: Proof of the Apostolic Preaching* (trans. Joseph P. Smith; Ancient Christian Writers 16; New York: Newman, 1952), 70. Used by permission of Paulist Press.

IV. Life-Nourishing Doctrines

[1] *St. Irenaeus: Proof of the Apostolic Preaching* (trans. Joseph P. Smith; Ancient Christian Writers 16; New York: Newman, 1952), 51. Used by permission of Paulist Press.

[2] Ibid., 69. Used by permission of Paulist Press.

[3] *Didascalia Apostolorum* (trans. R. Hugh Connolly; Oxford: Clarendon, 1929), 124, 127. Used by permission of Oxford University Press.

[4] Guy, Jean-Claude, *Recherches sur la tradition grecque des Apophthegmata Patrum* (Brussels: Société des Bollandistes, 1962), 231.

V. Christian Living

[1] Up to this point the translation is by D. M. Kay from the Syriac in *The Ante-Nicene Fathers* 10 (repr. Peabody: Hendrickson, 1994), 276. Used by permission. The remainder is my translation from the Greek.

[2] *St. Irenaeus: Proof of the Apostolic Preaching* (trans. Joseph P. Smith; Ancient Christian Writers 16; New York: Newman, 1952), 106. Used by permission of Paulist Press.

[3] *Gregory of Nyssa: The Life of Moses* (trans. Abraham J. Malherbe and Everett Ferguson; New York: Paulist, 1978), 119. Used by permission of Paulist Press.

[4] Ibid., 113–14, 117. Used by permission of Paulist Press.

[5] Ibid., 30–31. Used by permission of Paulist Press.

[6] Ibid., 116. Used by permission of Paulist Press.

[7] *The Odes of Solomon* (trans. James H. Charlesworth, Missoula: Scholars Press, 1977), 19. Used by permission of James H. Charlesworth.

[8] Ibid., 26–27. Used by permission of James H. Charlesworth.

[9] Ibid., 70–72. Used by permission of James H. Charlesworth.

[10] Ibid., 114. Used by permission of James H. Charlesworth.

[11] *The Sayings of the Desert Fathers: The Alphabetical Collection* (trans. Benedicta Ward, SLG; Kalamazoo: Cistercian Publications, 1975), 18–19. Used by permission of Cistercian Publications.

[12] Ibid., 35. Used by permission of Cistercian Publications.

[13] *Gregory of Nyssa*, 131–32. Used by permission of Paulist Press.

[14] Ibid., 114. Used by permission of Paulist Press.

[15] *The Sayings of the Desert Fathers*, 29. Used by permission of Cistercian Publications.

SOURCES CITED

OR MORE INFORMATION on the sources quoted in this anthology see the entries in Everett Ferguson, Michael McHugh, and Frederick Norris, eds., *Encyclopedia of Early Christianity*, 2d edition (New York: Garland, 1997; pb., 1998).

Ambrose—Bishop of Milan in Italy (374–397).

Apophthegmata Patrum—"Sayings of the Fathers," a collection of proverbs and anecdotes from monks of the fourth and fifth centuries, gathered together in several series (alphabetical, anonymous, and systematic).

Apostolic Constitutions—A collection of materials on church order that was compiled and edited from earlier documents in the late fourth century.

Athanasius—Bishop of Alexandria in Egypt (328–373).

Athenagoras—Author of a defense for Christianity written about 177.

Augustine—Bishop of Hippo in North Africa (354–430).

Basil of Caesarea—Bishop of Caesarea in Cappadocia (370–379).

1 Clement—A letter from the church at Rome to the church at Corinth, usually dated about 96 and traditionally ascribed to one of the Roman presbyter-bishops known as Clement.

2 Clement—A sermon from the early second century of uncertain authorship (not the same as *1 Clement*) and uncertain place (perhaps Corinth).

Clement of Alexandria—A teacher and perhaps a presbyter who lived ca. 160–215.

Cyprian—Bishop of Carthage in North Africa (248–258) and martyr.

Cyril of Jerusalem—Presbyter and then bishop (349–387).

Didache—"The Teaching of the Lord through the Twelve Apostles to the Nations," a manual of church life compiled probably in Syria around the beginning of the second century.

Didascalia—A church order produced in Syria in the first half of the third century.

Diognetus, Epistle to—An apology for Christianity of uncertain authorship, probably written in the second century.

Dorotheus of Gaza—Founder of a monastery near Gaza in Palestine about 540.

Eusebius—Bishop of Caesarea in Palestine (ca. 313–339), whose *Church History* quotes many earlier documents.

Gregory of Nazianzus—Bishop of Constantinople (379–381), orator, poet, and theologian.

Gregory of Nyssa—Bishop of Nyssa in Cappadocia (372–ca. 395) and philosophical and moral theologian.

Gregory Thaumaturgus (Wonderworker)—Missionary and bishop of Neocaesarea in Pontus (240s–260s).

Gregory the Great—Bishop of Rome (590–604) and moral theologian.

Hermas—A prophet who was active in the church at Rome in the first half of the second century.

Hippolytus—Presbyter and rival bishop in the church at Rome (died ca. 236), under whose name are preserved works of perhaps more than one author.

Ignatius—Bishop of Antioch in Syria, martyred in Rome perhaps about 117.

Irenaeus—Bishop of Lyons in Gaul (France) (ca. 178–202) and opponent of Gnosticism.

Jerome—Presbyter in Rome (382–385) and later monk in Bethlehem, Palestine (died ca. 420), Bible translator and commentator, and controversialist.

John Cassian—Founder of monasteries in Marseilles, France, and writer on monasticism (died ca. 433).

John Chrysostom—Presbyter in Antioch, Syria (386–398), bishop of Constantinople (398–404), and master of expository preaching.

John Climacus—Abbot of monastery in Sinai, Egypt, and writer on asceticism (d. 649).

John of Damascus—Monk at Mar Saba monastery and Orthodox theologian (died ca. 749).

Justin Martyr—Defender of Christianity against paganism and Judaism, martyred in Rome about 165.

Lactantius—Literary champion of Christianity from North Africa (ca. 250–325).

Martyrdom of Polycarp—Letter from the church at Smyrna of which he was bishop, relating his martyrdom probably about 156.

Maximus the Confessor—Monk, theologian, and ascetical writer (580–662).

Melito—Bishop of Sardis in Asia Minor (Turkey) in the late second century.

Methodius—Bishop of Olympus in Lycia, Turkey (died ca. 311).

Minucius Felix—Author of a dialogue that defended Christianity against paganism in the late second or early third century.

Novatian—Presbyter and then a rival bishop in Rome during the mid-third century.

Origen—Learned teacher and prolific writer in Alexandria, Egypt, and then in Caesarea, Palestine (ca. 185–ca. 251).

Pseudo-Clement—Fourth-century compiler who pretended to be Clement of Rome and incorporated into his work documents of the second and third centuries.

Pseudo-Cyprian—Author of third-century Latin works preserved under the name of Cyprian of Carthage.

Sentences of Sextus—Wise sayings compiled largely from pagan philosophical sources by a Christian who lived about 200.

Tatian—Defender of Christianity from Syria in the latter half of the second century.

Tertullian—Apologist, theologian, and moralist from North Africa who was active in the late second century and early decades of the third century.

Theodoret—Bishop of Cyrus in Syria (423–ca. 460), theologian, and historian.

Theonas—Bishop of Alexandria, Egypt (ca. 281–ca. 300).

Theophilus—Bishop of Antioch who wrote in defense of Christianity about 180.

INDEX OF SUBJECTS

INDEX OF SCRIPTURES

INDEX OF SOURCES CITED